The Fables of Reason

A Study of Voltaire's
'Contes Philosophiques'

ROGER PEARSON

CLARENDON PRESS · OXFORD
1993

Oxford University Press, Walton Street, Oxford OX2 6DP
Oxford New York Toronto
Delhi Bombay Calcutta Madras Karachi
Kuala Lumpur Singapore Hong Kong Tokyo
Nairobi Dar es Salaam Cape Town
Melbourne Auckland Madrid
and associated companies in
Berlin Ibadan

Oxford is a trade mark of Oxford University Press

Published in the United States
by Oxford University Press Inc., New York

British Library Cataloguing in Publication Data
Data available

Library of Congress Cataloging in Publication Data
Pearson, Roger.
The fables of reason : a study of Voltaire's "Contes
philosophiques" / Roger Pearson.
Includes bibliographical references.
1. Voltaire, 1694–1778. Contes philosophiques. 2. Fables,
French – History and criticism. 3. Philosophy in literature.
4. Reason in literature. I. Title.
PQ2125.P43 1993 848'.509—dc20 92-39575
ISBN 0-19-815880-7

Typeset by Rowland Phototypesetting Ltd.
Bury St Edmunds, Suffolk
Printed in Great Britain
on acid-free paper by
Biddles Ltd.
Guildford and King's Lynn

for
Samantha and Nicholas

J'aime les fables des philosophes, je ris de celles des enfants, et je
hais celles des imposteurs.

(318)

Tous ces contes-là m'ennuient [. . .] Ils ne sont bons que pour
être commentés chez les Irlandais

(553)

PREFACE

J'ai lu *Candide* vingt fois, je l'ai traduit en anglais et je l'ai encore
relu de temps à autre.

(Flaubert in a letter to Louis de Cormenin, 7 June 1844)

THIS book arises out of my recent translation of *Candide and Other
Stories* for the World's Classics series published by Oxford University
Press. Having spent many months shadowing Voltaire word for word
I came to see his *contes* in a quite different light from that in which I
had previously encountered them. In particular the experience of his
story-telling as an evolving process rather than as a series of ready-
made classics bred a strong sense in me that what Voltaire's *contes*
principally do is not so much to convey a number of alleged intellectual and moral truths in palatable form as to foster a spirit of
irreverence and to instil in the reader a habit of mind with which he or
she may embark upon the independent pursuit of wisdom.

Translation itself, of course, is a much debated activity. In more
self-important moments I felt it to be the supreme form of literary
interpretation: each act of linguistic transposition having to be undertaken in as full an awareness as possible of all the conceivable functions
of the unit to be rendered, not to mention the effects of one's
proposed rendition, with the final choice of the best of all possible
words being in itself literary commentary of the most authoritative
kind. But the implicitness of such commentary left me with a Panglossian desire to pronounce further.

I have therefore undertaken to present as succinctly as possible an
account of all Voltaire's twenty-six *contes*. On the eve of the tercen-
tenary of his birth it is surprising to note that no such comprehensive
study exists. Dorothy Madeleine McGhee's *Voltairian Narrative
Devices as Considered in the Author's 'Contes philosophiques'*, published in
1933, covers the whole corpus (with the exception of *Pot-pourri*) but
from the limited point of view indicated in her title. Jacques Van den
Heuvel's *Voltaire dans ses contes. De 'Micromégas' à 'L'Ingénu'* (1967)
considers some of the major stories in their biographical and historical
context, as well as commenting on a number of important narrative
techniques: but several stories are neglected, not only the minor ones.

The time is thus perhaps ripe for a full study of Voltaire's *contes philosophiques* which takes note of the extensive range of critical literature on the subject while also suggesting new ways of reading each individual *conte*.

I have incurred several debts of gratitude in the writing of this book, not least to the many scholars who have written on Voltaire, most notably W. H. Barber, J. H. Brumfitt, Frédéric Deloffre, Jacqueline Hellegouarc'h, Haydn Mason, René Pomeau, and Jacques Van den Heuvel. Once more I am particularly indebted to my friend and colleague Ian Maclean for his generous encouragement and clear-minded advice.

R.P.

The Queen's College, Oxford

CONTENTS

NOTE ON REFERENCES

THE following abbreviations have been used in the footnotes. For further bibliographical information see the Bibliography.

CAIEF:	*Cahiers de l'association internationale des études françaises*
CW:	*The Complete Works of Voltaire* (ed. Th. Besterman *et al.*)
D (and a number):	Voltaire's correspondence in vols. 85–135 of *The Complete Works of Voltaire*
Dict. phil.	*Dictionnaire philosophique* (ed. René Pomeau)
Lett. phil.	*Lettres philosophiques* (ed. Frédéric Deloffre)
Mélanges:	*Mélanges* (Bibliothèque de la Pléiade)
Mol.:	*Œuvres complètes* (ed. Louis Moland)
RC:	*Romans et contes* (Bibliothèque de la Pléiade, 1979)
SVEC:	*Studies on Voltaire and the Eighteenth Century* (ed. Th. Besterman (1955–76) and H. T. Mason (1977–), Geneva, Banbury, and Oxford, 1955– .

Note: all page references included parenthetically in the text are to *Romans et contes* (Bibliothèque de la Pléiade, 1979).

I
The Fables of Reason

Ah! s'il nous faut des fables, que ces fables
soient du moins l'emblème de la vérité!

(318)

I
The *conte philosophique* and its Readers

'. . . si j'ai fait des romans
j'en demande pardon à Dieu.'
(D11889 (24 May 1764, to Panckoucke))

It has sometimes been thought a paradox that Voltaire should owe his enduring place in the literary canon to his *contes* while those works from which he derived his literary reputation during his own lifetime, namely his tragedies and his epic verse, have since fallen into neglect. No less paradoxical, it would seem, is the fact that he should have written *contes* at all, and that he should have achieved some of his most persuasive feats of enlightenment in a genre which he associated with foolishness and deceit. For 'conte', 'fable', and 'roman' were all dirty words in the vocabulary of this empiricist *philosophe*, who used them variously to disparage the Old Testament, ancient historiography, and the metaphysics of anyone from Plato to Descartes. Nothing but old wives' tales, he would scoff, or worse even: 'des contes qu'une vieille femme de bons sens ne ferait pas à des petits enfants.'[1] 'La raison', on the other hand, 'consiste à voir toujours les choses comme elles sont.'[2]

But both paradoxes are superficial. In the case of his epic poem and his theatre, some of Voltaire's reputation was based on the ephemeral foundations of political polemic and a taste for sentiment, while the narrative verve of *La Henriade* and the dramatist's deft manipulation of audience response are also manifest in the *contes*. Here, as in the epic and the play, entertainment and enlightenment were Voltaire's aims, not the glorification of heroes or a purgation of the passions.[3] As to the *contes* themselves, it is not as if they

[1] *Dict. phil.*, 273 ('Martyrs').
[2] *Dict. phil.*, 177 ('Enthousiasme').
[3] 'je ne sais pas ce que c'est que cette médecine' (*Commentaires sur Corneille, CW*, lx. 1031).

brought their author no success or recognition during his own life-time. *Candide, L'Ingénu,* and *L'Homme aux quarante écus* were all best-sellers. On the other hand, only about eight *contes* out of a total of twenty-six can be said to have entered safely into the late-twentieth-century canon. Two-thirds of them, therefore, have sunk with the plays into relative oblivion, and probably for similar reasons. Either they are perceived as being unoriginal and mechanically repetitive, or else they are deemed to be so anchored in the polemics of the past that all point and pleasure have been lost.

It is indeed true that, like most eighteenth-century men of taste, Voltaire scorned prose fiction:

on est bien éloigné de vouloir donner ici quelque prix à tous ces romans dont la France a été et est encore inondée. Ils ont presque tous été, excepté *Zaïde* [by Mme de Lafayette], des productions d'esprits faibles, qui écrivent avec facilité des choses indignes d'être lues par les esprits solides. Ils sont même pour la plupart dénués d'imagination; et il y en a plus dans quatre pages de l'Arioste que dans tous ces insipides écrits qui gâtent le goût des jeunes gens.[4]

But he scorned 'romans' not so much out of a neo-classical sense of their generic vulgarity and illegitimacy as for the same powerful reason that he excoriated the Old Testament, ancient historiography, and metaphysics: they are fictions which allow and even encourage human beings not to see 'les choses comme elles sont'. There is no paradox in the fact that Voltaire should have achieved enlightenment through fiction, for, like some literary fifth columnist, he infiltrates the world of romance the better to destroy it and to replace it with fictions of a more authentic kind. In this respect Candide's garden stands in a direct line between Cervantes's Rosinante and Flaubert's parrot. Against not only the illusions of chivalric romance but also the foolish 'fables' of superstition and fanaticism and the 'romans' of rationalist metaphysics, Voltaire pits his own apologues of common sense, his own fables of reason.

Voltaire's enduring success as a story-teller is even less paradoxical when one considers not only that so many of his contemporaries speak of his natural talent as a raconteur[5] but also how central narra-

---

    [4] Art. 'Villedieu', in *Le Siècle de Louis XIV* (*Œuvres historiques*, ed. René Pomeau, Bibliothèque de la Pléiade (Paris, 1957), 1213).
    [5] See D1681 (9–11 Dec. 1738, Mme de Graffigny to Devaux); D6562 (1 Nov. 1755, Claude Pierre Patu to David Garrick); and William F. Bottiglia, *Voltaire's 'Candide': Analysis of a Classic*, 2nd edn. (Geneva, 1966 [= *SVEC* 7a]), 57–8. See also

tive is to so much of his work. He was, after all, a very considerable historian; and none other than Bolingbroke, one of Voltaire's most important mentors, observed that 'history is philosophy teaching by example'. That he should have devoted so much time to writing history is in itself evidence of what is perhaps the most important single thing about Voltaire: he thinks narratively. His plays tell stories; his epic tells a story; his histories tell stories; his *contes en vers* tell stories; his philosophical dialogues at least imply stories. In many of his polemical works he resorts to narrative as a means of argument,[6] sometimes even as a way of avoiding logical conclusion (for example, at the end of the *Poème sur le désastre de Lisbonne*), a facility which he will readily exploit in the *conte*. Moreover, not only does he think in narratives, he thinks in short narratives. As many commentators have pointed out, all his prose work from the *contes* and the *Essai sur les mœurs* to the *Lettres philosophiques* and the *Dictionnaire philosophique* is essentially cumulative and episodic: he is, in René Pomeau's telling phrase, 'interminablement bref'.[7]

Jacques Van den Heuvel has made the valuable point that Locke's philosophical method in the *Essay Concerning Human Understanding*, which so influenced Voltaire, is itself essentially narrative. Locke speaks of this method as being 'historical' and 'plain': 'historical' because ideas are not innate but arrived at by stages ('the steps by which the human mind attains several truths') and 'plain' because, in its uncorrupt state, the mind is untrammelled by prejudice and preconception.[8] Voltaire was almost 30 when he read Locke: did Locke make him think narratively, or did perhaps the already narrative cast of his mind make him warm to Locke? Be that as it may,

---

Yvon Belaval, 'Le conte philosophique', in W. H. Barber *et al.* (eds.), *The Age of Enlightenment. Studies Presented to Theodore Besterman* (Edinburgh and London, 1967), where Belaval argues that the *conte philosophique* has its roots in the conversational skills of salon and café society.

⁶ e.g. *Dict. phil.*, 272 ('Maître'): 'On a écrit sur ce phénomène un grand nombre de bons volumes; mais je donne la préférence à une fable indienne, parce qu'elle est courte.'

⁷ René Pomeau, *La Religion de Voltaire*, 2nd edn. (Paris, 1967), 471.

⁸ Jacques Van den Heuvel, *Voltaire dans ses contes. De 'Micromégas' à 'L'Ingénu'*, 3rd edn. (Paris, 1967), 82. See Locke's *Essay Concerning Human Understanding*, bk. 1, ch. 1, para. 2, and bk. 1, ch. 2, para. 15. Cf. the narrator's comment to the critic in *Tristram Shandy*: 'Locke's Essay upon the Human Understanding . . . is a history . . . a history book, Sir (which may possibly recommend it to the world), of what passes in a man's own mind; and if you will say so much of the book, and no more, believe me, you will cut no contemptible figure in a metaphysic circle' (bk. 2, ch. 2).

story-telling is central to Voltaire's work, and it is the perfect match between medium and mentality which accounts for the success of Voltaire's *contes philosophiques.*

Given this prevalence of narrative in his writing, it may seem arbitrary to restrict a study of Voltaire as story-teller to the twenty-six stories which are traditionally seen as constituting the corpus of his *contes philosophiques*; but there is sufficient evidence that he himself regarded them as distinct from his other writings to justify this narrowing of focus.[9] As to the term *conte philosophique*, convenient as it now is, it was rarely used by Voltaire himself. Indeed, over the thirty years between 1740 and 1770 during which the great majority of Voltaire's *contes* were written, it was used explicitly as a subtitle in only three *contes*, all by other writers.[10] However, in 1771, in the so-called Quarto edition of Voltaire's works prepared for publication in Geneva by Gabriel and Philibert Cramer, volumes 13 and 14 appeared under the title *Romans, contes philosophiques, etc.* Since then the label has stuck. It is true that Voltaire had added the subtitle 'Histoire philosophique' to *Micromégas* in 1754, but this was an isolated instance. For the most part he referred to his stories either simply as 'histoires' and 'petits ouvrages', or else dismissively as 'fadaises', 'rogatons', and 'petits pâtés'.

Did Voltaire invent the *conte philosophique*? In using fictional narrative for the illustration and discussion of philosophical and moral issues, Voltaire was following a well-established tradition stretching back to Lucian, though his immediate precursors included Montesquieu, Swift, Tyssot de Patot, Cyrano de Bergerac, and Rabelais. His originality lay in annexing the *conte* to this tradition by trading on its contemporary popularity[11] and thus, more especially, on his readers' familiarity with its principal features. He was able to write, as it were, against the *conte* and to exploit some of its more salient characteristics (particularly of the *conte oriental*) for his own polemical and entertaining ends. To say that Voltaire invented the *conte philosophique* implies that he created a genre which others subsequently exploited, but no one did.

⁹ See *RC*, pp. xi–xix.

¹⁰ See Angus Martin, *Anthologie du conte en France 1750–1799. Philosophes et cœurs sensibles* (Paris, 1981), 30.

¹¹ More than 7,500 fictional narratives (of 200 pages or less) were published in France during the 18th c., of which more than 6,500 numbered less than 100 pages. See Martin, *Anthologie du conte*, 10–11.

To say, on the other hand, as Gustave Lanson does, that Voltaire was really only doing what every other eighteenth-century polemicist did, only more so, is to err in the opposite direction.[12] Certainly the threatening presence of the censor, not to mention the Bastille, encouraged frequent recourse to parable and fable in eighteenth-century France, but Lanson's account obscures the way in which Voltaire's *contes philosophiques* differ from his other incidental narratives by their subversive engagement with the world of the 'romanesque'. The Voltairian *conte* is *sui generis*, a unique blend of fiction and philosophical debate which bears certain resemblances to the work of other writers but none the less was and has remained without close parallel.

Why and for whom was Voltaire a *conteur*? In the view of several influential critics the answer would seem to be: himself. When Voltaire's first *contes* were thought to date from 1747–8, René Pomeau saw them as the product of a crisis in Voltaire's thinking about theodicy and the problem of evil.[13] Similarly, Van den Heuvel's *Voltaire dans ses contes* approaches the *contes* essentially as a form of confession, revealing a 'vérité profonde . . . qui s'élabore sans cesse dans l'intimité du moi'.[14] This biographical approach, however, does insufficient justice to a writer who declared: 'j'écris pour agir'.[15] Voltaire was, if nothing else, a performer, and his *contes* were written to be read. Initially he wrote for his friends and well-placed acquaintances: his first two surviving *contes* were intended for the entertainment of the duchesse du Maine and her court at Sceaux, as were several subsequent stories; a first version of *Micromégas* was sent to Frederick of Prussia; and *Zadig* was published privately and circulated personally to a select readership. Beyond this intimate circle he aspired to delight and to encourage a growing intelligentsia who were receptive to the new ideas, a group drawn from the nobility and the bourgeoisie alike, from the magistrature of the Parlements and even from some enlightened clergy.[16] As the century progressed, of course, this potential readership increased, and

---

[12]   Gustave Lanson, *L'Art de la prose* (Paris, 1908), 179–81.
[13]   Pomeau, *La Religion de Voltaire*, 248. Cf. Laurence L. Bongie, 'Crisis and the Birth of the Voltairian *conte*', *Modern Language Quarterly*, 23 (1962).
[14]   *Voltaire dans ses contes*, 10.
[15]   D14117 (*c.*15 Apr. 1767, to Jacob Vernes).
[16]   See René Vaillot, *Voltaire en son temps. II. Avec Madame Du Châtelet 1734–1749* (Oxford, 1988), 144.

with the publishing coup of *Candide* and the popularity of *L'Ingénu*, Voltaire must have been read by a large section of literate Europe.

In emphasizing that Voltaire's *contes* are texts to be read, one must be careful not to exaggerate the extent to which they were intended to 'convert' readers from one way of thinking to another. Clearly Voltaire was writing for fellow *philosophes* and free-thinkers who would sympathize with his views and spot the myriad allusions with which his *contes* are filled. But, as with Stendhal's repeated dedications of his works to the Happy Few, this has led some to see Voltairian wit in terms of a rather cosy exclusivity: 'Cette forme de séduction . . . s'adresse moins au cœur qu'au bon sens. Sa ruse est une flatterie. Comment ne point se sentir fier d'entendre finesse? Elle appelle la complicité. On devient partie d'une élite. On est pris par le point d'honneur.'[17] Writers evidently adopt a wide variety of strategies in respect of their readers, from the rib-poking directness of Diderot in *Jacques le fataliste* to the seamless inscrutability of Flaubert and Mallarmé. But, while irony may be a particularly valuable and insidious weapon with which to beguile the reader over to one's side, its use should not lead the reader automatically to suppose that he or she alone has got the point. The flattering complicity is an illusion, and Voltaire, like Stendhal, hoped for as wide a readership as the gradual disappearance of readerly prejudice would permit. As Voltaire put it in a letter in 1766: 'il me paraît essentiel de se faire lire de tout le monde si on peut.'[18]

Thus, for all that Voltaire was writing for readers who would at least be sympathetic to his views, if not already persuaded, this very desire to be widely read points to a proselytizing purpose, a desire to foster Enlightenment attitudes and beliefs as generally as possible. As always with Voltaire one must be careful not to sum up a long life in easy generalizations. This expressed ambition for a wide readership dates from a time when his campaign against the Church and the Parlements was in full swing, and the letter reflects a particular concern to encourage tolerance and compassion.[19] But it also

[17]   Yvon Belaval, 'L'Esprit de Voltaire', *SVEC* 24 (1963), 151. Cf. also Henri Coulet, 'La distanciation dans le roman et le conte philosophiques', in *Roman et lumières au XVIIIe siècle* (Paris, 1970), 439.
[18]   D13641 (Oct./Nov. 1766, to Moultou).
[19]   'Ne pourrait-on point faire quelque livre qui pût se faire lire avec quelque plaisir, par les gens mêmes qui n'aiment point à lire, et qui portât les cœurs à la compassion?' (D13641). *L'Ingénu* was such a book.

echoes earlier statements. In the *Lettres philosophiques* (1734), for example, he reflects gloomily that nineteen twentieths of the human race are manual workers and will go to their graves never having even heard of Locke. Of the remaining twentieth hardly any of them read, and of those that do 'il y en a vingt qui lisent des romans, contre un qui étudie la philosophie'.[20] And the *Lettres philosophiques* themselves, of course, represented amongst other things an attempt to bring the ideas of Locke and Newton before a wider audience, as did the highly successful and influential *Elements de la philosophie de Newton* (1738).

One may suggest therefore that, while Voltaire's career as a *conteur* began as a form of court entertainment at Sceaux, he later grew more keenly aware of the propagandistic potential of the genre. Up until *Candide*, the content gradually became more and more explosive, but the readership remained comparatively restricted. In these *contes*, as Pomeau and Van den Heuvel have argued, Voltaire is indeed primarily concerned with finding a narrative solution to the problem of evil. Then, following the enormous success of *Candide*, the *conte* became a major weapon in the battle against 'l'infâme' as well as Voltaire's own special contribution to the contemporary debate about education. By writing within the genre of fiction he was gaining access to a non-philosophical readership, while the brevity and saleability of the *conte* might bring happiness, respectively, to his readers and his publisher. For similar reasons the first edition of the *Dictionnaire philosophique portatif* (1764) appeared, as *Candide* had, in user-friendly pocket-book format. Here was Voltaire's marketing answer to the problems of distribution facing the editors of the *Encyclopédie*, and hence his famous remark to D'Alembert: 'Jamais vingt volumes in-folio ne feront de révolution; ce sont les petits livres portatifs à trente sous qui sont à craindre. Si l'évangile avait coûté douze cents sesterces, jamais la religion chrétienne ne se serait établie.'[21]

While Voltaire was keen to achieve a wide readership, he was not nevertheless prepared to be meretricious. He had, for example, certain doubts on this score about Montesquieu's *De l'esprit des lois*, which he once accused of being all 'esprit' and little 'lois'.[22] As for

---

[20] *Lett. phil.*, 94.
[21] D13235 (5 Apr. 1766).
[22] Mol., xxvii. 321.

Fontenelle, who was in some respects the first major popularizer of the Enlightenment, Voltaire took exception to what he regarded as his peculiar blend of self-advertisement and circumspection.[23] Conscious of the paradox whereby this man who sought to spread knowledge more widely was also a keen believer in the social utility of ignorance, he dismissed Fontenelle's caution as 'prudente lâcheté'[24] and enjoyed repeating Fontenelle's apocryphal but probably authentic comment: 'J'aurais la main pleine de vérités que je ne l'ouvrirais pas pour le peuple.'[25]

Voltaire himself, of course, in common with many progressives of his age, was not notable for his desire to educate the masses. In 1763 he complimented La Chalotais on his recently published treatise on education and noted with particular gratitude that La Chalotais had not proposed anything which might prevent Voltaire's own gardeners at Ferney from getting on with their job.[26] Voltaire's view of enlightenment was, like D'Alembert's, essentially gradualist: 'les hommes ne s'éclairent que par degrés'.[27] The hand should release its clutch of 'vérités' finger by finger: the lessons and ideals of the Enlightenment should filter slowly down from the top. This process was likely to take so long that the question of allowing the filtering to reach 'le peuple' did not immediately arise. If it had, he would have opposed it. The penultimate paragraph of the preface to the *Dictionnaire philosophique* makes this clear:

Ce n'est même que par des personnes éclairées que ce livre peut être lu; le vulgaire n'est pas fait pour de telles connaissances; la philosophie ne sera jamais son partage. Ceux qui disent qu'il y a des vérités qui doivent être

[23] See D12660 (26 June 1765, to Helvétius).
[24] D13369 (22 June 1766, to the comte and comtesse d'Argental).
[25] D13355 (*c.*15 June 1766, to the comte d'Argental). But cf. D11418 (15 Sept. 1763, to Helvétius) for a more sympathetic interpretation. On the history and reception of Fontenelle's remark and for a rich account of eighteenth-century attitudes to the enlightenment of the masses, see Roland Mortier, 'Esotérisme et lumières. Un dilemme de la pensée du XVIIIe siècle', in his *Clartés et ombres du siècle des lumières. Etudes sur le XVIIIe siècle littéraire* (Geneva, 1969), 60–103 (esp. 63–4). See also Peter France, *Rhetoric and Truth in France. Descartes to Diderot* (Oxford, 1972), 74ff. For a fuller account of Voltaire's opinion of Fontenelle see Christiane Mervaud, 'Voltaire et Fontenelle', in Alain Niderst (ed.), *Fontenelle. Actes du colloque tenu à Rouen du 6 au 10 octobre 1987* (Paris, 1989).
[26] D11051 (28 Feb. 1763). Cf. France, *Rhetoric and Truth*, 74: 'Popularization stopped a long way short of the peasant, who might be inclined to abandon the soil, once he had eaten the forbidden fruit.'
[27] Mol., xxvii. 367.

cachées au peuple ne peuvent prendre aucune alarme; le peuple ne lit point; il travaille six jours de la semaine et va le septième au cabaret. En un mot, les ouvrages de la philosophie ne sont faits que pour les philosophes, et tout honnête homme doit chercher à être philosophe, sans se piquer de l'être.[28]

While Voltaire is here trying to placate potential enemies of the *Dictionnaire philosophique* by minimizing its incendiary qualities and by suggesting that he is merely preaching to a select band of the converted, it is difficult not to hear a genuine note of disdain for the beer-swilling masses.[29]

The 'prudente lâcheté' which Voltaire objected to in Fontenelle was not so much, therefore, his refusal to educate 'le peuple' as his reluctance to portray 'les choses comme elles sont'. In his *Dialogues des morts* (1683) Fontenelle had argued that the human mind is naturally inclined to illusion rather than truth. Hence, if one wished to impart the fruits of reason, one did well to cover them up in falsehood.[30] Voltaire rejects this view in the article 'Fraude' in the *Dictionnaire philosophique*:

Ouang: 'Il faudrait . . . ne point mêler une morale sage avec des fables absurdes, parce que vous affaiblissez par vos impostures, dont vous pourriez

---

[28]   *Dict. phil.*, 20. This ideal of the *philosophe* who does not appear to be a *philosophe* is reflected in Condorcet's *Vie de Voltaire*, where it is said to be best illustrated by the *conte philosophique* itself:

> Ce genre a le malheur de paraître facile; mais il exige un talent rare, celui de savoir exprimer par une plaisanterie, par un trait d'imagination, ou par les événements mêmes du roman, les résultats d'une philosophie profonde, sans cesser d'être naturelle et piquante, sans cesser d'être vraie . . . Il faut être philosophe, et ne point le paraître.
>
> En même temps peu de livres de philosophie sont plus utiles; ils sont lus par des hommes frivoles que le nom seul de la philosophie rebute ou attriste, et que cependant il est important d'arracher aux préjugés, et d'opposer au grand nombre de ceux qui sont intéressés à les défendre (Mol., i. 240–1).

[29]   For an examination of Voltaire's ambivalence in this area, see Mortier, 'Esotérisme et lumières', 73–9, and his 'Voltaire et le peuple', in W. H. Barber *et al.* (eds.), *The Age of Enlightenment: Studies Presented to Theodore Besterman* (Edinburgh and London, 1967).

[30]   'Vous vous imaginez [Homer says to Aesop] que l'esprit humain ne cherche que le vrai; détrompez-vous. L'esprit humain et le faux sympathisent extrêmement. Si vous avez la vérité à dire, vous ferez fort bien de l'envelopper dans des Fables, elle en plaira beaucoup plus . . . Ainsi le vrai a besoin d'emprunter la figure du faux pour être agréablement reçu dans l'esprit humain; mais le faux y entre bien sous sa propre figure, car c'est le lieu de sa naissance et de sa demeure ordinaire, et le vrai y est étranger' (Fontenelle, *Nouveaux dialogues des morts*, ed. Jean Dagen (Paris, 1971), 143–4).

vous passer, cette morale que vous êtes forcés d'enseigner.' Bambabef: 'Quoi! vous croyez qu'on peut enseigner la vérité au peuple sans la soutenir par des fables?' Ouang: 'Je le crois fermement.'[31]

Rather as Rousseau believed that virtue is natural, so Voltaire believed (as *L'Ingénu* shows) that straight-thinking is natural, provided the mind is free of prejudice and left to operate in Locke's 'historical' and 'plain' manner. If one is going to straighten out warped minds, then one does not begin by wrapping the truth in lies. Voltaire did not dispute that Aesop's fables were excellent, but he saw them as naïve, rather than artful, expressions of truth.[32]

In his *De l'origine des fables* (1724) Fontenelle had contended that 'fables' (here in the sense of myth rather than apologue)[33] were evidence of man's natural tendency to create fictions in the absence of knowledge: 'Ne cherchons donc autre chose dans les fables que l'histoire des erreurs de l'esprit humain.'[34] Fontenelle was arguing against the notion that pagan myths were a subsequent 'fabulous' transformation of the 'historical' events recorded in the Old Testament, a theory which had been advanced by Huet and Bochart and which Voltaire also rejects in both the *Essai sur les mœurs* and *La Défense de mon oncle*.[35] Fontenelle argues instead, from an empiricist standpoint and rejecting the Cartesian theory of innate ideas, that the history of human thought is a simple progression from error to truth (rather than a progression from Mosaic truth, through error, to the Christian revelation): 'Une des plus agréables histoires, et sans doute la plus philosophique, est celle des progrès de l'esprit humain.'[36] As Starobinski has shown, this was an important strategic

---

[31] *Dict. phil.*, 200. Cf. also the *Sermon des cinquante*: 'On nous dit qu'il faut des mystères au peuple, qu'il faut le tromper. Eh! mes frères, peut-on faire cet outrage au genre humain? . . . le peuple n'est pas si imbécile qu'on le pense' (*Mélanges*, 269).
[32] *Le Philosophe ignorant*, ed. J. L. Carr (London, 1965), 90.
[33] While 18th-c. French vocabulary contained the word 'mythologie', the first recorded use of 'mythe' dates from 1818, when it was doubtless coined to escape the pejorative connotation of 'fable' as Romantic interest in the 'truth' of primitive culture increased.
[34] *De l'origine des fables*, ed. J.-R. Carré (Paris, 1932), 39.
[35] *Essai sur les mœurs*, ed. René Pomeau (Paris, 1964), i. 97–100; and *La Défense de mon oncle*, *CW*, lxiv. 256–7. This theory was an extension of the then orthodox Christian view that pagan gods are a degenerate and plural reflection of the God of Genesis. See Jean Starobinski, 'Fable et mythologie aux XVIIe et XVIIIe siècles', in *Le Remède dans le mal. Critique et légitimation de l'artifice à l'âge des lumières* (Paris, 1989), 250–1.
[36] Quoted by Carré (ed.), *De l'origine des fables*, 48.

move since, where the Counter-Reformation had tolerated the 'errors' of pagan mythology both as a form of proof by counter-example of the truth of Christianity and as a kind of profane play-area for activities not directly subject to the prescriptions of the faith, Fontenelle and others were turning the very equation of 'fable' and error against the Church itself.

Voltaire himself played along with this strategy, as his repeated comparisons between the Old Testament and Ovid's *Metamorphoses* demonstrate (for example, in *Le Taureau blanc*). But, no less of an empiricist than Fontenelle and equally opposed to Cartesian metaphysics, he prefers to see pagan mythology as a series of 'allégories ingénieuses':

ainsi Janus a un double visage qui représente l'année passée et l'année commençante. Saturne qui dévore ses enfants est le temps qui détruit tout ce qu'il a fait naître. Les Muses filles de la Mémoire vous enseignent que sans mémoire on n'a point d'esprit, et que pour combiner des idées il faut commencer par retenir des idées.[37]

In the article 'Fables' in the *Dictionnaire philosophique* he concludes:

Les plus anciennes fables ne sont-elles pas visiblement allégoriques? . . . Il est impossible de ne pas reconnaître dans ces fables une peinture vivante de la nature entière. La plupart des autres fables sont ou la corruption des histoires anciennes, ou le caprice de l'imagination. Il en est des anciennes fables comme de nos contes modernes: il y en a de moraux, qui sont charmants; il y en a qui sont insipides.[38]

In short, Voltaire sees in Aesop's fables and ancient myths not error but a kind of truth, and thus two important models for his own *contes philosophiques.* Far from wishing to use fabulation as a means of exploiting man's taste for illusion — and this is what he holds against Fontenelle, Herodotus,[39] and all the *romans* of which he is so scornful — he sees story-telling strictly in terms of utilitarian allegory or symbolism. Literary devices are there to expound the truth, not to disguise it.[40]

---

[37] *La Défense de mon oncle, CW,* lxiv. 256. Cf. his own *Aventure de la mémoire* (1775).
[38] *Dict. phil.,* 188.
[39] *La Défense de mon oncle, CW,* lxiv. 257: 'Des fables qui ne disent rien du tout, comme Barbe bleue et les contes d'Hérodote, sont le fruit d'une imagination grossière et déréglée qui veut amuser des enfants, et même malheureusement des hommes.'
[40] For further discussion of the status and function of 'fables' within the context of 18th-cent. fiction, see Geoffrey Bennington, *Sententiousness and the Novel. Laying Down the Law in Eighteenth-Century French Fiction* (Cambridge, 1985), 80–90.

This explains how Voltaire, with his great admiration for the aesthetic achievements of the Grand Siècle, came to write *contes philosophiques* of an increasingly experimental kind. As a reading of any one of Voltaire's tragedies demonstrates, his pride in the glories of the past did not lead to slavish imitation, which in fact he explicitly denounced as the sure way to produce bad art.[41] Instead, with characteristic practicality, he investigated how the great plays of Corneille and Racine work (or fail to work) and sought to apply their principles rather than their specific methods. Like theirs, his model was 'nature'; and his ambition was to convince his theatre audience (and the readers of his *contes*) of the reality and plausibility of his own 'fables'. As the Ingénu discovers (320), the Racine of *Phèdre* and *Andromaque* rings true, where the Corneille of *Rodogune* fails to convince. Similarly, Voltaire would hope that *Candide*, for all its fantasy and artifice, rings true, where the grand manner of supposedly more realistic fiction like *La Nouvelle Héloïse* does not. Voltaire's *contes philosophiques* are modern allegories which, by seeking never to pull the wool of fiction over our eyes, promote the cause of reason and clear-sightedness.

Because of the elements of allegory and fable in these *contes*, there has traditionally been a tendency to see them in rather simplistic Horatian terms of entertainment and instruction. Many readers would seem to swallow Voltaire's stories like sugar-coated pills, the bitter kernels of intellectual or moral edification being agreeably covered in consumable narrative excitement. But, as will be seen in the following chapters, it may often be that the real lesson of a *conte* is conveyed by its narrative order while the supposed philosophical 'content' provides the laughter. Sequence may instruct while ideas delight. It is particularly important to guard against seeing 'messages' at every turn, since the decoding of such messages as may exist can cause the reader to foreclose on the humour. For Voltaire seeks to liberate his potentially free-thinking readers by fostering a spirit of irreverence as much as, if not more than, he wants to urge a particular point of view. Thus in *Candide*, for example, Jacques the Anabaptist doubtless provides evidence of the compatibility of non-conformist theology and true Christian charity (as a mirror-

---

[41]   D12100 (25 Sept. 1764 to the comte and comtesse d'Argental), D15876 (6 Sept. 1769, to Mme du Deffand). See David Williams, *Voltaire: Literary Critic* (Geneva, 1966) (= *SVEC* 48), 343.

image of the historical co-existence of orthodox theology and the cruelty of the Inquisition). But he is also, as Pangloss might have said, put there to be drowned: only death by involuntary and permanent immersion will do for a man who believes in the necessity of adult baptism. Similarly, in any discussion of Leibnizian Optimism in either *Candide* or *Zadig*, sober analysis may tend to blunt the amusing incongruity of lowbrow adventure story and highbrow German rationalism. Nor should one forget that Voltaire is quite capable of poking fun at something he agrees with if he happens to see the possibility of a good joke. Indeed, in the various personas which he adopts throughout his *contes*, he quite often laughs at himself.

Nor are the 'messages' themselves always, if indeed ever, unambiguous. Vivienne Mylne has written that 'Voltaire was never willing to trust to the story alone; the lesson had always to be made explicit'; and she has been quoted with approval by Haydn Mason, for whom '[Voltaire's] attitudes are generally not hard to define', and who argues that 'his irony is of the "stable" kind, whose point of departure is that a covert fixed meaning is possible and decipherable'.[42] Again as the following chapters will show, ambiguity is rife in Voltaire's *contes*. Indeed his meaning is sometimes at its most oblique when, as in the stories which end with an adage, it is apparently most explicit. Voltairian irony is 'stable' to the extent that, just as so many of the stories are themselves allegedly translations, so the reader is being invited to 'translate' an ironic text into the 'original' intention of an author. If the narrator of *Candide* writes of a 'bel auto-da-fé' (157), even the most 'ingénu' of readers is likely to spot the antiphrasis. But one would be wrong to think that each of Voltaire's *contes* contains a recuperable unambiguous lesson, and indeed one would be doing their author an injustice to think so.

For one is faced here with what is perhaps the central paradox of all Enlightenment literature: how does one assert the need to doubt assertions? how can one be dogmatic about the ills of other people's dogmas? how should one singlemindedly insist on broadmindedness?[43] So strong is the image of Voltaire the polemical wizard

[42]   Vivienne Mylne, 'Literary Techniques and Methods in Voltaire's *contes philosophiques*', *SVEC* 57 (1967), 1075; Haydn Mason, *Voltaire* (London, 1975), 85, and 'Contradiction and Irony in Voltaire's Fiction', in Robert Gibson (ed.), *Studies in French Fiction in Honour of Vivienne Mylne* (London, 1988), 188.

[43]   This problem has been perceptively analysed in relation to the *Lettres philosophiques* by Marsha Reisler, 'Rhetoric and Dialectic in Voltaire's *Lettres philosophiques*', *L'Esprit créateur*, 17 (1977).

campaigning ardently against the 'infâme', virulently opposed to intolerance and injustice, and determined to drag the world into the light of reason by the very scruff of its neck, that one may easily overlook just how much latitude he insisted on giving his reader. 'Les livres les plus utiles sont ceux dont les lecteurs font eux-mêmes la moitié', he declares in the preface to the *Dictionnaire philosophique*, and then issues periodic reminders, as in the articles 'Morale' and 'Sensation': 'Lecteur, réfléchissez: étendez cette vérité; tirez vos conséquences'; 'Que conclure de tout cela? Vous qui lisez et qui pensez, concluez.' He does not want a silent, passive reader who unthinkingly consumes what is put before him, but an active, vociferous reader who grasps the principles behind the polemic and is ready to put them into practice. 'Que de choses à dire sur tout cela', he remarks in the article on priests: 'Lecteur, c'est à vous de les dire vous-même.'[44] His ideal reader is thus someone who has the capacity to think for himself and to speak up with his own voice, rather like M. André in *L'Homme aux quarante écus* who reads *Candide* and turns out to be no mean story-teller.

Voltaire's ideal reader is the 'honnête homme' of the preface to the *Dictionnaire philosophique*, or the 'homme raisonnable' to whom the *Lettres philosophiques* are addressed in their first sentence — or the addressee of some of the *contes*. In the 'Épître dédicatoire à la sultane Sheraa' Sadi describes *Zadig* as an 'ouvrage qui dit plus qu'il ne semble dire' and begs the sultana 'de le lire et d'en juger'. Having depicted her as the female equivalent of the 'honnête homme', down to the 'petit fonds de philosophie qui m'a fait croire que vous prendriez plus de goût qu'une autre à cet ouvrage d'un sage', he then expresses the hope that she will resemble Sultan Ouloug who, unlike his feather-brained sultanas, preferred *Zadig* to the *Thousand and One Nights*. Like Sadi with Sheraa, Voltaire, too, hopes that each of us will be 'un vrai Ouloug'.

In this way Voltaire likes to put his reader on his or her mettle, and it may be instructive to look briefly at how this process is continued in the case of the *Lettres philosophiques* before considering further how Voltaire treats the reader of his *contes*. The opening letter begins: 'J'ai cru que la doctrine et l'histoire d'un peuple si extraordinaire méritaient la curiosité d'un homme raisonnable.' The 'homme raisonnable' is in the first instance the author himself, but

---

44 *Dict. phil.*, 299, 354, 324.

the clear implication is that if we readers want to consider ourselves reasonable, we had better take an interest in England. The letters on the Quakers, Anglicans, Presbyterians, and Socinians encourage us French Catholic readers of 1734 to trust the author and to join with him in superior mockery of these curious people across the Channel. But then, of course, the author-guide's views begin to diverge from the orthodoxy of his imagined reader. The topics treated become more central and vital – religious tolerance, politics, commerce, the health service – until finally in the eleventh letter, which concerns inoculation against smallpox, it is the French and not the English who are now extraordinary: 'Quoi donc? Est-ce que les Français n'aiment point la vie? est-ce que leurs femmes ne se soucient point de leur beauté? En vérité, nous sommes d'étranges gens.'[45] The author's patriotic adoption of the first person plural form does not conceal where his real allegiance lies, and, needless to say, the whole thrust of the polemic in the *Lettres philosophiques* points to France, not England, being the land of 'invraisemblance'. The absurdities of the Quakers or the unruly genius of Shakespeare's plays are as nothing compared with the fundamental and pernicious 'fables' by which the realm of Louis XV is governed.

   The *Lettres philosophiques* provide a good example of what Brecht later called the technique of 'Verfremdung', the rendering strange of familiar phenomena or 'myths' (Galileo, Hitler) the better to encourage a critical reappraisal of them. Voltaire's *contes* will proceed in a similar manner to the *Lettres philosophiques*. The initially extraordinary becomes gradually familiar and 'real' while the reality to which the *conte* allegorically relates becomes increasingly unreal. Important philosophical questions – ontology, the existence of God, the nature of Providence, the problem of evil, the soul and immortality, freedom and determinism, the mind–body relationship, etc. – are all subjected to this treatment, as are the contemporary phenomena of the Christian Church, court intrigue, the power struggle between the King and the Parlements, education policy, war, international politics, class relations, economics, and atheism.

   All along Voltaire is translating the real world into modern fables which the reader must translate back again. By this process of 'translation' the reader is actively implicated in the reshaping and mental restatement of the world which the reader conceptually and

45 *Lett. phil.*, 81.

empirically knows — or thought to know. By this process he or she is thereby instructed — and thereby entertained. For putting two and two together is the essence of wit:

> Ce qu'on appelle esprit est tantôt une comparaison nouvelle, tantôt une allusion fine: ici l'abus d'un mot qu'on présente dans un sens, et qu'on laisse entendre dans un autre; là un rapport délicat entre deux idées peu communes; c'est une métaphore singulière; c'est une recherche de ce qu'un objet ne présente pas d'abord, mais de ce qui est en effet dans lui; c'est l'art ou de réunir deux choses éloignées, ou de diviser deux choses qui paraissent se joindre, ou de les opposer l'une à l'autre; c'est celui de ne dire qu'à moitié sa pensée pour la laisser deviner.[46]

The notion of 'esprit', like its English equivalent 'wit', combines the two strands of entertainment and instruction, as do Voltaire's stories. Indeed Voltaire's definition of wit reads like a poetics of the *conte philosophique*: unexpected analogies and subtle allusions; wordplay and the foregrounding of polysemy; incongruous connection; striking images; defamiliarization; bold combination, disjunction, and antithesis; the power of the implicit.

Such wit is binary, not only in the relations upon which it internally depends, but in the relationship between author and reader. In his article for the *Encyclopédie* Voltaire gives the following definition of 'finesse': 'la finesse dans les ouvrages de l'esprit, comme dans la conversation, consiste dans l'art de ne pas exprimer directement sa pensée, mais de la laisser aisément apercevoir: c'est une énigme dont les gens d'esprit devinent tout d'un coup le mot.'[47] In his *contes* Voltaire undertakes just such a conversation with his reader, and one in which our response is no less important than the author's own fables of wit and reason. As Yvon Belaval nicely puts it: 'Je est un conte. Le regard d'autrui me compose.'[48]

Reading Voltaire's *contes* is itself, therefore, a form of translation; and no doubt all readers should be guided by the author's comment on his version of Hamlet's 'To be or not to be' speech in the *Lettres philosophiques*: 'malheur aux faiseurs de traductions littérales, qui en traduisant chaque parole énervent le sens! C'est bien là qu'on peut

---

[46]   Mol., xix. 3.
[47]   The article was reproduced in the *Dictionnaire philosophique*. See Mol., xix. 146.
[48]   'L'Esprit de Voltaire', 147.

dire que la lettre tue, et que l'esprit vivifie.'[49] In order to enliven the deadly predictability of a steady chronological progression through each of the *contes* in turn, and in order to defamiliarize the subject for readers of Voltaire who are familiar only with the better-known *contes*, it may be useful to look next at one of his most neglected yet 'witty' stories, *L'Homme aux quarante écus*. It is hoped that analysis of this story will establish it as a revealing paradigm of Voltaire's main procedures as a story-teller. It is particularly suitable for such a role since it is notoriously bereft of the 'romanesque' elements which are customarily thought essential to fictional narrative.

[49]   *Lett. phil.*, 126–7.

2

Statistics and Symposia

L'Homme aux quarante écus

Messieurs, allez souper chez M. André.

(467)

Written in 1767, *L'Homme aux quarante écus* was published anonymously in Geneva by the Cramers in February 1768. It went through at least ten editions within the first year and on 24 September was condemned and ordered to be burned by the Paris Parlement, who also sentenced two booksellers to three days in the pillory and subsequent despatch to the galleys for having had the audacity to purvey it. The Vatican authorities finally placed it on their Index of forbidden works on 29 November 1771. For one of Voltaire's books, therefore, a fairly standard launch. But this initial success and notoriety were soon replaced by comparative oblivion, and the work has come generally to be seen as a septuagenarian's rather rambling and stubbornly repetitious attack on all-too-familiar bugbears. For many readers it is indeed scarcely a *conte* at all, given its comparative lack of action and the absence of traditionally delineated protagonists.[1] By reputation, therefore, *L'Homme aux quarante écus* is no more than a hastily conceived and rather irritable outburst against the economic theories of the Physiocrats.[2]

Also known as the 'économistes', these pioneers in the study of political economy[3] argued against the prevailing orthodoxy of

---

[1] See Voltaire, *Romans et contes*, ed. Henri Bénac (Paris, s.d. [1949]), p. v; Nuçi Kotta, *'L'Homme aux quarante écus. A Study of Voltairian Themes* (The Hague and Paris, 1966), 15; Vivienne Mylne, 'Literary Techniques and Methods', 1056; and Van den Heuvel, *Voltaire dans ses contes*, 327.

[2] See Kotta, *'L'Homme aux quarante écus'*, 17; *Romans et contes*, ed. René Pomeau (Paris, 1966), 383; and *RC*, p. lxv. A worthy exception to this dismissive consensus is provided by Robert Ginsberg, 'The Argument of Voltaire's *L'Homme aux quarante écus*: A Study in Philosophic Rhetoric', *SVEC* 56 (1967).

[3] They included François Quesnay (1694–1774), who was the author of articles for the *Encyclopédie* ('Fermiers' in 1756, and 'Grains' in 1757) and a *Tableau économique* (1758) which became early Physiocrat manifestos; Dupont de Nemours (1739–1817),

mercantilism, which holds that a nation's wealth depends on a favourable balance of trade with other nations and on the extent of its gold and silver reserves. They advocated that the way forward for France in its economic war with England was to develop its agriculture and reform its tax system. In particular they believed that only land is productive of wealth and hence that an increase in the products of the soil is the only means to an increase in prosperity. Le Mercier de la Rivière developed the political aspects of the Physiocratic doctrine known as 'despotisme légal' and contended that it was 'natural' for there to be a hereditary ruler who combined executive and legislative functions and who was joint-owner of the land with his subjects. Such despotism was legal because the ruler governed not arbitrarily but according to laws which were empirically manifest in the 'natural order'. Le Mercier also proposed that France's old, cumbersome system of taxation be replaced by a single tax levied exclusively on income from land.[4] The term 'Physiocratie', coined by Dupont de Nemours, advocates etymologically that nature should rule: i.e. that 'market forces' should prevail. Hence its proponents sought to free competition from restrictive practices and to provide for the free movement of goods both nationally and internationally. Hence, too, their famous motto: 'laissez faire, laissez passer'. In short, the Physiocrats favoured a single market and looked forward to 1993.

Voltaire was not unsympathetic to these views. He accepted the need for taxes and advocated reform of the existing ones. He was in favour of the removal of restrictions on the movement of agricultural produce (eventually effected by Turgot), and in several previous works he had criticized some of the tenets of mercantilism.[5] On the

who gave the school its name by publishing a collection of Quesnay's essays under the title *La Physiocratie ou Constitution naturelle du gouvernement le plus avantageux au genre humain* (1767), and whose own *Origine et progrès d'une science nouvelle* appeared in 1768; and Le Mercier de la Rivière (1720–93), author of *L'Ordre essentiel et naturel des sociétés politiques* (1767), which, thanks to the intervention of an enthusiastic Diderot, brought him an invitation to Russia from Catherine the Great to help her draft a new constitution.

4 According to Kotta no one ever attempted to put this into practice except for the Margrave of Baden, and with disastrous results: 'It led to a sharp drop in the value of the land and to the multiplication of bars and taverns' ('*L'Homme aux quarante écus*', 68).

5 See Kotta, '*L'Homme aux quarante écus*', 38–45, 68–83. Kotta finds it puzzling that Voltaire should revert in *L'Homme aux quarante écus* to antiquated mercantilist views when he had shown himself more progressive (even than Adam Smith) in previous writings, especially in his *Dialogue entre un philosophe et un contrôleur général des finances* (1751). Broadly Kotta sees Voltaire as being initially impressed by Physiocrat

other hand, Le Mercier de la Rivière's ideas seemed to Voltaire quite simply risible. The proposed single tax on land income would exempt industrialists, merchants, and in many cases even the Church. As to royal joint-ownership of the land, the master of Ferney was not at all persuaded. Above all he was suspicious of the Physiocrats' system *qua* system, especially their axiomatic belief in the 'naturalness' of despotism. Instead of being the result of hasty vituperation, therefore, it is quite possible that the apparent disorder of this *conte* is intended as a riposte to the specious and dangerous tidiness of system-builders.

FROM MR AVERAGE TO M. ANDRÉ

What Voltaire has done in *L'Homme aux quarante écus* is to turn a statistic into a human being via the medium of the *conte*: narrative maketh man. For it is as if Voltaire had read that every family in Britain has 2.4 children and decided to write the biography of that 0.4 of a person. The Homme aux quarante écus is Mr Average. The population of France numbers twenty million; there are 130 million 'arpents' (roughly, acres) of which some 80 million are productive; and each 'arpent' brings in an annual income of 30 livres, or 10 écus. Mr Average will have four acres and thus an income of 40 écus per annum. By rights — or at least 'suivant les registres du siècle d'or' (424) — this would have been every person's 'portion égale' in a pre-lapsarian world of evenly distributed wealth, but now — since 'il faut compter suivant le siècle de fer' (424) — it simply means poverty, especially if Mr Average has to share half his annual income with 'la puissance législatrice et exécutrice . . . née de droit divin copropriétaire' (417) — i.e. the King.

The hero of Voltaire's *conte*, therefore, is a figment of the administrative imagination, a 'fable' of reason; and his function is twofold. The first, and more obvious, is to show up the impracticability and injustice of the Physiocrats' proposed single tax on land. The financier, or 'capitaliste',[6] would pay no tax because his capital is all in

---

theories, then revolting against the single tax and the idea of joint-ownership, and finally taking refuge in mercantilism but without renouncing the Physiocrats' central view that land alone was productive of wealth.

[6]   See *RC*, 1069, n. 1.

'contrats' and 'billets sur la place' (418). The Carmelite (sect. IV)[7] would pay no tax because the monks derive their wealth from donations of money on which tax has already been paid. But the Homme aux quarante écus, 'seigneur terrien' (418) that he is with his four broad acres, must pay his dues along with the wealthiest of the landed gentry. The latter, of course, could afford it, even if they did begrudge it, whereas half of forty écus leaves one with rather little to live on. Fortunately, in the end, the Contrôleur Général des Finances reveals that it was all a bad joke (sect. V).

In this first function the Homme aux quarante écus is complemented by the figure of the Géomètre who is, amongst other things, a surveyor with a sense of humour. As a practical man and not a system-builder, he represents the ideal *philosophe* and is Voltaire's answer to Fénelon's Mentor in *Télémaque* or the tutor in Rousseau's *Emile* (just as M. André is a wicker-worker rather than a joiner like Emile). Conscious that 'la véritable géométrie est l'art de mesurer les choses existantes' (419) the Géomètre takes a fairly cavalier attitude towards statistical computation. For ease of reckoning he is ready to round the figure for the amount of productive land in France up from 75 to 80 million acres; for 'on ne saurait trop faire pour sa patrie' (420). Likewise the average income per acre is rounded up to 'trente livres' (i.e. 10 écus) 'pour ne pas décourager nos concitoyens' (420–1). This means that the net annual national product is 2,400 million livres, which leaves him with something of a 'mystère' since there are only 900 million circulating in the economy (421). The Géomètre's statistical account of the average life-span is no less diverting. Given an average life expectancy in Paris of somewhere between twenty-two and twenty-three years, and having subtracted ten for childhood, and half of the remainder for sleep and boredom, one is left with six and a half in which to experience everything else — which leaves about three years of tolerable existence.

In these ways statistics are presented as being totally at variance

---

[7] The divisions of the *conte* may helpfully be numbered as follows: I ('Un vieillard . . .'); II ('Désastre de l'homme aux quarante écus'); III ('Entretien avec un géomètre'); IV ('Aventure avec un carme'); V ('Audience de monsieur le contrôleur général'); VI ('Lettre à l'homme aux quarante écus'); VII ('Nouvelles douleurs occasionnées par les nouveaux systèmes'); VIII ('Mariage de l'homme aux quarante écus'); IX ('L'Homme aux quarante écus, devenu père, raisonne sur les moines'); X ('Des impôts payés à l'étranger'); XI ('Des proportions'); XII ('De la vérole'); XIII ('Grande querelle'); XIV ('Scélérat chassé'); XV ('Le bons sens de M. André'); XVI ('D'un bon souper chez M. André').

with real experience, which leads on to the second function of the Homme aux quarante écus: he is to be the subject of what Voltaire in *L'Ingénu* (and in a different context in *Le Taureau blanc*) calls a 'métamorphose' (317). The statistical entity is to be fleshed out and given a reality by narrative which the inhumanity of demographic surmise has denied him. At the beginning he is simply the Homme aux quarante écus who exists by virtue of statistical calculation: and within the tale he has substance only in so far as he is its narrator. For the moment, like Candide and the Ingénu, he is a piece of white paper on which experience has yet to write itself. He is passive: he is spoken to by the 'vieillard', he is taxed, he is put in prison ('et on fit la guerre comme on put': 417), he is patronized by the fat financier. Mentally, however, he is beginning to be active: 'je commence à réfléchir' (416). Now he asks questions, of the financier, of the Géomètre, of the Carmelite. In section III he exists as both narrator and interlocutor: at the end of section IV he begins to tell stories to others. In section V he is active enough to petition the Contrôleur Général and achieves financial independence through being pardoned and awarded damages.

With this financial independence he emerges as a person in his own right: he ceases to be the first-person narrator and becomes the centre of other people's attention, at once a model (sect. VI) and a pupil (sects. VI, VIII–XII) and ultimately a much-admired, intimate friend (end of sect. XI, end of sect. XV, and sect. XVI). By the beginning of section VIII he is fully a member of the human race: 'L'homme aux quarante écus s'étant beaucoup formé, et ayant fait une petite fortune, épousa une jolie fille qui possédait cent écus de rente' (442: evidently his wife is worth two and a half average women). Moreover this wife is to bear him a child: the sterile statistic is to become a father. Upon achieving parenthood (exactly halfway through the story) 'il commença à se croire un homme de quelque poids dans l'Etat' (448). He is now maturely human in his response to events, both laughing with detached scorn at the idea that France should annually pay monetary tribute to the Vatican (453–4) and pleading with emotional involvement for a just and beneficent use of parish priests: 'ce digne homme s'attendrissait en prononçant ces paroles; il aimait sa patrie et était idolâtre du bien public' (454). He is reduced to tears of pity and outrage by the sight of an innocent miller being tortured for a confession and is now of one mind with his tutor the Géomètre (who has become the narrator): 'nous plaignions la nature humaine, l'homme aux quarante écus et moi' (457).

Once he has read *Candide* and spoken to a doctor (sect. XII), his education is almost complete: 'c'est ainsi que l'homme aux quarante écus se formait, comme on dit, "l'esprit et le cœur"' (464). He is now worthy of three accolades from his creator: description as 'notre nouveau philosophe' (465), a visit to Paris, and, above all, the humanity of a name: 'On l'appelait M. André, c'était son nom de baptême' (465). In Paris he becomes the ideal *philosophe*, and this — most importantly — by virtue of being a *conteur*. The dispute which has arisen as to whether or not Marcus Aurelius was an 'honnête homme' and whether he has gone to hell, purgatory, or merely limbo threatens to create 'un schisme, comme du temps des cent et un contes de ma mère l'oie' (466). But M. André, 'excellent citoyen' (466) that he now is, brings the opposing parties together for supper and achieves a reconciliation through narrative:

Il aurait fait souper gaiement ensemble un Corse et un Génois, un représentant de Genève et un négatif, le muphti et un archevêque. Il fit tomber habilement les premiers coups que les disputants se portaient, en détournant la conversation et en faisant un conte très agréable qui réjouit également les damnants et les damnés. (467)

For the first time in the story he is endowed with a physical feature: 'une physionomie ronde qui est tout à fait persuasive' (467). The statistic has a body; the round number has a round face. Not that the power to reconcile should be confused with indiscriminate tolerance: the despatch of the 'anti-philosophe' in Section XIV of the story shows that. His judgement is now almost impeccable: 'On ne peut guère tromper M. André. Plus il était simple et naïf quand il était l'homme aux quarante écus, plus il est devenu avisé quand il a connu les hommes' (468). This representative of 'un temps où la raison humaine commence à se perfectionner' (469) has become 'au fait de toutes les affaires de l'Europe, et surtout des progrès de l'esprit humain' (469). He can even treat the Parisian narrator to an allegory of the voyage of reason (469–70) which bears no little resemblance to Voltaire's own *Eloge historique de la raison* to be written seven years later.

His apotheosis comes in the final section where he presides over a supper-party which is the epitome of civilized living. This illustrates that the reconciliation of opposites should not be taken to mean a return to some presumed uniformity of opinion or experience. When the narrator speaks of a 'schisme, comme du temps des cent et un contes de ma mère l'oie', his mock-serious elaboration of the point suggests that this is just another 'fable' belonging to the 'siècle d'or': 'C'est une chose bien épouvantable qu'un schisme; cela signifie "division dans les opinions", et jusqu'à ce moment fatal tous les hommes avaient pensé de même' (466). How dull such a world must have been. The final supper-party shows that enlightened reconciliation tolerates and even encourages a plurality of opinion and experience. Like the community described at the end of *Candide*, M. André's guests are a decidedly mixed and international bag. French Catholic, Dutch Protestant, Swiss Calvinist, Portuguese Jew, and Greek Orthodox dine together as amicably as the lion lay down with the lamb.

THE CONVIVIAL *CONTE*

Contrary to the general view, therefore, there is a strong narrative line in *L'Homme aux quarante écus*. At the same time the diachronic development from statistic to ideal human being is complemented by a synchronic repetition of the opposition between system and reality. The satire focuses in turn on the systems of statistics, which posit phenomena that do not exist; of militarism, which spreads the pox and promotes a war in which nothing can be gained and much lost; of Christianity, which allows a monk both to withhold alms and to exact tithes; of agricultural theories that ruin; of biological and geological theories that reduce man variously to the level of a baboon or a cornflour eel, and even substantiate the 'fable' of the Flood; of metaphysics, with its monads, its *plenum*, and its *materia subtilis*; of genetics, which turns children into eggs, women into ambulant glands, and gestation into an ungainly jostle for position; of law, medicine, and theology, each with its own special absurdities.

In place of 'systems' we are offered the ethos of the Enlightenment: moderation, scepticism, discernment, and reading. 'Gardez le milieu en tout. Rien de trop' (432); 'il est fort sage de douter' (447); 'il faut en user avec eux [i.e. 'des livres'] comme avec les hommes, choisir les plus raisonnables, les examiner, et ne se rendre jamais qu'à l'évidence' (453). And we are offered the power of the *conte*. Where systems put people in prison, and torture them, and bankrupt the state (sect. X), the *conte* brings peace and harmony to troubled disputants. As the allegorical figure of 'la philosophie' points out, France is actually governed by the book, by 'l'ordonnance civile, le code militaire, et l'Evangile' (460).[8] Yet these are instruments of oppression, words to be accepted without question or challenge. Rather, Philosophy exhorts: 'que toute la France lise les bons livres' (459); and the clear implication of *L'Homme aux quarante écus* is that there is no better book than itself.

Just as the Homme aux quarante écus reaches perfection by becoming a *conteur* and hosting a supper-party that at once instructs and delights, so *L'Homme aux quarante écus* achieves perfection as a text of the Enlightenment by telling a story in the manner of a supper-party. It takes a symposium to beat the systems.[9] Just as 'c'est le sort de toutes les conversations de passer d'un sujet à l'autre' (474), so does this *conte*; just as the Parisian narrator at the end exclaims: 'De quoi ne parla-t-on point dans ce repas', so perhaps do we of the polemical feast which Voltaire has provided. For the fare is certainly copious, and Henri Bénac is not alone in having been reminded of the comic encyclopedism of Flaubert's *Bouvard et Pécuchet*.[10] The reader's reaction may well be that of M. André: 'il me prend quelquefois des envies de rire de tout ce qu'on m'a dit' (447). Every branch of intellectual enquiry, every country of consequence, every class of society, every walk of life is there: from alchemy to sociology, from Mexico to Russia, from king to convict, from theologian to basket-weaver, the Voltairian panorama stretches with comprehensive ease. But whereas Flaubert's two protagonists must complete the syllabus in order that their ultimate decision once more to become copyists should represent an indictment of all human aspiration to knowledge, Voltaire's Everyman must complete his education in order to be thoroughly up-to-date and poised on the very frontiers of knowledge. Only on such a basis can his rejection of academic quibbling in favour of urbanity and wit carry due conviction.

L'Homme aux quarante écus imitates a supper-party not only in its wide-ranging scope, but also in its polyphony. While we are denied

[8] Cf. the *Homélies prononcées à Londres en 1765* (1767): 'Les livres gouvernent le monde' (3ᵉ Homélie: 'Sur l'Interprétation de l'Ancien Testament', *Mélanges*, 1144).
[9] Moreover Voltaire envisaged this story as an after-dinner entertainment: 'Cependant, Monsieur, si vous jugiez qu'il y eût dans cette rapsodie quelque plaisanterie bonne ou mauvaise qui pût le faire digérer gaiement après ses tristes dîners [of the duc de Choiseul], je hasarderai de mettre à ses pieds, comme aux vôtres, l'homme aux quarante écus' (D14719: 3 Feb. 1768, to Chardon).
[10] *Romans et contes*, ed. Bénac, p. v.

the song with which M. and Mme André's evening is said to end, the story nevertheless provides an extraordinary gamut of narrative viewpoints, voices, registers, and intertextual echoes. Whereas the Establishment is said to govern despotically through the univocal texts of the Bible and the 'code militaire', Voltaire invites his reader to think independently by liberating his writing from generic affiliation and by devolving his authorial power. Hence the dialogic interplay of textual forms: pseudo-oral narrative, letter, manuscript extract, theatrical script, published 'discours', etc. Hence the bevy of narrators: the Homme aux quarante écus (I–V), a fellow-victim of newfangled notions (VI), a caricature of Voltaire himself (VII), a dead-pan, anonymous narrator for the delicate matter of how babies are made (VIII), the Géomètre (IX–XI/?XII), a further anonymous narrator (XII/?XIII–XIV), and lastly a like-minded Parisian (XV–XVI). Mediated through these narrators are the further voices of the reactionary 'vieillard' (sect. I), the 'avocat général de Dauphiné', the allegorical figure of 'Philosophie' (both in sect. XI), and the 'chirurgien-major' (sect. XII). Each is watched over by an unpredictable provider of footnotes rather as one might be interrupted by a pedant at the dinner-table.

Haunting the feast are a number of intertextual ghosts, whose words are quoted *verbatim* or to whom allusion is explicitly or implicitly made: Le Mercier de la Rivière, of course (417), but also Boileau (415) and Horace (431), St Matthew (435) and *Candide* (461), to name but a very few. As any annotated edition reveals, there is an abundance of such references, and their effect is further to erode Voltaire's privileged position as author and unique provider of sacred writ and to implicate this *conte* in a universal and eternal dialogue of reason. Moreover this dialogue is seen to take place at — and between — different linguistic registers. The participants contribute variously in Latin or the vernacular, in verse or in prose, in high rhetoric (of the 'avocat-général') or low colloquialisms (for example 'trigaud' (416), 'badaud' (419)), in the technical language of statistical calculation and the biological sciences, or in the easy, conversational manner of the Homme aux quarante écus at the beginning and the Parisian at the end.

Indeed attention is called to the slipperiness of language itself as a medium for dialogue: 'la "haute science" ' may be as full of charlatanry (419) as the lowest trick; the monk intent on exacting his 'dîmes' from the citizens in his parish refers to them feudally as 'ses paysans' (434); 'se sauver' (450) is all right for a monk but not for a soldier. Yet linguistic accuracy is of the utmost importance, as may be inferred from the humorous theory that the Jesuits were expelled from France because one of their number mistranslated a single verb in Horace (453).

MODERNITY

What *L'Homme aux quarante écus* demonstrates, therefore, is that in modelling the *conte* on the polyphonic disorder of a supper-party Voltaire was seeking to match his literary form to the Enlightenment values which the tale advocates. One of these values is modernity. Lurking among the many disputes which this *conte* seeks to contain lies the Querelle des anciens et des modernes. The opening section opposes a 'vieillard, qui "toujours plaint le présent et vante le passé"' and the Homme aux quarante écus, who is the man of the moment. The description of the 'vieillard' is a quotation from Boileau, and his sentiments are those of Fénelon, author of *Télémaque*. As has already been seen, the narrative line of *L'Homme aux quarante écus* leads from M. André's incipient scepticism ('Le raisonnement de ce vieillard, bon ou mauvais, fit sur moi une impression profonde … Je ne sais s'il avait raison en tout': 416) to his being sure in his judgement and bang up-to-date ('Il est aujourd'hui au fait de toutes les affaires de l'Europe, et surtout des progrès de l'esprit humain': 469). Unlike those of Ovid (439), M. André's is a thoroughly modern metamorphosis; and this coming up-to-date is reflected in the chronology of the story, which emerges at the end from a temporal penumbra and moves briskly from 'la semaine passée' (beginning of sect. XIV) to 'mardi dernier' (XV) to 'hier' (XVI).

At the final supper-party Boileau is mentioned again, and the conversation engages with the past/present opposition in the sphere of literature: 'On remarqua surtout avec beaucoup de sagacité que la plupart des ouvrages littéraires du siècle présent, ainsi que les conversations, roulent sur l'examen des chefs-d'œuvre du dernier siècle. Notre mérite est de discuter de leur mérite' (474). There is no little self-irony here on the part of the author of chapter 12 of *L'Ingénu* (let alone *Le Siècle de Louis XIV*), but the point is serious and one often made by Voltaire.[11] What *L'Homme aux quarante écus*

---

[11]   e.g. in *La Princesse de Babylone* (RC, 400).

does, however, is to break free of the literary past, to reject any sense of inferiority, and to assert the virtues of modernity. Just as M. André has no Latin but does have a brain, so this *conte* flouts the canonical in the cause of truth. The passage just quoted continues: 'Nous sommes comme des enfants déshérités qui font le compte du bien de leurs pères. On avoua que la philosophie avait fait de très grands progrès, mais que la langue et le style s'étaient un peu corrompus.' More self-irony, not to mention a possible pun on 'compte' (and even on 'bien'). The *conte philosophique* is a bastard genre, conceived outside the legitimizing prescriptions of neo-classical poetics and sinful in its disregard for the virtues of 'good taste'. It favours Tasso against Homer, the conscious absurdities of Rabelais against the revered nonsense of Greek myth, the flaws of Montesquieu against the 'fatras' of Grotius (473–4). And, as we have seen, it prefers itself to Plato's *Symposium*, not to mention the feasts of Atticus and Lucullus (472–3).

There is, of course, the danger that this rejection of the traditional canon leads to mere superficiality. But Voltaire is alive to the impending charge:

les esprits superficiels préfèrent l'héroïsme extravagant aux grandes vues d'un législateur; . . . la plupart des lecteurs aiment mieux s'amuser que s'instruire. De là vient que cent femmes lisent *Les Mille et une Nuits* contre une qui lit deux chapitres de Locke. (475)

Superficiality is in the mind of the reader. The aim of the *conteur* is to instruct as he pleases. The ancestry of the *conte* is popular and oral, not bookish and academic. Metaphysical, religious, and economic systems take themselves seriously and purport to be true, yet turn out to be pernicious fictions, sinister 'fables' of reason. The *conte*, on the other hand, like the literary figures it champions, flaunts its implausibility and punctures the pompous: it brings laughter, it breeds tolerance, it humanizes.

For all that the *conte* enjoys considerable structural freedom, however, this particular one (like all of Voltaire's) is held together by a unifying thread: here the story of M. André's education. As if to remind the reader of the distance travelled, the story comes full circle by ending as it began with references both to seventeenth-century literature and to the science of demography. But Boileau has been replaced by the *conte*, and a theory of population by a living human being. Common to both themes is the question of creation. At the beginning of the extract from the manuscripts 'd'un vieux solitaire', Voltaire's *alter ego* prefaces his onslaught on systems with the following remark:

Je vois que, si de bons citoyens se sont amusés à gouverner les Etats et à se mettre à la place des rois, si d'autres se sont crus des Triptolèmes et des Cérès, il y en a de plus fiers qui se sont mis sans façon à la place de Dieu, et qui ont créé l'univers avec leur plume, comme Dieu le créa autrefois par la parole. (439)

The systems he goes on to deride concern the origins of the earth, and the extract is followed by the section in which M. André and the Géomètre review theories of our human origins. In each case arrogant human minds are presuming to construct grandiose theories about the nature of God's creation. Has perhaps Voltaire, in *L'Homme aux quarante écus*, substituted for these arrogant rewritings of Genesis his own more humble, less dogmatic account of how to create a happy citizen? Cleaner air, a healthier diet, more exercise, breast-feeding, inoculation (423): it is an agenda that might have been written for the 'bien-pensants' of our own day, except that the programme also includes marriage and lots of children as the means to an increase in the male individual's material prosperity. For all that the openness of Voltaire's text may allow the reader to jib at the message of bourgeois liberalism if he or she wishes, it is nevertheless clear that the literary creation of the *conte* emerges from *L'Homme aux quarante écus* with rather more credit than the fantastical creations of the fashionable intellectuals whom it ridicules.

For these intellectuals, too, were bang up-to-date; and it is easy to lose sight of the fact from a late-twentieth-century perspective in which the medium of ridicule may seem only slightly less antiquarian than its objects. As the invitation from Catherine of Russia indicates, Le Mercier de la Rivière's ideas, and those of the Physiocrats generally, were potentially very influential: hence the urgent need to throw some cold water on them. In doing so Voltaire finds himself in a difficult polemical position, for he is having to counter the new as opposed to the old. The deist who wanted to 'écraser l'infâme' could present himself as a modern believer in progress and an enemy of superstition, tradition, institutions, and fusty scholarship. Even when the enemy was the contemporary, voguish thought of Leibniz and Wolff, he had managed to suggest that it belonged to the past (and anyway its authors were German: look how clever they had been to

(modernity)

start the Seven Years War). But how to oppose his fellow *philosophes*, indeed how to oppose the new generation of *philosophes* who were in many respects his intellectual heirs? Voltaire's answer is to send up both his own elderliness and his own impatience with scientific hypothesizing, to offer an oblique reminder of his activities as a champion of human rights (on behalf of Calas and Sirven), and to make the humane, level-headed, practical-minded Géomètre his principal spokesman and narrator. Those aspects of the contemporary Voltaire legend that might have made his reader resistant are thus neutralized by being wittily recuperated in the text (the 'vieillard' of sect. I, the experimental farmer of sect. VI, the 'vieux solitaire' of sect. VII). At the same time the urbane Parisian narrator who befriends M. André at the end is a portrait of Voltaire's ideal reader, a man who would have no more truck with systems than Voltaire himself, a man who shuns the controversy that destroys empires (473) in favour of the conversation that unites 'la bonne compagnie' (475). This man is struck by the thought that whereas those great empires 'd'Occident et d'Orient' are gone, 'les ouvrages de Virgile, d'Horace et d'Ovide subsistent' (473). So, doubtless, is Voltaire. Political regimes may come and go, but literature survives – and survives to invite future generations of readers to its feast. Therein lies the hoped-for modernity of *L'Homme aux quarante écus* even though it attacks some aspects of the modern. In the event, a work which questions the human consequences of economic theories and the justice of a single tax universally applied may not have dated quite as quickly as one might have imagined. Nor, indeed, has the écu.

3
Fallen Fables

Après cela, messieurs les savants, faites
des calculs et des systèmes, ils seront
aussi faux les uns que les autres.

(472)

The lesson of *L'Homme aux quarante écus* is the lesson of all Voltaire's *contes*, and indeed for many commentators the principal message of the Enlightenment. In *The Philosophy of the Enlightenment*, for example, Ernst Cassirer stresses the way in which 'the thought of the Enlightenment again and again breaks through the rigid barriers of system and tries, especially among its greatest and most original minds, to escape this strict systematic discipline'.[1] For Cassirer the real originality of the Enlightenment lies not so much in what it thought as in how it thought; and he offers an account of what the eighteenth century meant by 'reason' which is particularly helpful for an understanding of Voltaire's *contes*:

In the great metaphysical systems of [the seventeenth century] — those of Descartes and Malebranche, of Spinoza and Leibniz — reason is the realm of the 'eternal verities', of those truths held in common by the human and the divine mind. What we know through reason, we therefore behold 'in God'. Every act of reason means participation in the divine nature; it gives access to the intelligible world. The eighteenth century takes reason in a different and more modest sense. It is no longer the sum total of 'innate ideas' given prior to all experience, which reveal the absolute essence of things. Reason is now looked upon rather as an acquisition than as a heritage. It is not the treasury of the mind in which the truth like a minted coin lies stored; it is rather the original intellectual force which guides the discovery and determination of truth. This determination is the seed and the indispensable presupposition of all real certainty. The whole eighteenth century understands reason in this sense; not as a sound body of knowledge, principles,

---

[1] *The Philosophy of the Enlightenment*, tr. Fritz C. A. Koelln and James P. Pettegrove (Princeton, NJ, 1931), p. ix.

and truths, but as a kind of energy, a force which is fully comprehensible only in its agency and effects.[2]

Reason, then, is a process, the means to a systematic destruction of systems. The Voltairian *conte* is also a process rather than a 'treasury . . . in which the truth like a minted coin lies stored': his fables teach us not what the reason but how to reason. In *L'Homme aux quarante écus* this process is one of humanization and education, and its movement from the stupidity of systems to the 'sagacité' (474) of the supper-party is paradigmatic of the majority of Voltaire's stories. In this respect, at least, they may legitimately be seen as essentially repetitive in their principal polemical and ideological strategy — as indeed Voltaire makes humorously plain in *L'Homme aux quarante écus* in the concluding remarks of the 'vieux solitaire': 'Je suis bien vieux; j'aime quelquefois à répéter mes contes, afin de les inculquer mieux dans la tête des petits garçons, pour lesquels je travaille depuis si longtemps' (442).

Broadly speaking, the typical Voltairian *conte* begins by introducing a theory, prejudice, or complacent assumption. Through the eyes and experience of an initially innocent observer this 'system' is juxtaposed with the facts of life, with the result that the observer's outlook is gradually transformed and he is brought to adopt a provisional *modus vivendi* based on moderation and discernment and a scepticism which does not prevent useful, practical action. In Voltaire's hands the *conte* is thus an instrument of demythification, of 'defabulation', which inculcates a habit of mind more than it illustrates a series of aphoristic truths. Typically his *contes* demonstrate that systems are an unwarranted and unsustainable imposition of false order on the facts of life, and they trace a coming to terms: with human ignorance, with the contingencies of living (or is it providence?), with other people. They tend to depict an accommodation with reality, a movement from system to 'sagesse', from being 'philosophique' in the sense of being abstract and unemotionally logical to being 'philosophique' in the sense of being knocked about by life.

Protagonist and reader are, as it were, ejected from a fool's paradise, shown the lessons of experience, and left in a kind of sceptical

    [2] *The Philosophy of the Enlightenment*, 13. Cf. Peter Gay, *Voltaire's Politics. The Poet as Realist*, 2nd edn. (New Haven, Conn., and London, 1988), 26–8: 'The Enlightenment was not an Age of Reason but a Revolt against Rationalism' (27).

suspense. Paradoxically Voltaire uses fiction (in the sense of invented stories) to provide the empirical evidence, the facts of life, upon which the initial, illusory system founders, with the result that both protagonist and reader are brought to believe not in a theory or an abstraction but in the evidence of their own eyes (even if, like the 'crocheteur borgne', Memnon, or Pangloss, they have only one). They are subjected to what Jean Starobinski calls 'la riposte du monde à l'euphorie du système'.[3]

In narrative terms this process is reflected in a movement from 'fable', in the sense of what is fantastical, naïve, implausible, to *conte*, the Voltairian fable of reason which presents a veiled lesson of experience and ends with an invitation to a plural response. Thus, for example, *Zadig* opens with an assertion of its Oriental affiliations in the 'Epître dédicatoire' and proceeds to employ the structure of the Oriental tale as apparently corresponding to some providential order: all will be well in the end, though we cannot yet quite see how. But then the ending (of 1752) undermines this. The two appended chapters bring us, by their close approximation to the style of the *Thousand and One Nights*, stylistically full circle back to the register of the 'Epître dédicatoire'; but now the Oriental tale serves as an expression of perplexed uncertainty. The future is no longer full of Eastern promise, merely more of the same: the dirty tricks of destiny. Voltaire's sceptical *conte* has replaced the starry-eyed fable.

Similarly, in *Candide*, the marvellous world of chivalric romance is replaced by the sober realism of the garden suburb. The typical sequence of trial by ordeal — uncertain birth, capture, duel, disguise, abduction, chase, storm, shipwreck, piracy, captivity, recognition, release, and reunion — is shown to be no more bizarre than the manifold manifestations of man's (and God's) inhumanity to man and the systems used to justify it. The 'fables' of romance and Optimism become the *conte* of utilitarian survival.

What we see, therefore, in many of Voltaire's *contes*, is that the main part of the story, the process of disillusion and debunking, is a kind of Fall as protagonist and reader alike eat of the Tree of Knowledge. Such an analogy may not be entirely fanciful. As a genre the fable originated in primitive allegory which presented animals

---

[3] 'Sur le style philosophique de *Candide*', *Comparative Literature*, 28 (1976), 198; reprinted in *Le Remède dans le mal. Critique et légitimation de l'artifice à l'âge des lumières* (Paris, 1989), 129.

and plants speaking like human beings;[4] and this is exactly what one
finds in *La Princesse de Babylone*, where the phoenix belonging to
Amazan tells Formosante of this ideal place, the 'pays des Gangarides', where men and animals still converse to their mutual educational benefit. Mocking the naïvety of ancient fable, Voltaire here
sends it up by taking its allegories as literally true. Thus the phoenix
reveals that animals have stopped talking in the rest of the world
because 'les hommes ont pris enfin l'habitude de nous manger, au
lieu de converser et de s'instruire avec nous' (363). If Formosante
does not believe him, she has only to read 'Les fables de votre ancien
Locman, traduites en tant de langues' which provide 'un témoignage
éternellement subsistant de l'heureux commerce que vous avez eu
autrefois avec nous. Elles commencent toutes par ces mots: "Du
temps que les bêtes parlaient"' (363–4).

The fable, then, is associated with a mythical realm and a mythical
age ('du temps que les bêtes parlaient'); it represents the fantastical
epoch before the Enlightenment, of which Voltaire's own *contes* are
the modern, fallen fables. Locman has given way to the new man,
Locke. And this will be the lesson of *Le Taureau blanc*. Like *La
Princesse de Babylone* it takes fables literally, here the many 'fables'
contained within the Old Testament. In this ancient Egyptian world
the local fauna are positively garrulous, but the heroine belongs to
the Age of Enlightenment. Amaside prefers Locke to Locman, and
when the Serpent tells her stories, she insists on 'vraisemblance'
(553–4). Like the Serpent's ensuing tale, the Voltairian *conte* is an
onslaught on taboo. Wielded as an invaluable weapon in Voltaire's
long campaign against bigotry and intolerance and in favour of open-
minded enquiry and debate, it is a 'fallen' fable in the sense that,
whereas the fable of old appealed to a childlike credulity and fostered
the passive acceptance of incontrovertible moral truths, the *conte
philosophique* is like an apple plucked from the Tree of Knowledge
and handed to us by the Serpent himself that we should gorge ourselves and feel the nakedness of our prejudice. We should eat, question, and consider.

In summary, the Voltairian *conte* mocks and undermines systems,
those 'fables' of reason concocted by metaphysicians, theologians,
economists, and rationalists of every sort. It substitutes the authentic

---

[4]   See Alex Preminger (ed.), *Princeton Encyclopedia of Poetry and Poetics*, 2nd edn.
(London and Basingstoke, 1975), 269.

fable of reason, which is the story of how the human mind gathers evidence, weighs it, and reaches conclusions which are acceptable only because they are provisional. It provides not *the* answer, but the means to *an* answer. Like Flaubert, Voltaire believed that 'la bêtise consiste à vouloir conclure'.[5] True human 'esprit' means an open mind and the wit that comes from an awareness of the surprises, paradoxes, and ironies of the human condition. System-building derives from a nostalgic desire for the unity of a prelapsarian world in which all were of one mind: Enlightenment 'sagesse' lies in the recognition that it takes all sorts, and that it is usually better, whatever the issue, to be in two minds. In the cause of humanity the supper-table is altogether more salutary than the drawing-board.

I now propose to trace Voltaire's career as a *conteur* in chronological order, paying detailed attention to each individual story in turn. Interestingly, a similar pattern will emerge. His earlier stories tend to be more schematic and one-tracked in their presentation: *Micromégas* is 'about' relativity, *Zadig* is 'about' goodness defeated, *Le Monde comme il va* is 'about' mixture. Gradually they fill out with the hurly-burly and muddle of human experience, and *Candide* and *L'Ingénu* both conceal considerable complexity beneath their easy-going surfaces. From *L'Homme aux quarante écus* onwards the moral complexity begins to be matched by an increasing complexity of form such that the Voltairian *conte* comes to resemble nothing more than that 'ragoût exquis' which so delighted Flaubert.[6] Moreover, just as each story breaks down a system on the anvil of the facts, so too the Voltairian *contes* hammer away successively at the hallowed clichés of narrative before proposing a new form of story-telling that is all apparent improvisation, orality, disjointed textual fragments. The *conte* of ingenious allegory gradually becomes the *conte* of conversation. In so doing it approximates more and more closely to the eighteenth-century ideal of good manners which the narrator of *Tristram Shandy* so eloquently describes:

Writing, when properly managed (as you may be sure I think mine is), is but a different name for conversation. As no one who knows what he is about in good company would venture to talk all; so no author who understands the just boundaries of decorum and good breeding would presume to think all.

5 Letter of 4 Sept. 1850 (to Louis Bouilhet) and *passim*.
6 Letter of 7 June 1844 (to Louis de Cormenin).

The truest respect which you can pay to the reader's understanding is to halve this matter amicably, and leave him something to imagine, in his turn, as well as yourself.[7]

[7] Bk. 2, ch. 11.

II
The Voyage of Reason and the Problem of Evil

Mais en philosophie il faut se défier de ce qu'on croit entendre trop aisément, aussi bien que des choses qu'on n'entend pas.

(*Lett. phil.*, 102)

4
Party Games

Le Crocheteur borgne and *Cosi-Sancta*

. . . ce n'est que par des contes
qu'on réussit dans le monde.

(551)

Given that Voltaire recited verse at the age of 4 and had written his
first tragedy by the age of 12, there is no reason to suppose that he
was not already telling tales before the seventeenth century was out.
Of his surviving *contes*, however, it is now believed that *Le Crocheteur
borgne* and *Cosi-Sancta* were the first to be composed.[1] Although
neither was published until the posthumous Kehl edition in 1784,[2]
both are now believed to date back to the period between October
1712 and December 1718 during which, when he was not being
banished from the capital or thrown into the Bastille, Voltaire was
a regular guest of the duchesse du Maine at Sceaux.

Despite her diminutive stature, the blonde Louise de Bourbon,
granddaughter of the Grand Condé and married to Louis XIV's
eldest legitimized son (by Mme de Montespan), was far from diminutive in either her self-regard or her political ambitions. As a princess
of the blood she liked to hold court in authoritative and regal style,
and for her gratification she had founded her own Ordre de la
Mouche à miel in 1703. She was the self-styled 'reine des abeilles'
and 'dictatrice perpétuelle' of this order, to whom newly inducted
members would swear an oath of allegiance before being presented

---

[1] See Jacqueline Hellegouarc'h, 'Mélinade ou la duchesse du Maine. Deux contes
de jeunesse de Voltaire: *Le Crocheteur borgne* et *Cosi-Sancta*', *Revue d'histoire littéraire
de la France*, 78 (1978), and 'Genèse d'un conte de Voltaire', *SVEC* 176 (1979). Her
findings have been unconvincingly challenged by R. Galliani, 'La date de composition
du *Crocheteur borgne* par Voltaire', *SVEC* 217 (1983).

[2] Apparently unbeknownst to the Kehl editors a bowdlerized version of *Le Crocheteur borgne* had been published in the *Journal des dames* in 1774. This version is
reproduced in *RC*, 677–81.

with a medal bearing her profile and attached to a yellow ribbon. Infringements against the rules of her elegant dictatorship were duly punished, one particular forfeit being the telling of a story. The resulting improvised tale, generally involving the duchesse and others of the company, would be read out and copies of it subsequently distributed among the interested parties. Such were the origins of *Le Crocheteur borgne* — and the reason why a manuscript version survived to be published.

The duchesse's high life reached its zenith in a series of sixteen all-night parties known as the Nuits blanches, which were held between 31 July 1714 and 15 May 1715. To while away the small hours the house-guests were required to put on entertainments for their hostess, the genre — and perhaps the subject also — occasionally being determined by a ballot arranged by the duchesse herself. Thus it fell to Mme de Montauban, mother of one of the duchesse's ladies-in-waiting, to produce not a comedy, or an opera, or a ballet, but a 'nouvelle' or 'proverbe';[3] and the theme was 'Un petit mal pour un grand bien'. Having perhaps heard Voltaire regale the company with *Le Crocheteur borgne* but in any case presumably aware of his skills as a story-teller, the lady delegated her task. And such were the origins of *Cosi-Sancta*.

In the first instance, therefore, both works were clearly 'œuvres de circonstance', and even 'œuvres à clé'. In *Le Crocheteur borgne* the name and attributes of Mélinade, 'la grande princesse', reflect a scarcely veiled tribute to the duchesse, while Voltaire's implicit self-portrait as a drunken one-eyed porter from Baghdad who wishes he could be a handsome prince is a piece of urbane 'galanterie' and self-deprecation. *Cosi-Sancta* was in part intended to mock the duchesse's husband, who liked to spend his time compiling the sayings of St Augustine;[4] and both the heroine's husband Capito and her lover Ribaldos may well have been knowingly named and characterized.[5] Evident also, and particularly in *Le Crocheteur borgne*, are allusions of a literary kind, designed to put an audience flatteringly on its mettle: the magic ring which recalls Ariosto's *Orlando furioso*,

    [3] See René Pomeau, *Voltaire en son temps. I. D'Arouet à Voltaire 1694–1734* (Oxford, 1985), 87, n. 55 for this last suggestion.
    [4] See Christiane Mervaud, 'Voltaire, saint Augustin et le duc du Maine, aux sources de *Cosi-Sancta*', SVEC 228 (1984). Pomeau describes the duc du Maine as 'boiteux et pied-bot, mou, veule' (*D'Arouet à Voltaire*, 82).
    [5] See Pomeau, *D'Arouet à Voltaire*, 88.

the parallel with Charles Perrault's *La Belle et la bête*, the several similarities with Hamilton's *Zénéyde*, and, most obviously, the pastiche of the *Thousand and One Nights*.[6] In *Cosi-Sancta* the use of prophecy and the emphasis on the number three recall both the *Thousand and One Nights* and the world of Perrault, while the explicit allusion to St Augustine and the *City of God*, together with the implicit reference to Pierre Bayle's *Dictionnaire historique et critique* add philosophical spice.[7]

In essence *Le Crocheteur borgne* is a titillating tale of how a great lady may enjoy multiple orgasms should she chance to be waylaid by a man of the people;[8] while *Cosi-Sancta* urbanely asserts the veniality of adultery, even if one's parents do happen to be Jansenists. But such crudity is veiled in an ambiance of debonair worldliness which expresses itself in the guise of Oriental fatalism. Mesrour is no proto-revolutionary sexual athlete but the very model of a well-regulated existence. One-eyed he may be, but he is 'content de son état' (3):

L'argent et l'appétit lui venaient toujours en proportion de l'exercice qu'il faisait; il travaillait le matin, mangeait et buvait le soir, dormait la nuit, et regardait tous ses jours comme autant de vies séparées, en sorte que le soin de l'avenir ne le troublait jamais dans la jouissance du présent. Il était (comme vous le voyez) tout à la fois borgne, crocheteur et philosophe. (3)

When his erotic dream is terminated by a literal bucket of cold water, he is not filled with regret or dissatisfaction with his humble lot, but rather with renewed affection for the 'eau-de-vie' which brought him such a vision of bliss. Not for him the Proustian notion that 'les vrais paradis sont les paradis qu'on a perdus'. Rather he is an early representative of the ethos of *Le Mondain* (1736): 'le vrai paradis est où je suis'. And so too, it seems, is the Princess. Raped she may have been: 'mais, comme elle était juste, elle bénissait sûrement le destin de ce que toute infortune porte avec elle sa consolation' (6). In similar manner Cosi-Sancta may swear at her priest and find it difficult to envisage how she will be canonized for a triple infidelity, but she too decides to take life as it comes: 'Mais, ayant

---

[6] Antoine Galland's French translation was published between 1704 and 1717.

[7] Voltaire derived the plot of *Cosi-Sancta* from the article 'Acindynus' in the *Dictionnaire*, where Bayle refers to St Augustine's *De sermone Domini in monte*. In *Cosi-Sancta* the story is considerably adapted, and St Augustine's version is recorded more faithfully by Père Toutatis in *L'Ingénu* (330).

[8] 'Les faiblesses de Mélinade lui reprenaient à chaque instant, et à chaque instant son amant reprenait des forces' (6).

bien fait réflexion qu'on ne peut vaincre sa destinée, elle s'abandonna à la Providence, qui la mena au but par les chemins du monde les plus honnêtes' (12).

Voltaire's first two stories may seem, therefore, no more than witty entertainments of a mildly risqué but ultimately unproblematic kind. Yet they contain further features which give them greater edge than one might expect from the average party game and which point forward to the narrative techniques of the later, more overtly philosophical *contes*. Mesrour's dream in *Le Crocheteur borgne* is at one level an entirely conventional narrative 'excuse' for implausibility and the means to a climactic 'twist' at the end. As later in *Le Blanc et le noir*, with which it shares several similarities, the dream also contributes to the Oriental flavour of the work (such dreams being a regular feature of the *Thousand and One Nights*). At another level, doubtless, it lends itself readily to a symbolic reading: the beautiful blonde princess driving her own carriage drawn by six white steeds (ostensibly to preserve her virtue but perhaps endangering it); the hunted wild animal which makes the horses bolt, the bit between their teeth; the dirty, one-eyed man who carries things on a long stick with a hook and cuts the traces of the horses' harness — saving the lady from one plunge into the abyss only to subject her to another. The duchesse du Maine and her less obtuse guests would have needed no magical foreknowledge of Freud to divine their story-teller's oblique bawdry.

More subtle, perhaps, is the dream within a dream which sees Mesrour transformed into a scantily-clad, two-eyed Adonis and his 'crochet' into a golden and bejewelled quiver ('le plaisir faisait seul sonner ses flèches': 7). Entry into the 'palais brillant' may not automatically suggest the sexual act, but when the princess is forbidden entry on her own and Mesrour is told: 'Frappe sans crainte' ('Il frappa, et aussitôt les portes s'ouvrirent d'elles-mêmes avec un grand bruit': 7), we are surely reminded of the rape: 'il fut brutal et heureux' (6). Paradise for Mesrour is to be 'maître de l'anneau' with a host of genies hastening, in blatantly symbolic terms, to 'baiser le doigt sacré auquel il le portait' (7).

The second part of Mesrour's dream thus retells the action of the first in more elevated (or displaced) terms. Unduly phallocentric as such an allegory may be, the fact remains that this part of the dream contains a secret message. In it the genies come also to 'prêter serment de fidélité' (7), a clear reference to the custom whereby eligible male guests swore an oath of allegiance to the duchesse du Maine upon being accepted into her Ordre de la Mouche à miel. Possession of the Princess is not enough: to occupy her queenly position of power would be paradise indeed. When Mesrour prays to Mohammed to grant him the 'faveur . . . d'être aux yeux de Mélinade ce qu'elle serait à mon œil s'il faisait jour' (6), Voltaire is giving himself the opportunity to portray the duchesse du Maine and her court in flattering terms. But he is also indulging in the presumptuous fantasy of being her master, and even possibly in the suggestion that a man's sexual power over a woman is a more authentic road to bliss (for both parties) than a woman's recumbent ascendancy 'sur sa chaise longue au milieu d'une foule de petits-maîtres' (5).

Temporarily reluctant to be a mere worker-bee to the duchesse's queen, Voltaire briefly reveals — as he always will in his *contes* — that there is a sting in his tale. But at once he covers his impertinence beneath an effusive profession of (Mesrour's) contentment with his lot. Voltaire, here in his very early twenties, was conscious of his starring role in such a gathering, but also willing to play the courtier and even to declare himself happy once more 'd'être au service de tous les bourgeois de Bagdad après avoir régné sur tous les génies' (8). The man who read his own *Œdipe* to the very same audience was no doubt mindful of his dependence on audience response.[9]

The bucket of water which puts an end to Mesrour's grandiose vision contains the holy water used by a devout Muslim for his fifth ablution before his fifth prayer. This passing sally at religious ritual strikes the first note of anti-clericalism in Voltaire's *contes*. The same tune is taken up again in *Cosi-Sancta*, where St Augustine, Jansenism, and the customs of the Early Church are the butt of Voltaire's satire. But the tune is as yet muted. The prophecy of the priest at Hippo is equated with oracles and fortune-telling (priestly prophecy in any case not being an everyday activity on the part of a 'curé'): and thanks to saving the lives of her husband, brother, and son by sleeping with a pro-consul, a brigand chief, and a rather unhippocratic doctor, Cosi-Sancta emerges as an implausible martyr to the demands of family life ('on trouva qu'une pareille femme était fort nécessaire dans une famille': 14) and is duly canonized for what is deemed, in

---

[9] Cf. Jacques Barchilon's alternative view that *Le Crocheteur borgne*, by showing sexual attraction to be potentially stronger than class barriers, is 'valid as social criticism'. See his 'Uses of the Fairy Tale in the Eighteenth Century', *SVEC* 24 (1963), 126–7. On the reading of *Œdipe* see Pomeau, *D'Arouet à Voltaire*, 102.

a deft Voltairian version of casuistical piety, to be mortification of the flesh.

The main thrust of the story, however, concerns destiny and — in clear anticipation of *Zadig* — the extraordinary turns that events may take against even our most considered expectations. Moreover, as also in *Zadig*, the point is made that virtue may as likely be rewarded with disaster as alleged vice may prove beneficial. Even in this early *œuvre de circonstance*, therefore, one has the makings of a *conte philosophique*; and, both in *Cosi-Sancta* and *Le Crocheteur borgne*, one can perceive, in embryonic form, the scheme of the Voltairian *conte* as described in the preceding section. Each story begins with a commonplace notion or habit which is then put to the test of experience and found wanting. *Le Crocheteur borgne* opens thus:

Nos deux yeux ne rendent pas notre condition meilleure; l'un nous sert à voir les biens, et l'autre les maux de la vie. Bien des gens ont la mauvaise habitude de fermer le premier, et bien peu ferment le second; voilà pourquoi il y a tant de gens qui aimeraient mieux être aveugles que de voir tout ce qu'ils voient. Heureux les borgnes qui ne sont privés que de ce mauvais œil qui gâte tout ce qu'on regarde! Mesrour en est un exemple. (3)

Here the youthful and successful Voltaire takes issue with the human tendency to wallow in gloom and despondency and, by implication perhaps, with the Christian doctrine of original sin and with Jansenist, or Pascalian, pessimism. Better, he argues, to look on the bright side, to turn a blind eye. The message may not be profound, nor the illustrative example greatly persuasive; but the Voltairian recipe is already at work. On the road to happiness, maturity is thought to entail the open-eyed dispelling of illusion: *Le Crocheteur borgne* queries that unthinking assumption.

Similarly, and even more explicitly, *Cosi-Sancta* begins: 'C'est une maxime faussement établie, qu[e] ...'. All Voltaire's *contes* could open with those words. In this case the alleged maxim runs: 'il n'est pas permis de faire un petit mal dont un plus grand bien pourrait résulter' (9). Obviously this raises the question of ends and means, as well as that of whether evil is absolute or quantifiable. Like *Le Crocheteur borgne*, therefore, *Cosi-Sancta* is also a debate about the appropriate human response to the problem of evil. Once more the message may seem glib and the illustration absurd; but again the formula is at work, this time with the central issue highlighted as the subtitle and repeated at the very end in the form of Cosi-Sancta's epitaph.[10] Here, however, the formula is reinforced by being repeated at the level of the plot itself. Cosi-Sancta's strict Jansenist upbringing has rendered her particularly set in her theological ways, so that she is — not surprisingly — prejudiced against the very possibility of her predicted canonization for a triple marital infidelity. Her beliefs allow her but one way of coming to terms with the incomprehensible: 'elle en demanda l'explication, croyant que ces paroles cachaient quelque sens mystique' (10). Only real life will provide the answer.

The main joke in *Cosi-Sancta* is at the expense of Jansenism, that doctrine espoused by Voltaire's hated father and despised elder brother and to which his own education at the Jesuit college of Louis le Grand had scarcely made him any more sympathetic. Being in some respects the Catholic equivalent of Calvinism in that it repudiated the efficacy of the human will, held that the bestowal of divine grace is predetermined, and was characterized by the moral austerity of its adherents, such a doctrine was anathema to Voltaire, who, at this stage, believed that human beings have free will and was himself a voluntary and enthusiastic participant in the pleasures which life has to offer, especially at Sceaux. He rejected the pessimism of its followers, notably Pascal, and considered their mental outlook to be one of sterile and inhumane narrow-mindedness. How better to ridicule their closed minds than to have a young girl from St Augustine's birthplace be predestined to sainthood for selfless promiscuity? In *L'Ingénu* he would later treat the same issue in greater depth and, to some extent, with pathos. For the moment the *conteur* was content to save Mme de Montauban the bother of making up a story for herself and to play on the anti-Jansenist sentiments of his audience for a sophisticated laugh.

Thus party games set Voltaire on the path to *Candide*, and many of the characteristics of his more 'serious' *contes philosophiques* are evident from the outset. The elegant and economical style; the witticisms ('il aurait fallu être aveugle pour ne pas voir que Mesrour était borgne': 3); the portrayal of sexual relations to comic ends; the reliance on national stereotype (Cosi-Sancta's husband is 'jaloux . . . comme un Vénitien': 9); the narrative subversion of abstract 'idées reçues'; the incongruous juxtaposition of the highbrow and the

---

[10] A similar narrative device is employed in *Le Crocheteur borgne*, where the final phrase recalls the opening sentence.

lowbrow; and, above all perhaps, the clear sense that beneath the easy surface of the story is another, more complex text which is constantly inviting not only the duchesse du Maine and her company but also future readers to play a hermeneutic game of hide-and-seek. Moreover, the two stories were composed as contributions to a bee; and the microcosmic society of Sceaux in which all joined together to instruct and entertain each other will be reflected, *mutatis mutandis*, at the end of *Zadig*, of *Candide*, and of *L'Homme aux quarante écus*, in the handpicked company with which the eponymous heroes surround themselves. Central to this vision of ideal human concourse is, from the outset, the supper-party. There is more to Mesrour's dream of paradise than sex:

Les deux amants entrèrent, au son de mille voix et de mille instruments, dans un vestibule de marbre de Paros; de là ils passèrent dans une salle superbe, où un festin délicieux les attendait depuis douze cent cinquante ans sans qu'aucun des plats fût encore refroidi: ils se mirent à table, et furent servis chacun par mille esclaves de la plus grande beauté; le repas fut entremêlé de concerts et de danses. (7)

5
Man in the Universe

Micromégas

Je peux porter une vue rapide sur tous les siècles,
tous les pays, et par conséquent sur toutes les
sottises de ce petit globe.

(Traité de métaphysique (1734))

Any account of Voltaire's development as a *conteur* is beset by the problem of dating, particularly for the period up to 1750. In the light of Jacqueline Hellegouarc'h's findings it has been possible to situate the first stages of this development with some conviction. But where next? Thanks to the memoirs of Longchamp, his secretary, it used to be thought that Voltaire's story-telling career did indeed begin in the company of the duchesse du Maine, but in 1746–7 and not *c*.1715.[1] But Longchamp's reminiscences have increasingly been contested: *Memnon ou la sagesse* and the *Histoire des voyages de Scarmentado*, for example, are now thought to have been written later, while *Le Monde comme il va* has been seen to date back, in conception at least, to 1739.

Nevertheless there is reason to suppose that renewed contact with the duchesse du Maine after the Jeu de la Reine affair[2] may have prompted a revival of Voltaire's interest in the writing of *contes*. Nostalgia would have played its part as the elderly 'dictatrice perpétuelle' sought to relive the heyday of the Ordre de la Mouche à miel; and Voltaire, like Micromégas only 'médiocrement affligé d'être banni d'une cour qui n'était remplie que de tracasseries et de petitesses' (20), may well have indulged his hostess with enthusiasm. It is plausible to suppose, for example, that *Zadig* began as a story created especially for the duchesse in 1746; that in it Voltaire took up the pastiche of the *Thousand and One Nights* where he had left off

---

[1]   Longchamp et Wagnière, *Mémoires sur Voltaire*, 2 vols. (Paris, 1826), ii. 140.
[2]   See Vaillot, *Avec Madame Du Châtelet*, 289–97.

in *Le Crocheteur borgne*[3] and used it once more to convey a secret story (in this case how Voltaire/Zadig, having forsaken his quiet life of philosophical contemplation at Cirey, had encountered both flattering success and eventual disgrace at the royal court); and that then, at the duchesse's instigation, he published a first version of the story in 1747.[4] By the same token *Le Monde comme il va* may have begun as an elegant report to the duchesse on the nature of life in contemporary Paris.

The question remains: what should one regard as Voltaire's third *conte*?[5] The most profitable answer is the *Voyage du baron de Gangan*, which subsequently became *Micromégas* and was first published in mid-April 1751.[6] Voltaire sent a copy of the *Voyage du baron de Gangan* to Frederick of Prussia in June 1739, though it may date from a year or two earlier. No manuscript of this story has survived, and Voltaire's own description of it in his accompanying letter is characteristically dismissive: 'C'est une fadaise philosophique qui ne doit être lue que comme on se délasse d'un travail sérieux avec les bouffoneries d'Arlequin.'[7] But Frederick's reply makes clear the similarities with the published version of *Micromégas*.[8]

What is not clear, however, is how much of the *Voyage* survives in *Micromégas*, nor when, and how extensively, Voltaire revised it. Much has been written on the subject,[9] but definitive answers are impossible on the basis of the available evidence. The most plausible hypothesis is that *Micromégas* originated some time during the late 1730s and already contained the central device whereby human pre-

---

3   Thus the first chapter is entitled 'Le Borgne'. There is perhaps also an intentional echo of *Cosi-Sancta* in the observation that knowing lovers are able to conceal their emotions and so appear innocent, while innocent ones have yet to acknowledge the need for concealment and so reveal their 'guilt'. Cf. *RC*, 11 and 77.

4   See Longchamp et Wagnière, *Mémoires*, ii. 151–3.

5   *RC* has *Songe de Platon* next, for reasons given in Van den Heuvel's 'Notice' but which have since been powerfully challenged by R. Galliani, 'La date de composition du *Songe de Platon* par Voltaire', *SVEC* 219 (1983). Galliani concludes that 'le *Songe de Platon* n'a pu être conçu avant 1752–1753' (56). Galliani's arguments leave Van den Heuvel unmoved in his recent edition of *Songe de Platon* (1991): see *CW*, xvii. 539–42.

6   See D. W. Smith, 'The Publication of *Micromégas*', *SVEC* 219 (1983). Only two copies of this first edition were in fact sold (before it was withdrawn).

7   D2033 (*c.*20 June 1739).

8   D2042 (7 July 1739). For an analysis of these see *RC*, 694–5.

9   See in particular Ira O. Wade, *Voltaire's 'Micromégas'. A Study in the Fusion of Science, Myth, and Art* (Princeton, NJ, 1950), W. H. Barber, 'The Genesis of Voltaire's *Micromégas*', *French Studies*, 11 (1957), and the 'Notice' in *RC*.

tensions are exposed from the perspective of a celestial traveller; that Voltaire later returned to the story in order to entertain the duchesse du Maine at Sceaux in 1746–7 and/or because, from September 1750 or a little earlier, he was selecting new material for Walther's second collected edition of his works; and that some time before 12 January 1751, when the finished *conte* was dispatched from Prussia, he omitted and incorporated ideas and allusions in the light both of new circumstances and possibly of certain developments in his own outlook. This last factor should not, however, be overemphasized. One reason why it is profitable to regard *Micromégas* as being, to all intents and purposes, Voltaire's third *conte* is that it expresses an attitude of mind which is altogether more sanguine than that reflected in the stories which follow. The voyage of reason has begun, but the problem of evil is as yet but a tiny blot on the landscape.

'HISTOIRE PHILOSOPHIQUE'

Being a short story with a long pedigree and broad implications, *Micromégas* is well titled. And subtitled. This 'histoire philosophique' is indeed the first (as well as one of the half-dozen most important) of Voltaire's stories to present a broad range of intellectual issues within a fictional setting. It is the only one to be specifically dubbed 'philosophique' (from the 1754 edition onwards), and the tag accords well with the circumstances in which it was originally conceived. Following the furore created by the publication of the *Lettres philosophiques* and its public burning by the Paris Parlement, Voltaire had gone to live with Mme du Châtelet in a civilized *ménage à trois* at her home at Cirey in Champagne (which, for a man on the run, was conveniently situated near the border with Lorraine). After the upheaval of his exile in England (1726–8) and his busy involvement in Parisian cultural life (1729–33), a period of study and seclusion in the company of Emilie must have seemed particularly welcome. For Voltaire it was the quiet life which began at 40, and it brought the opportunity to devote himself more thoroughly to the life of the mind. He could now be a full-time *philosophe* in the special eighteenth-century sense of one engaged upon intellectual enquiry, free of religious or political constraint, across the whole range of human thought from mathematics to metaphysics.

A particular enthusiasm of Voltaire and his mistress was the 'natural philosophy' of Isaac Newton (1642–1727), which Voltaire had first encountered during his stay in England and subsequently introduced to the French in the *Lettres philosophiques*. Newton's *Principia Mathematica* (1687) had made a deep impression on him, with its theory of planets revolving round the sun in empty space and kept within their orbits by the force of gravity. For Voltaire, as a deist, the *Principia* seemed to offer irrefutable evidence to sustain the 'argument from design' (i.e. that the order in the universe points to the existence of an intelligent Creator, as the workings of a clock to the presence of a clockmaker). Here, too, was a valid method of scientific enquiry, based on observation and induction, and thus directly comparable with the philosophical method of Locke as expounded three years later in the *Essay Concerning Human Understanding* (1690). Newton's physics filled the emptiness of interplanetary space with the order and harmony of gravitational law, where, for example, Pascal had seen only the void left by a God who had withdrawn from Creation, and Descartes a system of 'tourbillons' or vortices consisting of ethereal fluid (*materia subtilis*) which supported and conveyed the celestial bodies within a *plenum*. From this study of Newton came Voltaire's *Eléments de la philosophie de Newton* (1738) and Mme du Châtelet's *Institutions de physique* (1740). From it, too, derived their considerable interest in the expedition led by Pierre-Louis Maupertuis to Lapland in 1736–7 to take measurements of a meridian line within the Arctic Circle. These measurements, replacing earlier, inaccurate ones taken in France itself, proved a resounding vindication of the Newtonian theory that the Earth was flat at its two poles.

Physics led in turn to metaphysics. While the two intellectual voyagers at Cirey did not neglect the ancients, notably Plato, they warmed more readily to the philosophical Optimism which had been expressed in Alexander Pope's *Essay on Man* (1733–4). For Pope and the English Optimists (Shaftesbury, Bolingbroke, King) God's work is admirable, and any apparent shortcomings are the result of our imperfect understanding. As the famous lines have it:

> Submit. In this, or any other sphere,
> Secure to be as blest as thou canst bear:
> Safe in the hand of one disposing pow'r,
> Or in the natal, or the mortal hour.
> All nature is but art, unknown to thee;
> All chance, direction, which thou canst not see;

All discord, harmony not understood;
All partial evil, universal good.
And, spite of pride, in erring reason's spite,
One truth is clear, 'Whatever is, is right.'[10]

Later, in less Optimistic mood, Voltaire would have only to quote part of this last line in the abbé du Resnel's translation ('tout est bien') in order to suggest the inadequacy of this view.[11] But at this stage, as his seven *Discours en vers sur l'homme* suggest, he accepted much of Pope's approach to the problem of evil.

As well as Pope the two *philosophes* encountered Leibniz, to whose ideas they were first introduced by Frederick of Prussia in 1736–7 via the work of Leibniz's disciple Christian Wolff. It might seem from *Micromégas* that Leibniz was nothing but a figure of fun for Voltaire. After all, the Leibnizian philosopher's attempt to explain the mind–body relationship in terms of the theory of pre-established harmony (not to mention the chiming clock and the mirror-frame) makes him appear equally as foolish as the Cartesian or the Malebranchist. And indeed it is true that Voltaire never did manage to swallow either the pre-established harmony or the monadology.[12] But Leibniz's theodicy was a different matter, and the key part which it plays in at least two of Voltaire's major *contes*, *Zadig* and *Candide*, is testimony to its importance.[13]

[10] *Essay on Man*, Epistle i. 285–94. Cf. iv. 113–16: 'God sends not ill; if rightly understood, / Or partial ill is universal good, / Or change admits, or nature lets it fall, / Short, and but rare, till man improv'd it all.'

[11] e.g. the subtitle of the *Poème sur le désastre de Lisbonne* and the article so entitled in the *Dictionnaire philosophique*. See *Les Principes de la morale et du goût* (i.e. the *Essay on Man*), tr. abbé du Resnel, 2nd edn. (London, 1750), 20: 'La Nature n'est pas une aveugle puissance, / C'est un art qui se cache à l'humaine ignorance, / Ce qui paraît hasard est l'effet d'un dessein, / Qui dérobe à tes yeux son principe et sa fin. / Ce qui dans l'Univers te révolte et te blesse, / Forme un parfait accord qui passe ta sagesse; / Tout désordre apparent est un ordre réel; / Tout mal particulier, un bien universel; / Ainsi malgré tes sens, malgré leur imposture, / Conclus que tout est bien dans toute la Nature.' Voltaire himself translated the key line correctly as 'tout ce qui est est bien' (D1039: 18 Mar. 1736), as did Rousseau in his so called 'Lettre sur la Providence' in response to the *Poème sur le désastre de Lisbonne* (see Rousseau, *Œuvres complètes*, ed. Bernard Gagnebin and Marcel Raymond, 4 vols. (Paris, 1959–69), iv. 1068).

[12] See the *Métaphysique de Newton* in which Voltaire gives a lucid, critical account of both (Mol., xxii. 425–7), essentially as a reply to Mme du Châtelet's *Institutions de physique*.

[13] Cf. W. H. Barber, *Leibniz in France from Arnauld to Voltaire. A Study in French Reactions to Leibnizianism, 1670–1760* (Oxford, 1955), p. xi: 'Of the major literary figures of the age, Voltaire alone in France is deeply and continuously involved in the Leibnizian controversies.'

Leibniz himself coined the term 'théodicée' (from the Greek for 'god' and 'justice') in his *Essais de théodicée*, thus confusing some early readers who thought it was a man's name. The *Essais* were essentially a reply to Bayle's *Dictionnaire historique et critique*,[14] in which Bayle the sceptic had sought, among other things, to show that the demands of human reason and the content of the Christian revelation are not to be reconciled. As part of his argument he expounded the heresy of Manicheism as an example of a 'solution' to the problem of evil which is plausible to human reason but which is at odds with the revelation. Leibniz, on the other hand, seeks in his *Essais* to demonstrate that Christian faith can be reconciled with rationalism. His God is 'la suprême raison des choses': 'Dieu est tout ordre, il garde toujours la justesse des proportions, il fait l'harmonie universelle.'[15] Unlike Pascal's 'gouffre', Leibniz's universe is susceptible of successful rational exploration and is presided over by an intelligence whose hand is ubiquitous. Had Voltaire ever had to invent a God, this is just the sort of God he would have chosen: hence his great interest in Leibnizian theodicy, and hence in part the astronomical vision of an intelligent creator in *Micromégas*.

But what does Leibniz argue? After the preface, in which he sets out the nature of his purpose, there comes a 'Discours de la conformité de la raison avec la foi' in which he asserts, first, that the truth which God supernaturally revealed to man is not in conflict with the truths which human intelligence 'peut atteindre naturellement'. For Leibniz, what Bayle considers as being contrary to reason is simply beyond reason.[16] Second, he distinguishes between necessary and contingent truth: that is, between 'les *vérités éternelles*, qui sont absolument nécessaires, en sorte que l'opposé implique contradiction' — i.e. truths 'dont la nécessité est logique, métaphysique ou géométrique' — and truths which are '*positives*, parce qu'elles sont des lois qu'il a plu à Dieu de donner à la nature, ou parce qu'elles en dépendent'.[17]

---

[14] For a full account see Barber, *Leibniz in France*, 70–89.

[15] Leibniz, *Essais de théodicée sur la bonté de Dieu, la liberté de l'homme et l'origine du mal*, ed. J. Brunschwig (Paris, 1969), 28 and 27 respectively.

[16] Ibid. 50 and 87 respectively.

[17] Ibid. 51. Cf. his subsequent distinction between 'le *principe de la contradiction*, qui porte que de deux propositions contradictoires, l'une est vraie, l'autre fausse', and 'celui de la *raison déterminante*: c'est que jamais rien n'arrive, sans qu'il y ait une cause ou du moins une raison déterminante, c'est-à-dire quelque chose qui puisse servir à rendre raison *a priori*, pourquoi cela est existant plutôt que non existant, et pourquoi

The heart of Leibniz's theodicy, and particularly those aspects which Voltaire was later to ridicule so mercilessly in *Candide*, is to be found in the Première Partie of the *Essais*. Two questions pose themselves: how can an omnipotent and beneficent God permit evil? and how can one reconcile the concept of human free will with the existence of an omnipotent God? In answer to the first question Leibniz begins by arguing that, since the known universe[18] is a demonstrably contingent assembly of temporal, spatial, and material features which could have combined to make any number of other sorts of universes, whatever caused this particular assembly must have been intelligent, since a choice was involved and choice implies intelligence. To bring this universe into being, this First Cause had also to have a will and the power to carry out its will. The exercise of its will involved discrimination and thus value judgements. In short:

La puissance va à l'*être*, la sagesse ou l'entendement au *vrai*, et la volonté au *bien*. Et cette cause intelligente doit être infinie de toutes les manières et absolument parfaite en *puissance*, en *sagesse* et en *bonté*, puisqu'elle va à tout ce qui est possible. Et comme tout est lié, il n'y a pas lieu d'en admettre plus d'une. Son entendement est la source des *essences*, et sa volonté est l'origine des *existences*. Voilà en peu de mots la preuve d'un Dieu unique avec ses perfections, et par lui l'origine des choses. (para. 7)

It follows that, if God is infinitely wise and infinitely good, then he must have chosen to create, from among 'une infinité de mondes possibles' 'le meilleur (*optimum*)' (para. 8).[19] Why? Because 'il ne fait rien sans agir suivant la suprême raison'. In other words God is bound by the 'vérités éternelles' of logic, so that an infinitely wise

---

cela est ainsi plutôt que de toute autre façon' (*Essais*, 128). Elsewhere in his work, particularly in his correspondence with Clarke (1716), Leibniz refers to the latter principle as that of 'la raison suffisante'. Further references to the *Essais* will be included in the text in the form of parenthetical paragraph numbers relating to the Première Partie.

[18] Leibniz uses the term 'monde' but defines this in para. 8 as 'toute la suite et toute la collection de toutes les choses existantes . . . ou si vous voulez . . . un univers'. The famous Leibnizian phrase to which this is all leading thus means 'the best of all possible universes', and its satirical application exclusively to life on Earth constitutes a Voltairian sleight of hand comparable with his repeated use of du Resnel's inadequate 'tout est bien'.

[19] The term 'optimisme' first appeared in a review of the *Essais de théodicée* in the *Journal de Trévoux* in 1737.

and good being must necessarily choose to create the best possible universe available.[20]

But there is an obvious objection to be made (which Zadig will later put to the angel Jesrad): why did God not choose a universe without sin and suffering (para. 9)? Leibniz's answer is simple. Such a universe would not have been the best possible one:

Car il faut savoir que tout est lié dans chacun des mondes possibles: l'univers, quel qu'il puisse être, est tout d'une pièce, comme un océan; le moindre mouvement y étend son effet à quelque distance que ce soit, quoique cet effet devienne moins sensible à proportion de la distance ... Ainsi, si le moindre mal qui arrive dans le monde y manquait, ce ne serait plus ce monde, qui, tout compté, tout rabattu, a été trouvé le meilleur par le créateur qui l'a choisi. (para. 9)

Leibniz acknowledges that one can imagine universes without sin and suffering, just as one can think up 'des romans, des utopies' (para. 10), but they would be 'fort inférieurs en bien au nôtre'. This raises the interesting possibility that a comparison of Eldorado with life in the Turkish 'métairie' in *Candide* may reveal a Voltaire who is in fact illustrating rather than refuting Leibniz's philosophy.

For the moment, though, we have reached the nub of Leibnizian Optimism: 'Nous savons d'ailleurs que souvent un mal cause un bien, auquel on ne serait point arrivé sans ce mal' (para. 10). The nub is also something of an Achilles' heel, however, for Leibniz is unable to come up with convincing examples at this point. Instead, having recourse to rather trivial analogies, he remarks that a bitter taste may sometimes be welcome in place of sweetness, and continues:

les ombres rehaussent les couleurs et même une dissonance placée où il faut donne du relief à l'harmonie. Nous voulons être effrayés par des danseurs de cordes qui sont sur le point de tomber, et nous voulons que les tragédies nous fassent presque pleurer. Goûte-t-on assez la santé, et en rend-on assez grâces à Dieu sans avoir jamais été malade? et ne faut-il pas le plus souvent qu'un peu de mal rende le bien plus sensible, c'est-à-dire plus grand. (para. 12)[21]

---

[20]   Leibniz's words are 'n'a pu manquer de choisir le meilleur' (para. 8), but he argues that God's choice is not necessary in the strict sense because it is a choice between contingent possibilities.
[21]   Cf. *Candide*: 'Mais un sage ... m'apprit que tout cela est à merveille; ce sont des ombres à un beau tableau' (205–6).

Complaints about the evil in the universe are, therefore, without foundation: 'c'est murmurer en effet contre les ordres de la Providence' (para. 15).[22]

Physical and moral evil, then, are not necessary as such, but in so far as they are possible, then they are potential ingredients in the 'mondes possibles' from which God has chosen 'le meilleur'; 'c'est ce qui a déterminé Dieu à permettre le mal' (para. 21). It is part of the 'vérités éternelles', part of the logic of things, that the best possible universe is one containing evil: over that logic God, being himself 'la suprême raison', has no control. In principle God seeks the good, but in practice he can but choose the best (para. 23). Or, put another way:

il manquerait à ce qu'il se doit, à ce qu'il doit à sa sagesse, à sa bonté, à sa perfection, s'il ne suivait pas le grand résultat de toutes ses tendances au bien, et s'il ne choisissait pas ce qui est absolument le meilleur, nonobstant le mal de coulpe qui s'y trouve enveloppé par la suprême nécessité des vérités éternelles. (para. 25)

It is all a matter of what Leibniz elsewhere calls 'compossibility'. The 'vérités éternelles' dictate that only certain combinations of ingredients are possible. Because the sufficient reason for the Creation was God's desire to manifest his perfection to the greatest possible extent (para. 78), then he sought the most beneficial possible combinations of ingredients, as well as the greatest possible number of such combinations. This aspect of Leibniz's theodicy is important to an understanding of *Micromégas* and *Zadig*, since in both *contes* mention is made of the extraordinary variety within uniformity which obtains within the universe.[23] This variety is a manifestation of divine power and an important characteristic of the design which Voltaire, like Leibniz, finds so compelling a proof of God's existence.

Ultimately Leibniz's answer to the problem of evil is that God is not omnipotent, but he obscures this fundamental weakness in his solution by insisting on an infrangible logic which he has asserted a priori. As to the question of human freedom, again the 'vérités

---

[22] Cf. *Zadig*: 'Il lui échappa enfin de murmurer contre la Providence' (109).

[23] *RC*, 23, 114. Cf. the account of this aspect of Leibniz in the *Métaphysique de Newton*: 'Nous ne connaissons point deux corps entièrement semblables dans la nature, et il ne peut en être: car s'ils étaient semblables, premièrement cela marquerait dans Dieu tout puissant et tout fécond un manque de fécondité et de puissance. En second lieu, il n'y aurait nulle raison pourquoi l'un serait à cette place plutôt que l'autre' (Mol., xxii. 411).

éternelles' have their part to play, for Leibniz argues that the will
(of God, of man) is free in so far as it is choosing between contingent
possibilities and is not therefore subject to necessity. There may,
indeed certainly shall, be a 'raison suffisante' why a given choice is
made, but this is not to say that the act of choice is itself not free:
'il y a toujours une raison prévalente qui porte la volonté à son choix,
et il suffit pour conserver sa liberté que cette raison incline, sans
nécessiter' (para. 45).

In the final pages of this 'Première Partie' Leibniz seeks to reconcile determinism with the doctrine of free will. For him it is true
that 'Tout est donc certain et déterminé par avance dans l'homme,
comme partout ailleurs, et l'âme humaine est une espèce d'*automate
spirituel*.' Because each contingent future event will be dictated by a
'raison prévalente', those events are predetermined and known to
God; but the events in themselves do not cease to be contingent
(para. 52). Leibniz allows that there is a kind of 'nécessité hypo-
thétique' (para. 53) at work in that God, having once chosen His
'meilleur des mondes possibles', thereby sets in train a chain of cause
and effect whose outcome is known to Him. But for the human
being there are still choices to be made. We are, therefore, morally
responsible for our actions, and it behoves us as God's creatures to
use our reason to try to understand God's purpose and then to carry
it out to the best of our ability (para. 58). Or, as a University Lecturer
in Philosophy has more recently summarized the matter: 'We have
not been endowed with a miraculous freedom, but God has at least
granted us the gift of Philosophy, which enables us to understand
how all is ultimately for the best in the best of all possible worlds.'[24]

Micromégas clearly reflects much of this intellectual background,
and it has been shown how deeply the text is imbued with both the
conclusions and the inductive methods of Lockian empiricism and
Newtonian physics.[25] Micromégas and his travelling-companion are
an illustration of human understanding taking up a position outside
itself (in Lockian fashion) and examining the available evidence with
impartial eye. Such a procedure had already been mooted in the
Traité de métaphysique,[26] and here we see it in action as 'nos deux
curieux' embark on their voyage of discovery. Taking over the device

[24] G. MacDonald Ross, *Leibniz* (Oxford, 1984), 112.
[25] See Van den Heuvel, *Voltaire dans ses contes*, 79–100.
[26] Ed. H. Temple Patterson (Manchester, 1937), 2.

of the interplanetary journey, as used, for example, in Godwin's *Man in the Moon* (1638) and Cyrano de Bergerac's *Etats et empires de la lune* (1657), and combining it with elements of the imaginary journey used in the quasi-scientific, Utopian travel literature of the seventeenth and early eighteenth centuries (such as Bacon's *Nova Atlantis* of 1627), Voltaire adds the technique of the alien visitor which Montesquieu had put to such good use in the *Lettres persanes* (1721) and which he himself had employed in the *Lettres philosophiques*.

His further originality in *Micromégas* consists partly in having beings from other planets come to have a 'close encounter' with us (in the hope of finding Utopia . . .), and partly in using this visit as a demonstration of the merits of empiricism. The two travellers proceed by trial and (comic) error, with the visitor from the Sirian planet proving more judicious in his reasoning than his solar counterpart. Finally they identify man, only to find him in thrall to the 'trifling' metaphysics of the soul which Locke himself had sought to supersede. Their journey ends with an equally Lockian acknowledgement of the limits of human understanding.

At the same time the celestial journeys of Micromégas to Saturn and then of Micromégas and the Saturnian to Earth are based on the very latest cosmology. As well as Newton's *Principia*, this included the work of Christiaan Huygens — especially his *Systema saturnium* (1659) but also his *Cosmotheoros* (1698) — as well as the work of Kircher, Keill, and Wolff. There is nothing intrinsically fantastical about these journeys, for Micromégas has a sure knowledge of 'les lois de la gravitation et toutes les forces attractives et répulsives' (21), and he is so well organized that he never has to run for a comet. Saturn's ring provides a convenient comet-stop (25), and the Milky Way is quickly traversed; but there is absolutely no sign of 'ce beau ciel empyrée que l'illustre vicaire Derham se vante d'avoir vu au bout de sa lunette' (21). On the terrestrial level Newton is implicitly present also in the use of Maupertuis's Lapland expedition as a forum for human philosophical intercourse. Again, nothing was less fantastical, except in its fictional appearance, than this real journey to provide hard evidence to support a valid Newtonian theory.

As for Pope and Leibniz, the story reflects many of the central ideas of the *Essay on Man* and the *Essais de théodicée*. In Popean fashion man is ousted from his supposed place at the centre of the universe and demoted within the Great Chain of Being to a more humble level, while the universe which Micromégas and the Saturnian traverse would seem to support the view that 'Whatever is, is right'. At the same time the Leibnizian vision of divine perfection is evident in the maximal combination of variety and uniformity which so impresses Micromégas and in the nugatory role of moral evil within the universal scheme of things.

Such is *Micromégas. Histoire philosophique*. Van den Heuvel has argued that *Micromégas* shows Voltaire discovering a 'formule' whereby he is able to translate symbolically his own intellectual experiences of the moment.[27] Certainly this 'histoire philosophique' does reflect a specific philosophical and scientific background, but such an approach underrates the importance of the relationship between text and reader. For what *Micromégas* most clearly reveals is precisely that 'formule' which has been demonstrated in *L'Homme aux quarante écus*: a narrative which consists in the metamorphosis of a mathematical calculation into an ideal of humanity. In *Micromégas* the metamorphosis is less gradated than in the later work, but the effect is the same: to persuade the reader of the validity of this ideal less by explicit harangue than by insidiously involving him or her in a process of reading which itself puts the ideal into practice. It is thus an 'histoire philosophique' also in the more fundamental domain of its narrative order.

FROM FANTASY TO FACT

In common with D'Alembert's *Discours préliminaire* (1751) to the *Encyclopédie*, *Micromégas* makes plain the *philosophes'* aversion to system-building and the empiricists' suspicion of the extrapolations of the 'algébristes'.[28] It does so by turning silly numbers into sensible, sentient beings. The process begins with the laboured arithmetic of chapter 1 in which the various numbers involved in the dimensions of Micromégas and of his planet near Sirius, in his age and the duration of his court case, and in the size of Saturn and its inhabi-

[27] *Voltaire dans ses contes*, 109–10.

[28] There are several textual parallels between *Micromégas* and the *Discours préliminaire*, and one wonders if Voltaire may have changed 'géomètres' to 'algébristes' in the second paragraph of the 1754 (definitive) edition in the light of D'Alembert's disparaging remarks in the *Discours* about the abuse of algebra in physics: 'Au défaut d'expériences propres à servir de base à leur calcul, ils [les algébristes] se permettent des hypothèses les plus commodes, à la vérité, qu'il leur est possible, mais souvent très éloignées de ce qui est réellement dans la Nature' (p. vii).

tants, lend the two celestial protagonists an air of absurd unreality. The idea that there may be a precise mathematical relationship between the size of a planet and that of its (supposed) inhabitants occurs in the work of various cosmologists, including Huygens; but Voltaire's main target is Christian Wolff's calculation of the height of a putative Jupiterian in his *Elementa Matheseos Universae* (1735), a dimension arrived at by comparing the amount of sunlight on Earth and on Jupiter, assessing the consequent size of the pupil in a Jupiterian eye, and then measuring the size of the body in (earthly) proportion to the eye. Far from confirming a vision of cosmic harmony such calculations struck the Cirey household as a decidedly daft example of how *not* to think about the universe. Facts were needed, not wild Germanic surmise.[29]

The strategy of *Micromégas* consists in turning these monstrous projections of a fevered mathematical brain into empirical entities. Following the introductory spate of calculations, Micromégas and the Saturnian soon take on the attributes of 'êtres réels' by being endowed with familiar features which relate them to the world we know. Where Micromégas proclaims in Leibnizian vein that 'l'auteur de la nature ... a répandu sur cet univers une profusion de variétés, avec une espèce d'uniformité admirable' (23), the story demonstrates this in practice by revealing a wonderful similarity between philosophers everywhere, whatever their size and planetary provenance. Thus the pursuit of truth is universally accompanied by the more physical pursuit of feminine beauty: the Sirian wins the ladies over to his side in his dispute with the mufti (20); the Saturnian, always less successful than his taller colleague, has secured the favours of his mistress after some difficulty; and the earthling scientists are bringing back not only a vindication of Newtonian physics but a catch of 'filles lapones'. Mathematical expertise, too, is universal: from the Sirian prodigy's discovery of fifty Euclidian theorems to the young Pascal's paltry thirty-two. (The second-rate Saturnian simply 'faisait passablement ... de grands calculs': 21). The study and dissection of insects occupies the Sirian (20) as much as the

---

[29]   See D2526 (10 Aug. 1741, to Maupertuis): 'Il y avait longtemps que j'avais vu, avec une stupeur de monade, quelle taille ce bavard germanique assigne aux habitants de Jupiter ... Cet homme-là ramène en Allemagne toutes les horreurs de la scolastique surchargée de "raisons suffisantes", de "monades", d' "indiscernables", et de toutes les absurdités scientifiques que Leibnitz a mis [*sic*] au monde par vanité, et que les Allemands étudient parce qu'ils sont Allemands.'

shipbound *philosophes* (34), but not the Saturnian who merely writes 'de petits vers' and summarizes the 'inventions des autres' (21). Scientific advance is hampered by muftis and inquisitors, on earth as it is in heaven (20, 25). Nowhere are people ever satisfied: 'Il faut que ce soit une loi universelle de la nature' (23). Everywhere the tendency is to jump to premature conclusions: just as the mariners believe they have been struck by a hurricane, so the Saturnian believes the earth to be inhabited solely by whales.

At every level of *Micromégas* the reader is repeatedly subjected to a progression from the unreal to the real, from unthinking assumption and wild guess to a consideration of facts and the reserving of judgement. At the level of narrative invention itself, *Micromégas* is a parody of the imaginary voyage tradition (Lucian, Cyrano de Bergerac, Swift, Tyssot de Patot's *Voyages et aventures de Jacques Massé* (1710)). Voltaire mocks this tradition partly by exaggerating some of its stock devices, as when he attributes to Micromégas and his companion a Pentecostal 'don des langues' (30), but mainly by denying these devices their fantastical character. He defictionalizes fiction. Thus the basic narrative sequence employed in this tradition (as a convenient series of pegs for improbable fantasies) is still present: childhood, study, departure, wanderings, shipwreck, meetings with strange peoples and customs, misapprehension, revised assessment, separation, and return. In *Micromégas* this becomes: a prodigious gift for mathematics and science, exile for irreligion, Newtonian navigation, Saturn, needing a bed for the night, meeting man, empiricism, and a flight from human presumption.

At the level of the narrator, too, one finds a similar insistence on the move from myth to truth. Derham's empyrean is not there: 'je ne veux contredire personne'; 'mais Micromégas était sur les lieux' (21). Père Castel will say that Mars has not got two moons, but it has (25). The papers say that Maupertuis was shipwrecked, but 'je vais raconter ingénument comme la chose se passa' (28). In this last case, of course, Voltaire would claim he was substituting the greater truth of his own philosophical fable for the banality of a 'fait divers'.

FONTENELLE AND PASCAL

One of the principal truths which the fable of *Micromégas* asserts is the importance of the mean. In particular it attacks all preconceptions, prejudices, or systems which serve either to conceal or to

Schumann = Fontenelle

exaggerate the limits of human understanding; and these poles are represented by the two principal targets of Voltaire's satire in *Micromégas*: Fontenelle and Pascal.

In some respects the biggest joke of all in *Micromégas* is on man himself. But just as *Le Crocheteur borgne* is in essence a parody of the *Thousand and One Nights*, and *Cosi-Sancta* pokes fun at St Augustine, so the target in *Micromégas* is first and foremost Fontenelle and his *Entretiens sur la pluralité des mondes* (1686).[30] This may now seem a rather obscure target, but it was one of the principal bestsellers of its day, at least twenty-eight editions being published during the author's (admittedly protracted) lifetime. Following its publication Fontenelle was elected to the Académie Française in 1691, and in 1697 the model for Voltaire's Saturnian was appointed Perpetual Secretary to the Académie des Sciences.

At first sight Fontenelle may seem an odd target to have chosen. He was a friend of the Jesuits rather than Voltaire's despised Jansenists. He was an important precursor of the Enlightenment in several ways,[31] not least in his ambition to bridge the gap between the academic and the 'honnête homme'. To this end the *Entretiens* are conducted in a tone of mild flirtation with an anonymous marquise, the idea being evidently that if even a woman can understand all this stuff about astronomy, then so should the very dimmest of 'honnêtes hommes'. Moreover one might have expected Voltaire to warm to one so sceptical about much that passes for philosophical truth, and who declared that 'Toute la philosophie ... n'est fondée que sur deux choses, sur ce qu'on a l'esprit curieux et les yeux mauvais.'[32]

To some extent he did. But Fontenelle was a Cartesian and, as Robert Shackleton has shown, he abused his position as Secretary of the Académie des Sciences in the furtherance of his cause.[33] For Voltaire, therefore, Fontenelle was a representative of the French intellectual establishment at its worst: he was the unscrupulous defender of a home-grown theory of astrophysics arrived at by deductive surmise against the inductive reasoning and empirical evidence of a foreigner. At the heart of the *Entretiens* lies an account

---

[30] On the withdrawal of the first edition of *Micromégas* after representations by Fontenelle's friends, see Smith, 'The publication of *Micromégas*', 68–71.
[31] See Fontenelle, *Entretiens sur la pluralité des mondes. Digression sur les anciens et les modernes*, ed. Robert Shackleton (Oxford, 1955), 28–40.
[32] Ibid. 62. See also Mervaud, 'Voltaire et Fontenelle'.
[33] Fontenelle, *Entretiens*, 20–8.

of Descartes's theory of vortices, and in 1738 Voltaire's attitude to Fontenelle's work is categoric:

les dialogues des Mondes qui n'apprennent pas grand'chose et qui d'ailleurs sont trop remplis de la misérable hypothèse des tourbillons, sont pourtant un livre charmant, par cela même que le livre est d'une physique peu recherchée et que rien n'y est traité à fond.[34]

For Voltaire, Fontenelle the popularizer and polemicist had gone too far in making these things appear simpler than they are. In *Micromégas* Voltaire sets about the author of the *Entretiens* with relish. His most telling move is to portray Fontenelle as a Saturnian, for in the *Entretiens* itself the inhabitants of Saturn are described as being 'assez misérables, même avec le secours de l'anneau':

Ce sont gens qui ne savent ce que c'est que de rire, qui prennent toujours un jour pour répondre à la moindre question qu'on leur fait, et qui eussent trouvé Caton d'Utique trop badin et trop folâtre.[35]

Living as they do on what was then thought to be the planet most distant from the sun, these hypothetical Saturnians are not only used to the cold but are, of course, furthest from the light. Accordingly these inhabitants of a dim world are as 'lents' as the inhabitants of Mercury are said to be 'vifs'.[36] Such is Voltaire's own mercurial wit, therefore, that he has only to invent a Secretary of the Saturnian Academy of Sciences for his opinion of Fontenelle's own humour and wisdom to be plain.

Comparable with this first move in that it uses Fontenelle's own material against him, Voltaire's second move is to satirize Fontenelle's special brand of reasoning from analogy, which Voltaire regards as a travesty of inductive reasoning. Fontenelle describes it thus in the *Entretiens*:

Vous convenez que quand deux choses sont semblables en tout ce qui me paraît, je les puis croire aussi semblables en ce qui ne me paraît point, s'il n'y a rien d'ailleurs qui m'en empêche. De là j'ai tiré que la lune était habitée, parce qu'elle ressemble à la terre; les autres planètes, parce qu'elles

[34] D1502 (14 May 1738, to Berger). For Voltaire's similar attitude to Fontenelle in 1751, see D4486 (5 June 1751, to Frederick) and Barber, 'The Genesis of *Micromégas*', 5–7.
[35] Fontenelle, *Entretiens*, 127.
[36] Ibid. 127.

ressemblent à la lune. Je trouve que les étoiles fixes ressemblent à notre soleil, je leur attribue tout ce qu'il a.[37]

By implicitly comparing Fontenelle with a Saturnian, Voltaire is already employing this second move. More blatantly, the various analogies which the Saturnian puts to Micromégas at the beginning of chapter 2 are taken from Fontenelle;[38] while the narrator's insistence in chapter 3 on the fact that Mars has two moons is reinforced by an explicit appeal to 'ceux qui raisonnent par analogie' (25). Fontenelle's predilection for explaining potentially difficult scientific ideas in terms of simple comparisons clearly irritated Voltaire and struck him as both foolish and patronising. Hence his absurd use of the same technique in *Micromégas* when pointing to disparities of size (19–20, 26).[39]

Beyond these satirical ploys lie a number of other allusions to Fontenelle's life and work which were, one assumes, intended to delight an informed audience or readership by their obliquity as much as to point up the differences in philosophical beliefs between Voltaire and his target. Indeed in considering the philosophical content of *Micromégas* it is always necessary to bear in mind that modern editorial scholarship runs the risk of lending a more recondite air to the story than its author may have wished or than its first readers would have sensed. For *Micromégas* is above all a comedy, and its seven short chapters are packed with jokes. Life at Cirey had its lighter side, and Voltaire's third *conte* is as much, if not more, a reflection of this sophisticated gaiety than of the happy couple's weightier deliberations.

Deeply inimical to this gaiety, of course, was the pessimism of Pascal. Here Micromégas himself is the principal means for Voltaire's attack, and this is signalled from the outset in the Sirian's

[37] Ibid. 132.
[38] The comparison of nature with a flower-bed and a gathering of blondes and brunettes come from his *Lettres diverses de M. le chevalier d'Her* (1683). The comparison with an art gallery may echo the allusion to paintings in the *Entretiens* (112), where at the very beginning one also finds daylight likened to a 'beauté blonde' and night-time to a 'beauté brune' (60). Given Voltaire's scorn for Fontenelle's 'prudente lâcheté' (see above, Ch. 1) it is surprising that he did not make something of Fontenelle's final analogy in the book: 'les vrais philosophes sont comme les éléphants, qui, en marchant, ne posent jamais le second pied à terre, que le premier n'y soit bien affermi' (156).
[39] Cf. also: 'comme un oiseau voltige de branche en branche' (21); 'comme une goutte d'eau dans un océan' (23); 'comme deux voyageurs qui [. . . etc.]' (25–6).

precocious mathematical genius in working out fifty of Euclid's theorems all on his own: 'C'est dix-huit de plus que Blaise Pascal, lequel, après en avoir deviné trente-deux en se jouant, à ce que dit sa soeur, devint depuis un géomètre assez médiocre et un fort mauvais métaphysicien' (20). At the end Micromégas and the Saturnian fall about with helpless gigantic mirth on hearing the Sorbonne theologian's advocacy of the profoundly anthropocentric thought of Aquinas; and the Sirian is 'un peu fâché dans le fond du cœur de voir que les infiniment petits eussent un orgueil presque infiniment grand' (37). The allusion to the celebrated fragment of the *Pensées* entitled 'Disproportion de l'homme' is plain. Between these two references which frame the story, the whole of *Micromégas* is a categoric rejection of the Pascalian view of man's place in the universe.

At the beginning of the letter on Pascal which closes the *Lettres philosophiques*, Voltaire had declared: 'J'ose prendre le parti de l'humanité contre ce misanthrope sublime.'[40] In *Micromégas* it may seem that mankind could have had a better champion: we humans may be quite good at measuring things, it appears, but we wage pointless and murderous wars and we talk a lot of nonsense about things we know absolutely nothing about. But when it comes to the central question in the 'Disproportion de l'homme': 'Qu'est-ce qu'un homme, dans l'infini?',[41] the Voltairian answer is very different from Pascal's. For the latter, famously, scientific knowledge has shown us to be vertiginously poised 'entre ces deux abîmes de l'infini et du néant': man is

Un néant à l'égard de l'infini, un tout à l'égard du néant, un milieu entre rien et tout, infiniment éloigné de comprendre les extrêmes; la fin des choses et leurs principes sont pour lui invinciblement cachés dans un secret impénétrable.

Any attempt to understand the universe, or nature, is doomed by disproportion:

Manque d'avoir contemplé ces infinis les hommes se sont portés téméraire-ment à la recherche de la nature comme s'ils avaient quelque proportion avec elle.

C'est une chose étrange qu'ils ont voulu comprendre les principes des choses et de là arriver jusqu'à connaître tout, par une présomption aussi

---

[40] *Lett. phil.*, 156.
[41] L. 199. Reference is to the numbering of the *Pensées* in *Œuvres complètes*, ed. Louis Lafuma (Paris, 1963).

infinie que leur objet. Car il est sans doute qu'on ne peut former ce dessein sans une présomption ou sans une capacité infinie, comme la nature.

Pascal looks up to heaven and sees only vast, empty space: 'Dieu s'est voulu cacher.'[42]

In *Micromégas* Voltaire makes fun of Pascal's conclusions by inverting the process and substituting, in effect, 'l'homme caché'. Thus, in chapter 4, when Micromégas and the Saturnian are reconnoitring the earth:

Ils se baissèrent, ils se couchèrent, ils tâterent partout; mais, leurs yeux et leurs mains n'étant point proportionnés aux petits êtres qui rampent ici, ils ne reçurent pas la moindre sensation qui pût leur faire soupçonner que nous et nos confrères les autres habitants de ce globe avons l'honneur d'exister. (27)

But, of course, the two explorers subsequently overcome the problems of disproportion through microscopy and the advanced technology of the ear trumpet, and so are led to surer conclusions in respect of the existence of man. The Saturnian may still be prevented by 'l'extrême disproportion' (36) from embracing the follower of Locke, but at least there has been a meeting of minds. And such a meeting has been possible because the Saturnian has been persuaded — by experience — of the merits of empirical methods: 'Je n'ose plus ni croire ni nier, dit le nain; je n'ai plus d'opinion. Il faut tâcher d'examiner ces insectes, nous raisonnerons après' (31).

Similarly, Micromégas at first regards mankind in a thoroughly Pascalian light as being sunk 'dans ce misérable état si voisin de l'anéantissement' (32). But when human beings measure him, he is ready to believe the evidence of his own eyes, and he uses the language of Pascal to assert a profoundly un-Pascalian, deist message:

Je vois plus que jamais qu'il ne faut juger de rien sur sa grandeur apparente. Ô Dieu, qui avez donné une intelligence à des substances qui paraissent si méprisables, l'infiniment petit vous coûte aussi peu que l'infiniment grand; et, s'il est possible qu'il y ait des êtres plus petits que ceux-ci, ils peuvent encore avoir un esprit supérieur à ceux de ces superbes animaux que j'ai vus dans le ciel, dont le pied seul couvrirait le globe où je suis descendu. (33)

For Voltaire, Pascal is prejudiced by his Christian faith, and the deist regards as profoundly anti-humanitarian the Jansenist's

---

[42] L. 242.

defeatist attitude to intellectual enquiry as expressed in the *Pensées*: 'Curiosité n'est que vanité. Le plus souvent on ne veut savoir que pour en parler, autrement on ne voyagerait pas sur la mer pour ne jamais en rien dire et pour le seul plaisir de voir, sans espérance d'en jamais communiquer.' [43] It is thus deeply ironic that Micromégas should set off on his celestial Grand Tour 'pour achever de se former "l'esprit et le cœur", comme l'on dit' (20). This reference to the pedagogical treatise of the Jansenist Charles Rollin[44] is an incongruous starting-point for a journey which encounters divine order and proportion at every turn and which teaches the traveller so many useful lessons. Compared with the Pascalian void, Micromégas's universe resembles a rather busy thoroughfare.

THE VOYAGE OF REASON

In *Micromégas*, as Candide will later remark, 'il est certain qu'il faut voyager' (188). The Sirian travels, the Saturnian travels, earthly philosophers travel: it is the only way to discover anything — by a change of perspective. As a story *Micromégas* approaches its pedagogical task by taking the reader on a journey of discovery — to effect a change of outlook. The purpose of the journey is not so much to show us *what* we should think, but *how* we should think. Indeed it demonstrates the impossibility of providing answers to major metaphysical questions: Micromégas's 'beau livre de philosophie' in which the earthlings 'verraient le bout des choses' is famously blank. And to this extent Voltaire agrees with Pascal that the eternal mysteries are beyond human understanding. What he disagrees with is the Pascalian conclusion that curiosity is vain. Micromégas's book may be blank, but Voltaire's 'histoire philosophique' is full of pages, pages which demonstrate in every line the value of an enquiring and, above all, open mind. Whereas Pascalian space is silent, the universe of *Micromégas* is filled with the sound of conversation. Views are exchanged between Sirian and Saturnian, between giants and men, between narrator and reader: 'figurez-vous', 'concevez, je vous prie', 'vous croyez bien', etc. As Ira O. Wade first pointed out,[45] *Micromégas* is notable for the degree to which not only the first person

[43] L. 77.
[44] *Traité des études. De la manière d'étudier et d'enseigner les belles-lettres par rapport à l'esprit et au cœur* (1726–8).
[45] *Voltaire's 'Micromégas'*, 104–5.

singular is present in the story, but more especially – and more than
in any other Voltairian *conte* – the first and second persons plural.
This 'histoire philosophique' is presented as urbane and civilized
dialogue, not with Fontenelle's marquise nor even Pascal's 'roseau
pensant', but with 'atomes intelligents' (33).
   And how should we atoms react? On opening Micromégas's book
the Secretary of the Académie des Sciences is not surprised. But on
reading *Micromégas* we should be, constantly. For, like so many of
Voltaire's *contes*, this one takes us on a voyage of disorientation,
or 'defamiliarization', which seeks to liberate the mind from the
automatic response. Thus *Micromégas* presents *homo sapiens* in two
ways: reduced, as if seen through the wrong end of a telescope, in
the guise of the mite-size *philosophes*; and enlarged, as if under a
microscope, in the guise of a Saturnian and, even more enlarged, in
the guise of one from a planet near Sirius. In this way the narrative
technique of the story imitates the scientific instruments it extols
within its pages.
   Further, it disorientates by challenging our usual yardsticks of
measurement. Again as Ira O. Wade points out, Voltaire makes great
play with the terms 'grand' and 'petit' throughout the story, as well
as 'peu' and 'beaucoup', 'fort' and 'guère', etc., such that what we
might normally regard as 'grand' is 'petit' and vice versa.[46] As Wade
goes on to show, this makes *Micromégas* 'a story of proportionate
devaluation of extremes or of revaluation of means',[47] in which a
further favoured device is the binary epithet. Thus, for example, the
mufti is 'grand vétillard et fort ignorant' (20), and the 'raisonne-
ments' of the two travellers are 'fort ingénieux et fort incertains'
(23). Here, as in many other cases, an assumption is encouraged
which is then undermined. At this *micro* level of the text, therefore,
the central move from myth to truth, or from fantasy to fact, is
endlessly repeated.
   As well as exploiting the traditional Rabelaisian or Swiftian comedy of size, *Micromégas* is also one big comedy of measurement. It
is full not only of Fontenellian analogies but of every unit of measure
from the 'toise' and the 'lieue' to the 'pas géométrique' and the 'pied

---

[46]   Ibid. 94–100. See also Dorothy Madeleine McGhee, *Voltairian Narrative
Devices as Considered in the Author's 'Contes Philosophiques'* (Menasha, Wis., 1933), 129,
and Jean Sareil, 'Le Vocabulaire de la relativité dans *Micromégas* de Voltaire', *Romanic
Review*, 64 (1973).
[47]   *Voltaire's 'Micromégas'*, 101.

de roi'. Yet what do these measurements signify? Nothing essential: simply, that everything is relative. Including language. For *Micromégas* also serves as a pre-Saussurian illustration of the shifting relationship between signifier and signified. Not only do the words 'grand' and 'petit' change their sense according to context, so too do all manner of other words in the story. The huge Saturnian is a dwarf; Derham is 'illustre' but wrong; a ferruled walking-stick driven into the finger merely tickles; and, remarkably, the Saturnian 'vit quelque chose d'imperceptible' (28). This aspect of the story is signalled right at the beginning in the punning introduction of the hero: 'il s'appelait Micromégas, nom qui convient fort à tous les grands'. As to *Micromégas*, this title too is most appropriate for a story which proclaims the limits of human understanding and the inherent ambiguity of language. Why use a Greek name? Because, as the Aristotelian remarks: 'il faut bien citer ce qu'on ne comprend point du tout dans la langue qu'on entends le moins' (35).

Le Crocheteur borgne suggested playfully that it was best to turn a blind eye. In *Micromégas*, on the other hand, monocular vision is the province of the microscopist alone. Now Voltaire asserts the need to use both eyes and to focus them properly. The soldiers involved in the Russo-Turkish War slaughter each other without ever having seen either the land or the rulers they are fighting for. The legal experts condemn Micromégas's zoological paper without reading it. Human folly and injustice are a form of blindness, as are conjecture and vague speculation. Enlightenment requires accurate observation: with a microscope, a diamond, a quadrant, or indeed the naked eye. Seeing is all, as long as one is careful not to be deceived by appearances: 'ce qui n'arrive que trop, soit qu'on se serve ou non de microscopes' (30). Newtonian physics may seem fantastical, but it is borne out by the facts: metaphysical speculation about the soul may seem profound, but it reveals itself as pure fantasy.

Micromégas, for its part, may seem like a *conte fantastique*, but its lesson is a real one. The universe exhibits a wonderful profusion of difference and variety within a framework of orderly proportion and harmony. The Great Chain of Being extends from the *mega* to the *micro*, and man, much further down this chain than he imagines, can see only a small part of it (just as the Saturnian cannot see several stars which are visible to the Sirian). Ridiculous in his *mega*, anthropocentric pride (especially the person in academic dress), and absurdly wretched in his warring, man may be physically *micro* but his capacity for precise scientific observation (with a quadrant and microscope) suggests *mega* potential for discovery. But only if he will learn humility, and to eschew metaphysical absurdities about the soul. He should not jump to conclusions, like the muddle-headed Saturnian, but proceed in the judicious manner of the Sirian — and of the little follower of Locke. *Micromégas* is a eulogy of Newtonian physics and Lockian epistemology, of divine power and man's potential for enlightenment. As its moral lesson it teaches the virtues of a measured response; and it teaches it through comedy. If man can learn to laugh at himself, then he can aspire to higher things; for 'ce rire inextinguible . . . selon Homère, est le partage des dieux' (37). We must laugh, and withhold judgement. The Sirian's nice book of philosophy may be blank, but we have the pages of *Micromégas* itself. Comedy and fiction have provided their own kind of answer where metaphysical logic fails. Where reason falls short, the fable provides.

6

Man in the World

Le Monde comme il va, Zadig, Memnon,
and *Lettre d'un turc*

Tâchons de nous éclairer ensemble.

(*Essai sur les mœurs*, i. 3)

By 1744 Mme du Châtelet's enthusiasm for Leibniz had abated, and Voltaire's attitude had become uncompromising. He writes to Martin Kahle, a professor at Göttingen who had attacked his *Métaphysique de Newton*: 'Quand vous aurez aussi démontré en vers ou autrement, pourquoi tant d'hommes s'égorgent dans le meilleur des mondes possibles, je vous serai très obligé.'[1] To this question Voltaire himself, of course, had no ready answer. On the contrary, his jibe to Kahle shows that he is becoming more and more aware of the difficulty. So do *Le Monde comme il va* and *Zadig*. The problem of evil is now firmly on the Voltairian intellectual agenda, and both Pope and Leibniz are set to become favourite targets of his sceptical satire. Nevertheless Voltaire will remain enough of an Optimist never totally to lose faith in a rational God. He may mock 'la raison suffisante' in *Candide*, but he can still write in the *Dictionnaire philosophique* some five years later: 'Dieu ne peut rien faire sans raison.'[2] He may even have re-read the *Essais de théodicée* between 1768 and 1770;[3] and his last *conte*, the *Histoire de Jenni*, bears the marks of an enduring sympathy with the Leibnizian conception of a benevolent and rational God who has done His best.

The voyage of reason which Voltaire first depicted in *Micromégas* continues to be the central narrative device in almost all his *contes* up to and including *Candide*. After *Micromégas* the cosmic dimension receives less emphasis (until *Songe de Platon*), and the voyage becomes predominantly an exploration of human destiny and an attempt to

[1] D2945 (? March 1744).
[2] *Dict. phil.*, 289 ('Miracles').
[3] See Barber, *Leibniz in France*, 241 and 214, n. 4.

find some solution to the problem of evil here on Earth. Physics and metaphysics give way to ethics and anthropology. It is true that the Scythian hero of the first of these *contes*, *Le Monde comme il va*, is sent to Persepolis by a celestial visitor, but his brief is decidedly *terre-à-terre*: and whereas Micromégas proceeds on his interstellar way in the manner of an elegant young gentleman engaged upon his Grand Tour, Babouc resembles a Foreign Office envoy gradually going native.

LE MONDE COMME IL VA

Le Monde comme il va first appeared in 1748, and therefore after the first version of *Zadig* was published as *Memnon, histoire orientale* in 1747. Although one of the stories with which Voltaire entertained the duchesse du Maine in 1746 or 1747, its origins may date back to late 1739 when Voltaire and Mme du Châtelet visited Paris together. On the other hand, as with *Micromégas*, further details in the text suggest that later events in the capital have also been included. Whenever it was written, it is clear that the main subject of the *conte* is not only Persepolis/Paris but 'le mal moral' which, in the *Traité de métaphysique*, Voltaire had blithely declared to be a 'chimère'.[4]

Babouc, like Micromégas, is a representative of Lockian under-standing. He has been born with 'discernement'; never having been to Persia, he can be impartial; and he readily absorbs Ituriel's lesson in empirical free-thinking ('marche, regarde, écoute, observe, et ne crains rien': 39). His journey of discovery, in which (like the Ingénu later) he complements personal experience with the reading of books, provides a familiar checklist of Voltairian 'bêtes noires': war; religious practices; ecclesiastical, legal, and conjugal hypocrisy; the buying of military commissions and legal offices; tax-farmers and money-lenders; dull preachers; the low condition of actresses; mon-astic luxury; Jansenism; the 'glitterati'; bitchy lampoons and vapid novels; bureaucracy.

The technique of the alien observer in the manner of Montes-quieu's *Lettres persanes* is put to repeated use as an instrument of demystification: a requiem mass and a theatrical production are thus almost unrecognizable, while one can quite see why a tragedy is

---

[4] Ed. Temple Patterson, 16.

more likely to persuade its audience than a sermon its congregation. The progression from religion to commerce to the arts is particularly reminiscent of a similar sequence in the *Lettres philosophiques*. But there is a laborious repetitiveness about the narrative which is only partly excusable as contributing to a pastiche of the formulaic *conte oriental*. (Thus in ch. 1 Babouc visits the soldiers, the officers, and the satraps before the battle; and then, during battle, he observes them in the reverse order.) Likewise, considerable heavy-handedness is evident in the way in which the central message of the *conte* is conveyed, namely that the human condition reveals surprising moral contrasts. Thus in chapter 1 the counterweight to the authentic Voltairian satire on war and its political causes is based on a distinctly inauthentic lack of evidence:

S'étant ensuite informé plus en détail de ce qui s'était passé dans l'une et l'autre armée, il apprit des actions de générosité, de grandeur d'âme, d'humanité, qui l'étonnèrent et le ravirent. 'Inexplicables humains, s'écria-t-il, comment pouvez-vous réunir tant de bassesse et de grandeur, tant de vertus et de crimes?' (41)

Usually Voltaire narrates the 'détail', but here we are fobbed off with generality, albeit with a clear allusion to the Pascalian view of the human condition as a combination of 'grandeur et misère'.

Subsequently one of the most striking features of the story is the way in which the evils of Persepolis continue to be demonstrated 'in action', in both narrative and dialogue, while the 'good side' is merely reported but not demonstrated. Thus, in the case of religion, Babouc's first impression (based on his experience in the poorest quarter of Persepolis) is corrected on seeing the rest of the city: 'il vit d'autres temples mieux bâtis et mieux ornés, remplis d'un peuple poli, et retentissants d'une musique harmonieuse' (43). But the brevity and generality of this account are insufficient to outweigh the impression of ugliness, cacophony, and nauseous putrefaction created by the earlier, and longer, episode. This imbalance persists throughout the story until, in chapter 9, Babouc's acceptance of the fact that evil conceals good is summarized and presented without evidence or substantiation:

Il conçut à la fin que ces grands corps [i.e. the armies of Persia and India], qui semblaient en se choquant préparer leurs communes ruines, étaient au fond des institutions salutaires; que chaque société de mages était un frein à ses rivales; que si ces émules différaient dans quelques opinions, ils

enseignaient tous la même morale, qu'ils instruisaient le peuple et qu'ils
vivaient soumis aux lois, semblables aux précepteurs qui veillent sur le fils
de la maison tandis que le maître veille sur eux-mêmes. Il en pratiqua
plusieurs, et vit des âmes célestes. (50)

Similarly, in chapter 10 the judges (who owe their positions to
wealth and rank rather than legal training) reach the right judgement, and in so doing illustrate two ideas: that 'les lumières de la
raison' are a surer guide than books; and that 'il y [a] souvent de très
bonnes choses dans les abus' (51). But again the reader is not allowed
to judge for him- or herself: 'la cause était connue de tout le monde'
(51) but not by us.

Admirers of a radical Voltaire may be surprised to see the second
of these ideas, particularly as Voltaire seems to signal his agreement
by making one of his Hitchcock-like appearances in the guise of the
'sage lettré' who expounds it to Babouc: ' "Vous êtes étranger", lui
dit l'homme judicieux qui lui parlait; "les abus se présentent à vos
yeux en foule, et le bien, qui est caché et qui résulte quelquefois de
ces abus mêmes, vous échappe" ' (50). The lack of persuasiveness
with which it is conveyed throughout *Le Monde comme il va* may,
however, put one in mind of the first idea: trust reason, not the
book. For to what extent can we trust *Le Monde comme il va*? Perhaps
we should think for ourselves and, accepting the evidence for evil,
question the value of the mere assertion of a hidden 'good'. Perhaps
the *conte*'s explicit statement of its message is reminiscent of the
preacher whose sermon Babouc hears. He too, like *Le Monde comme
il va* itself, 'parla longtemps du vice et de la vertu', but his effort is
pointless and inauthentic: 'Ce mage divisa en plusieurs parties ce qui
n'avait nul besoin d'être divisé; il prouva méthodiquement tout ce
qui était clair, il enseigna tout ce qu'on savait. Il se passionna froide-
ment, et sortit suant et hors d'haleine' (45). The result of his effort
is a congregation which has not used its brain and yet believes itself
edified: 'Toute l'assemblée alors se réveilla et crut avoir assisté à une
instruction' (45). This is just the sort of readership Voltaire himself
does not want, as we have already seen him make plain in the preface
to the *Dictionnaire philosophique*: 'les livres les plus utiles sont ceux
dont les lecteurs font eux-mêmes la moitié'.

This question of how best to convey a message is the very issue
with which the story ends. Required from the outset by Ituriel to
'rendre un compte fidèle' (39), Babouc comes to the moment when
he must finally do so. Yet 'il craignait même le compte qu'il allait

rendre' (54), clearly because he wants to present the evil of Persepolis in such a way that the city will not be condemned. He himself has tended to jump to (usually unfavourable) conclusions throughout the story and he does not want Ituriel to do the same. Persisting with what it is tempting to see as a pun on 'conte', the final paragraph of the story begins:

Voici comme il s'y prit pour rendre ce compte. Il fit faire par le meilleur fondeur de la ville une petite statue composée de tous les métaux, des terres et des pierres les plus précieuses et les plus viles; il la porta à Ituriel: 'Casserez-vous, dit-il, cette jolie statue, parce que tout n'y est pas or et diamants?' Ituriel entendit à demi-mot; il résolut de ne pas même songer à corriger Persépolis, et de laisser aller 'le monde comme il va'.

Babouc has proved an able 'compteur/conteur' by preferring question to explicit statement and by using a symbolic object to produce the desired response in his 'destinataire'. The nature of this response ('à demi-mot') is that which Voltaire encourages in his own readers in other stories, but not, it seems, in *Le Monde comme il va*. For the passage continues: 'Car, dit-il [i.e. Ituriel], "si tout n'est pas bien, tout est passable"'. With this 'translation' of the statue the story ends weakly, despite the final witty reference to the trying experience of being three days in the belly of a whale.[5]

Le Monde comme il va thus offers an object lesson in the problems of didactic literature. Like Voltaire himself, Babouc prefers to trust to the allegorical and the implicit, and one has only to compare the banality and clichéd character of Ituriel's aphorism with the comparative, if unsustained, subtlety and ambiguity of Voltaire's portrait of Persepolis. Just as Ituriel understands the significance of the statue 'à demi-mot', so Voltaire's audience at Sceaux and his subsequent readers would have spotted the not-so-hidden analogies between Persepolis and Paris.

The main point at issue in this particular piece of didactic literature is the problem of moral evil. This problem is not susceptible of easy resolution, but a narrative of examples can lead its reader to reserve judgement and accept the essentially Optimistic notion that good may come of evil more persuasively than any abstract, sweeping generalization (clichéd or not). Ituriel's moralizing sentence severely

---

[5] The last two sentences of *Le Monde comme il va* (added in 1752) effect a frame for the story since the language with which Ituriel dispatches Babouc to Persepolis at the beginning pastiches the Book of Jonah.

weakens the impact of Babouc's allegorical statue not only by being blatant and thus patronizing the receiver, but also because, by being an abstraction, it lays itself more open to immediate refutation and rejection. Hence the reference to Jonah. Put generally, the sentiments 'laisser aller "le monde comme il va"' and 'si tout n'est pas bien, tout est passable' may immediately make the reader think of exceptions to the rule; and Jonah is thus a kind of representative or spokesman for those who would contest the generalization. But any desire to disagree with the message of *Le Monde comme il va* is then tolerantly but firmly disallowed as being the result of the (understandable) ill-humour consequent upon the discomforts of cetacean engorgement. Babouc's symbolic conclusion, on the other hand, remains open to interpretation: the idea of a mixture of good and bad is left vague, being indeterminate as to the relative amounts involved, and as to the precise nature of the ingredients. It is thus easier to accept, and each reader can, as it were, mix his or her own.

What Ituriel does is to turn Babouc's subtle message into a system. But Babouc's essential point (and Voltaire's) is that the nature of life, the muddle of reality, cannot be reduced to, or contained within, a system; and so the story duly ends on an affirmation of urbanity and sophisticated accommodation. Unlike Jonah, Babouc the Scythian[6] is 'de bonne humeur' because he has been to the opera and the theatre and has 'soupé en bonne compagnie'. The more effective solution to the problem of moral evil in *Le Monde comme il va* is a life-style, not an aphorism: a supper-party, not a saw.

But is it a solution? The end of *Le Monde comme il va* has evident parallels with the end of *Micromégas*, though the celestial–terrestrial positions are reversed. A question is 'answered' not explicitly but by the presentation of a text – be it bookish or statuesque – to be interpreted, and the process of interpretation is relatively simple. The Secretary of the Académie des Sciences and Ituriel, neither of them much given to irony or ambiguity, take their respective points at once. In *Micromégas* the reader, too, gets the point and, metaphysical enquiry having drawn a blank, is left with a story which demonstrates the merits of looking at the facts. The reader of *Le Monde comme il va*, on the other hand, may get the point but when, treating

---

[6] For Voltaire and his contemporary readers the Scythians were representative of a primitive, barbarous people. In Voltaire's tragedy *Les Scythes* (1767) they represent Genevan moral austerity in comparison with the less virtuous but more flexible and humane Persians (i.e. the French).

the story itself as a mixture of precious and base metals, he looks for 'le bien', he finds himself at a loss because of the marked narrative imbalance in the presentation of good and evil. *Le Monde comme il va* proclaims a message which its evidence fails to sustain, and not all the urbanity in the world can conceal the fact. Voltaire the 'mondain' has come to an awareness of the problem of evil which is greater than he wishes to admit and, like Babouc, he fears that it may show: 'Il craignait que Persépolis ne fût condamnée; il craignait même le compte qu'il allait rendre' (54).

ZADIG OU LA DESTINÉE

In *Zadig* Voltaire faces up more squarely to the problem of moral evil. But what does one mean by '*Zadig*'? The first version of *Zadig*, entitled *Memnon, histoire orientale*, appeared in 1747, comprising fifteen chapters. Three further chapters were then added ('Le Souper', 'Les Rendezvous', and 'Le Pêcheur'), and the name of the eponymous hero changed: the resulting *Zadig ou la destinée, histoire orientale* appeared on 10 September 1748. Subsequently, for the 1756 edition, chapter 6 (then entitled 'Les Jugements') was expanded and became chapters 6 ('Le Ministre') and 7 ('Les Disputes et les audiences').[7] Meanwhile, probably just after the Walther edition of 1752 and shortly before Voltaire's departure from Berlin in March 1753, the two chapters 'La Danse' and 'Les Yeux bleus' were written, but these were not published until the posthumous Kehl edition of 1784. Given the note which follows these two additional chapters, it is clear that Voltaire envisaged both them and the note itself as constituting a new ending to his story. By *Zadig*, therefore, one ought to mean the 1756 edition together with an 'Appendice' consisting of 'La Danse', 'Les Yeux bleus', and the final translator's note.[8]

The central subject of the story is man's pursuit of happiness. More broadly, it considers the question of divine providence: is there such a thing as providence or are events governed by blind chance? is such providence benevolent? how free is man to seek his own

---

[7] For an analysis of these revisions see Ursula Schick, *Zur Erzähltechnik in Voltaires 'Contes'* (Munich, 1968), 26–46.

[8] *Zadig ou la destinée*, ed. Georges Ascoli, edn. rev. Jean Fabre, 2 vols. (Paris, 1962) and *RC* provide such versions. Less satisfactory editorial decisions appear in *Romans et contes*, ed. Pomeau, and *Zadig and Other Stories*, ed. H. T. Mason (Oxford, 1971).

happiness? To debate these issues, *Zadig* confronts an idealized representative of Enlightenment values with the world of moral evil and then imports an angel, in the manner of a *deus ex machina*, to provide some metaphysical answers to the hero's resulting perplexity. These answers are received with the famous Zadigian 'Mais . . .', and the story (in its final version) closes with a non-ending. Foreshadowing Gide's *Les Faux-Monnayeurs*, 'pourrait être continué' is the message of its final sentences: 'C'est ici que finit le manuscrit . . . On sait qu'il [Zadig] a essuyé bien d'autres aventures qui ont été fidèlement écrites. On prie messieurs les interprètes des langues orientales de les communiquer, si elles parviennent jusqu'à eux' (123).

The 1748 version ends happily like a fairy-tale: 'ce fut le plus beau siècle de la terre: elle était gouvernée par la justice et par l'amour. On bénissait Zadig, et Zadig bénissait le ciel.' The final version ends with Zadig still the powerless plaything of fate: 'partons, et voyons à quoi me réserve ma triste destinée' (123). Living happily ever after becomes life as continuing uncertainty, life as an endless journey of experience. There is a note of Stoic acceptance now, and heaven is no longer to be blessed and glorified. One must simply grin and bear it; or rather just bear it. The grin is absent from the end of the final *Zadig*, and the emphasis is on the word 'triste'. In some ways, therefore, *Zadig* is a less optimistic story than *Candide*.

Zadig is notable in that, for the first time in a Voltairian *conte*, the voyage of reason assumes a temporal dimension, and anticipation and retrospect play an important part in the structure of the story. On the one hand, this temporal element is still essentially a function of the philosophical issues in question (the possibility of prediction; the value, if any, of remembering the lessons of the past; etc.) rather than part of any study of psychological development; and one could say that, once the initial disillusion has taken place, Zadig undergoes no further change in outlook — even when he submits to providence and swallows his 'Mais . . .'. On the other hand, it is an exaggeration to see no development in the hero at all.[9] The innocent optimism of the young bachelor in chapter 1 is quite different from the wisdom of the angelically tutored king at the end of chapter 19, let alone from the dogged, uncomprehending perseverance of the royal right-hand man at the end of the 'Appendice'.

[9]   See Nancy Senior, 'The Structure of *Zadig*', *SVEC* 135 (1975) for a brief survey of critical response to this question.

The characteristics of a 'roman de formation' may not be numerous in *Zadig*, therefore, and Zadig does not undergo a metamorphosis in quite the gradated way that Candide, the Ingénu, and the Homme aux quarante écus do. But there is a forward progression in the work which counterbalances the self-containedness of each individual chapter and lends the whole story considerable artistic and philosophical unity. It may be useful to trace this progression in detail before assessing how this *conte* employs fiction to treat the problem of evil.

Zadig's name being derived from the Hebrew word 'Zadik' for the 'just one', or the Arabic 'Saddyk' for the 'truthful' one,[10] Voltaire's hero is self-evidently the embodiment of reason and virtue: 'Zadig, avec de grandes richesses, et par conséquent avec des amis, ayant de la santé, une figure aimable, un esprit juste et modéré, un cœur sincère et noble, crut qu'il pouvait être heureux' (58). Here, from the outset, Voltaire situates his latest *conte philosophique* within a central eighteenth-century debate: do reason and virtue lead to happiness?[11] The naïve assumption that they do constitutes the 'system' which Voltaire proceeds to subject to the test of experience in *Zadig*.

At the beginning Adam has already met his Eve in the person of Sémire, but there is no question yet of any forbidden fruit: his attachment to her is 'solide et vertueux', though Sémire, potential instrument of Satan that she is, 'l'aimait avec passion' (58). But Zadig's innocence is soon disabused: his 'grâces' and 'vertus' are powerless against the 'jalousie' and 'vanité' of Orcan and the 'caprice' of Sémire (58–9). His first lesson is that woman is fickle, and that social class makes no difference to this apparently universal trait: Azora the 'citoyenne' displays a 'légèreté' to match the shallow loyalty of the 'premier parti de Babylone'.

Having proved his point (in ch. 2) Zadig withdraws to his own Garden of Eden (on the banks of the Euphrates) to eat of the Tree of Knowledge in solitary calm: 'Rien n'est plus heureux, disait-il,

[10] Several of the names in the text derive from Hebrew: e.g. Almona (widow); Coreb (royal adviser); Ogul (round); Azora (helpmeet); Balzora (house of Baal, house of false idols). See Pauline Kra, 'Note on the Derivation of Names in Voltaire's *Zadig*', *Romance Notes*, 16 (1975). As with Zadik and Saddyk some of these names are also similar or identical in Arabic (e.g. Almona), which is more in keeping with a pastiche of the *Thousand and One Nights*.

[11] See Robert Mauzi, *L'Idée du bonheur dans la littérature et la pensée françaises au XVIIIᵉ siècle* (Paris, 1960), chs. 12 and 13. On *Zadig* see pp. 64–7.

qu'un philosophe qui lit dans ce grand livre que Dieu a mis sous nos yeux' (62). But his intelligence leads to an excess of reason (in respect of the dog and the horse), which brings his first accusation of guilt and his ejection from this paradise. And yet this fallen hero cannot apply the lesson of experience (by pretending not to have seen the escaped prisoner) without getting into further trouble: 'qu'il est difficile d'être heureux dans cette vie!' (65). In chapter 4 sagacity proves no match for theological dispute; social charm provokes envy; and valorous patriotism in time of war is no shield against a smear-campaign in time of peace. But, thanks to royal favour: 'Zadig commençait à croire qu'il n'est pas si difficile d'être heureux' (69); and when virtue is royally rewarded: 'Zadig disait: "Je suis donc enfin heureux!" Mais il se trompait' (70). The wisdom of Solomon (chs. 6 and 7) is not proof against love nor the wrath of a jealous husband. For the second time this Babylonian Adam is ejected from paradise; and a lover's self-denial and a Prime Minister's loyalty are rewarded with impending death: 'Le malheur de Zadig vint de son bonheur même, et surtout de son mérite' (75).

Chapter 8 was the middle chapter of the 1748 *Zadig*, and in the final version the end of chapter 8 remains the halfway point in terms of the plot. Indeed it represents a kind of temporal pivot, with chapters 1–8 being dominated by prolepsis[12] while the remainder of the story is studded with retrospective summaries. Thus, too, the anticipatory leitmotif of 'être heureux' is replaced by an incessant recapitulation of past calamities and their illogical causes.[13] At this halfway point the forward momentum of the hero's quest for happiness carries him to a zenith of ministerial achievement and amorous delight, which is immediately followed by a nadir:

Qu'est-ce donc que la vie humaine? O vertu! à quoi m'avez-vous servi? ... Tout ce que j'ai fait de bien a toujours été pour moi une source de malédiction, et je n'ai été élevé au comble de la grandeur que pour tomber dans le plus horrible précipice de l'infortune. Si j'eusse été méchant comme tant d'autres, je serais heureux comme eux. (79)

The original naïve assumption has been replaced by another equally

[12] See the anticipations of future events at the end of chs. 4 and 5, in the middle of ch. 7 (when Zadig fails to replace the garter), and at the end of ch. 7.
[13] At the end of ch. 8, midway through ch. 10, and at the end of chs. 13, 14, 15, and 17.

simple and equally erroneous equation: vice, not virtue, is the means to happiness.

At this pivotal point the hero himself is at his least balanced, and his mood oscillates wildly between visions of cosmic sublimity and earthly wretchedness in terms which recall *Micromégas*:

Il admirait ces vastes globes de lumière qui ne paraissent que de faibles étincelles à nos yeux, tandis que la terre, qui n'est en effet qu'un point imperceptible dans la nature, paraît à notre cupidité quelque chose de si grand et de si noble. Il se figurait alors les hommes tels qu'ils sont en effet, des insectes se dévorant les uns les autres sur un petit atome de boue. Cette image vraie semblait anéantir ses malheurs en lui retraçant le néant de son être et celui de Babylone. Son âme s'élançait jusque dans l'infini, et contemplait, détachée de ses sens, l'ordre immuable de l'univers. Mais lorsque ensuite, rendu à lui-même et rentrant dans son cœur, il pensait qu'Astarté était peut-être morte pour lui, l'univers disparaissait à ses yeux, et il ne voyait dans la nature entière qu'Astarté mourante et Zadig infortuné. (79–80)

This passage is at once an echo of Zadig's earlier ambition to be a 'philosophe qui lit dans ce grand livre que Dieu a mis sous nos yeux' (62) and a foretaste of the meeting with the angel, and as such fulfils an important structural function at this middle point in the *conte*.

Just as the story began with examples of the fickleness of women, so the second half begins with the tale of Missouf, 'la belle capricieuse'. In chapter 6 it was said that Zadig's 'principal talent était de démêler la vérité, que tous les hommes cherchent à obscurcir' (71); but he is still no nearer coming to terms with the fickleness, not so much of women (for Astarté has shown her loyalty and even Missouf wishes Clétofis were alive) but of fate. This hero of the Enlightenment spends the remainder of the story very much in the dark, and until his meeting with Jesrad he is but a bewildered plaything of providence. Not that he ceases to be an active champion of deism and Enlightenment values. He attacks false religion and superstition (Sétoc's worship of the sun, moon, and stars, the practice of self-immolation) and exposes professional charlatanry (the medical treatment of Ogul); he secures justice (Sétoc's debtor is unmasked); he puts an end to division (at the Balzora world trade fair); he educates (Almona); he brings solace and material comfort (to the fisherman). But throughout his campaign of virtue it is evident that each case must be treated on its merits; and not even the simplest moral rules are of much help. A damsel in distress neither wants to be saved nor deserves to be; a slave-master is reasonable; a brigand is generous.

Zadig is a compendium of virtue and vice. The four cardinal virtues (justice, prudence, temperance, fortitude) are displayed by Zadig himself, while Sétoc's fairmindedness, Otame's valour and integrity, and the exploits of the contestants in the 'combat de générosité' complement the depiction of virtue through the central character. The reformed Almona is said to be a 'femme charitable et prudente' (91), though the manner in which she demonstrates this improvement may not normally be associated with the cardinal virtues. The seven deadly sins are equally in evidence: avarice (Arbogad, Sétoc's debtor, the applicants for the post of Nabussan's treasurer); anger (Clétofis); envy (l'Envieux); gluttony (Ogul); pride (Yébor, the Almona who wishes to commit suttee); sloth (the fisherman who has given up fishing, Babylon itself); lust (the priests whom Almona seduces). Zadig is shown to be immune from each of these vices: 'Il ne prétendait pas en savoir plus que les artistes; il les récompensait par des bienfaits et des distinctions, et n'était point jaloux en secret de leurs talents' (74). Thus, in one sentence, he is exonerated from avarice, envy, and pride. Just once his virtue slips when he is insulted while wearing the villainously named Itobad's armour: 'La patience lui échappa' (108); but this occurs very shortly before he is 'saved' by Jesrad.

This systematized Christian catalogue of morality is thus demonstrated to be plainly wanting. Here is Zadig with all the virtues and none of the vices, and yet he is not happy. On the other hand, Arbogad the brigand is 'le plus heureux de tous les hommes', not least because he knows that temperance may keep one awake at night (95). Nor does such a simple list of moral 'dos' and 'don'ts' serve in the slightest to explain the relationship between good and evil, or whether, and in what way, evil is necessary in the world: 'Les hommes, dit l'ange Jesrad, jugent de tout sans rien connaître' (113). For answers to these questions supernatural agency is required, or at least the philosophy of Leibniz and Pope. As chapter 17 comes to a close, Zadig has reached the end of his tether, wandering along the banks of the Euphrates 'rempli de désespoir, et accusant en secret la Providence, qui le persécutait toujours' (109). This is blasphemy, and the angel Jesrad redeems the sinner by an act of Enlightenment grace: 'tu étais celui de tous les hommes qui méritait le plus d'être éclairé' (113). Why? Presumably because he doubted.[14] Jesrad's redeeming gospel owes much to Leibniz and Pope. He gives the sufficient reason for the existence of evil people ('ils servent à éprouver un petit nombre de justes répandus sur la terre': 114)[15] and asserts the necessary interdependence of good and evil ('il n'y a point de mal dont il ne naisse un bien'). When Zadig asks why not a world without evil, the answer derives from the theory of possible worlds:

Alors . . . cette terre serait une autre terre; l'enchaînement des événements serait un autre ordre de sagesse; et cet autre ordre, qui serait parfait, ne peut être que dans la demeure éternelle de l'Etre suprême, de qui le mal ne peut approcher;

and Jesrad goes on, in terms which again are reminiscent of *Micromégas*, to cite the well-ordered diversity of the universe as evidence of God's power:

Il a créé des millions de mondes dont aucun ne peut ressembler à l'autre. Cette immense variété est un attribut de sa puissance immense. Il n'y a ni deux feuilles d'arbre sur la terre, ni deux globes dans les champs infinis du ciel, qui soient semblables.

Everything is as it has to be, as it should be: 'tout ce que tu vois sur le petit atome où tu es né devait être dans sa place et dans son temps fixe, selon les ordres immuables de celui qui embrasse tout.' Above all there is moral order in the universe. To man, who judges by appearance, events may seem contingent: 'mais il n'y a point de hasard: tout est épreuve, ou punition, ou récompense, ou prévoyance.'

Jesrad's pronouncements are evidently drawn from the philosophy of Optimism. To say that Optimism is being satirized at this point, however, would be an exaggeration. The manner of presentation is obviously comic, what with white-bearded hermits clutching books

---

[14]   Cf. the second *Discours en vers sur l'homme*: 'et ton âme sincère, / Puisqu'elle sait douter, mérite qu'on l'éclaire' (ll. 25–6). The similarity of the names Jesrad and Jesus reinforces the parallel between the angel's intervention and the Christian redemption.

[15]   Jesrad's statement that 'les méchants . . . sont toujours malheureux', on the other hand, derives more from Pope. See Barber, *Leibniz in France*, 221. Barber tends to underrate the presence of Leibnizianism in *Zadig*. For a different view see *Zadig*, ed. Ascoli, vol. i, pp. xlii–xlvii.

of destiny and turning into angels, and the various punning references to Jesrad's supernatural powers (his 'lumières supérieures' and
'charme invincible' (110), how he 'parlait avec tant d'ascendant sur
Zadig' (111), and how the latter's freedom of action is suspended by
'l'ascendant de l'ermite' (113)). But this genial idiocy is in keeping
with the rest of the story. Moreover, when Optimism is satirized
elsewhere in the story, the point is made quite plain. Thus, in the
episode (added in 1752) of the lady who must choose a father for
her priest-begotten child, Zadig prefers the one who will try to
render his child 'juste et digne d'avoir des amis' rather than the
paternal pedagogue who will teach him, *inter alia*, 'les monades et
l'harmonie préétablie' (72). As in *Micromégas*, Voltaire ridicules specific aspects of Leibnizian metaphysics without rejecting it all out of
hand: in respect of German theodicy, at least, he believes that partial
evils do not vitiate the whole.

But are Jesrad's arguments Voltaire's? Or, less biographically put,
does the context of *Zadig* as a whole suggest that these arguments
are the most satisfactory solution to the mystery of moral evil which
the story displays? Many readers have felt that there is something
unsatisfactory about the imported, supernatural character of the
spokesman. *Zadig* has stressed the human aspect of the problem of
evil (physical evil being more the domain of *Candide*), and a solution
to this problem is being sought throughout the story by the light of
human reason. But Jesrad's message is superhuman, and susceptible
of acceptance or rejection only on irrational grounds: either genu-
flexion or a speechless 'Mais . . .'. This 'unsatisfactoriness', though,
is part of the point of the story.

Voltaire's originality in *Zadig* is to use the structure of the *conte
oriental* as a model for the providentialist view of human history. On
the face of it, events in the narrative seem random and haphazard:
the worlds of Babylon, Egypt, and Arabia appear fantastical and
absurd. Chance and coincidence rule. This is the realm of fickle fate,
of Missouf 'la belle capricieuse'. And yet there is order: the teleology
of the narrative is such that events are all leading, by a roundabout
route, to that Happy Ending which is a necessary part of the genre.
As readers we are given a strong sense of inevitability: we may feel
that the author is playing with us, as fate plays with Zadig, but in
the end all will be well. And, sure enough, every character in the
story does get his or her just deserts. This is the world of divine
providence, of the ever-loving, faithful Astarté.

All is well that ends well: or is it? In its final version *Zadig* has in effect two endings, corresponding to the hero's two reactions to Jesrad's pronouncements, namely acceptance and doubt. According to one reading, Zadig submits to providence and the story ends with the chapter 'Les Enigmes'. Zadig wins through and marries Astarté; justice and love prevail: 'On bénissait Zadig, et Zadig bénissait le ciel'. The 'Appendice' does not alter this interpretation, but simply reminds the reader of the original fiction of a 'discovered manuscript' in a rather laboured fashion.

According to a second reading, what matters is that Zadig says 'Mais . . .': Jesrad's explanation is inadequate and cannot be verified. We note the irony that Zadig wins Astarté by solving the riddles, but these riddles (about time and life) are silly party games. He has been unable to solve the riddle that matters: i.e. the nature of providence and the reason for evil. And the text continues after the happy ending, just as the three dots after 'Mais' leave one in a state of suspense (like the 'blank pages' ending of *Micromégas*). The two chapters which figure as an 'Appendice' are perhaps, of all the chapters in *Zadig*, those which most resemble the *Thousand and One Nights* (because of the mechanical and contrived nature of the stratagems which they describe). As such they refer the reader back to the 'Epître dédicatoire' preceding chapter 1, since it too is a blatant pastiche of the *Thousand and One Nights* (in style as well as content). The 'Appendice' thus provides a measure of formal order to offset the relative disorder which it brings to the plot by detracting from the tidiness of the happy ending. It reminds us of Zadig when he was a plaything of fate, and the final words of the second appended chapter put the emphasis back, once and for all, on his ignorance and uncertainty: 'partons, et voyons à quoi me réserve ma triste destinée.' Following these words the final translator's note further detracts from the textual completeness of *Zadig* by exposing it as a manuscript with gaps that have yet to be filled.

This second reading is altogether more satisfactory, especially when one is reminded of the 'Epître dédicatoire' in which 'l'histoire de *Zadig*' is described as an 'ouvrage qui dit plus qu'il ne semble dire'. The story is announced from the outset as having gaps to be filled by the reader, lines to be read between. Indeed the 'Approbation' with which *Zadig* begins suggests that the only way to get the truth across is to say not just half of what you mean, but actually to state the opposite of what you mean. The imaginary author of a report for M. le Cadi-Lesquier (in charge of censorship) likes *Zadig* and pans it. One may now be further reminded, this time of the incident with the broken tablet on which Zadig writes some occasional verse in chapter 4. The four-line text speaks of the power of love and implies praise for the King: split in two, its left-hand side reads like treason. Incomplete texts are a danger to life.[16]

Or rather life is an incomplete text. History, or 'destinée', is itself a book, and it comes in two halves: the past and the future. Jesrad has read both halves, while Zadig has read only one (his past) and 'ne put déchiffrer un seul caractère du livre' (109) which Jesrad hands him. As we have seen, *Zadig ou la destinée* is itself a 'livre des destinées', being divided into two sections, the first proleptic and the second retrospective. Moreover the two halves seem to share certain similarities, almost as if it might have been possible to predict the second from the first. Already it has been seen that each section begins with the unreliability of women. In each half, Zadig's attempts to demythify legendary creatures (the griffin, the basilisk) endanger his life. In chapter 4 the Epicurean stage of his development is marked by 'soupers délicats' (66), which constitute a model of civilized living; while in chapter 12, entitled 'Le Souper', the supper-party at Balzora becomes (as in *L'Homme aux quarante écus*) the model of unity in diversity. Differences of nationality, religious belief and practice, diet, linguistic register, and capacity to drink are subsumed under a shared belief in one Creator and, by a nice paradox, in the unanimity of the guests who unite in rejecting Zadig's assertion that 'vous êtes tous du même avis' (90).

Beyond these and other parallels between the two sections (for example between Moabdar and Sétoc), further connections emerge from the text, tantalizing the reader with hints of some overall plan into which they can all be recuperated. Thus the first half (chs. 1–8) contrasts the disloyalty of Sémire at the beginning with the loyalty of Astarté at the end; just as the second half (chs. 9–19) begins with Zadig the gallant knight rescuing Missouf and ends with him win-

---

[16] Incomplete texts are also a guarantee against publishers' malpractice. In order to limit the print run of *Zadig* to a thousand copies (and to avoid pirated editions) as well as to keep distribution in his own hands and preserve his anonymity, Voltaire had the first 144 pages printed by one publishing house (Prault in Paris) and the remaining 51 pages printed by another (Lefèvre in Nancy). He then had the pages sewn and bound by two women under the supervision of his secretary Longchamp. See the latter's *Mémoires*, ii. 154–8; *Zadig*, ed. Ascoli, vol. i, pp. x–xiii; and Vaillot, *Avec Madame Du Châtelet*, 350–1.

ning the hand of Astarté in a tournament. In each case the contrast is also a contrast in literary register between the burlesque and, respectively, the tragic and the epic. Thus Sémire's aversion to one-eyed men is opposed to Moabdar's murderous jealousy; and Zadig's final jousting in the manner of chivalric epic is humorously adumbrated by his unseemly fight with Clétofis. In the course of the latter combat his unworthy opponent exploits Zadig's gallant offer to spare him (note the direct parallel with the overcoming of Otame, who accepts Zadig's mercy and proclaims him king like a true gentleman: 108); while Missouf falls equally short of the champion's ideal lady as she plonks herself on the grass and 'rajuste sa coiffure' (81). One might be forgiven for wondering if, in this story which mixes good and evil in surprising and unfathomable ways, there is not also a kind of literary Manicheism at work. Compare also Astarté, the beautiful queen whom Zadig worships and who traces his name in the sand with her 'main divine'; but who is also a comic goddess as, from her place of refuge within a statue in the temple of Orosmade, she booms out an oracle that scares her husband witless (102).

When it comes to 'livres des destinées', therefore, *Zadig* may be no less ambiguous than the book of life itself. The sublimity of the stars and the wretchedness of the earth are matched by the corresponding elements of 'high' and 'low' literature which are so skilfully juxtaposed and interwoven in the texture of the story. In fact this parallel between reading life and reading a book is but one of the many examples of self-reference in *Zadig*, all pointing to the perils of communication and understanding. What medium can one trust to convey one's thoughts? What medium can one trust to receive another's?

Throughout the story verbal language is contrasted unfavourably with the non-verbal. At the very outset the ideal figure of Zadig is juxtaposed with the Babel that is Babylon:

On était étonné de voir qu'avec beaucoup d'esprit il n'insultât jamais par des railleries à ces propos si vagues, si rompus, si tumultueux, à ces médisances téméraires, à ces décisions ignorantes, à ces turlupinades grossières, à ce vain bruit de paroles, qu'on appelait 'conversation' dans Babylone. (57)

The way in which this sentence itself reflects the linguistic tumult which it describes alerts the reader to the important fact that 'truth' may often lie as much, if not more, in how something is said than in what is said. In the course of the story verbal language repeatedly figures as an instrument of deceit, be it in Sémire's protestations of undying love, or the book which the great doctor Hermès writes to 'prove' that Zadig should not have recovered from his eye injury (59), or the 'annales secrètes' of Babylon which merely 'prétendent' that Zadig succumbed to the sexual temptations of high office (74). 'Natural' language is safer, from the 'ce grand livre que Dieu a mis sous nos yeux' (62) to the looks and blushes which reveal Astarté's love: 'les passions ont des signes auxquels on ne peut se méprendre' (77). Objects may not always convey the right message: the blue garter sent by 'l'Envieuse' bespeaks an excessive intimacy between Zadig and Astarté, and Itobad's borrowed armour proclaims him temporarily a champion. But blue babouches and yellow ribbons are faithful, and unwitting, 'indices' (77). Sétoc's lying debtor is outwitted by a rock: 'Eh bien! s'écria Zadig, je vous avais bien dit que la pierre porterait témoignage' (84); and the dwarf mute (a trusted servant for his very incapacity to speak) can convey what he wants in symbolic pictures.

Verbal language may not always be untruthful: Astarté's tracing of ZADIG reveals where her heart lies (100), and Zadig himself is capable of ensuring 'conversations charmantes' at supper (66) and of composing a 'discours éloquent' to demonstrate that 'le Dieu du ciel et de la terre, qui n'a acception de personne, ne fait pas plus de cas de la jambe gauche que de la jambe droite' (73). But this latter incident is instructive. Zadig is clearly *Zadig* 'mis en abyme' since in his advocacy of a rational God he has eschewed the excesses of the Oriental style. 'L'envieux' and his wife take on the role of Voltaire's potential critics:

L'envieux et sa femme prétendirent que dans son discours il n'y avait pas assez de figures, qu'il n'avait pas fait assez danser les montagnes et les collines. 'Il est sec et sans génie, disaient-ils: on ne voit chez lui ni la mer s'enfuir, ni les étoiles tomber, ni le soleil se fondre comme la cire; il n'a point le bon style oriental.' (73)

In seeking to persuade, Voltaire has not employed the flowery rhetoric that might be thought 'de rigueur' for orators and polemicists. Not for him the fine periods of a Bossuet, but rather the unadorned 'style de la raison'. But, alas, this is not what wins Zadig's congregation over: 'Tout le monde fut pour lui, non pas parce qu'il était dans le bon chemin, non pas parce qu'il était raisonnable, non pas parce qu'il était aimable, mais parce qu'il était premier visir.' For language to convince it has to speak with political authority, but how should Voltaire the *conteur* acquire that authority? He is 'dans le bon chemin', his thinking is 'raisonnable', and his wit 'aimable', but with what power can he win us readers over? By the power of example. Later, as has already been seen, *L'Homme aux quarante écus* will show the *conte* replacing the 'codes' of authority as the proper guide for the ideal citizen. At this stage what we find is *Zadig* taking up the problem of literary persuasion which is highlighted at the end of *Le Monde comme il va* and figuring a solution in a more sophisticated way than Babouc's statue. Zadig's sermon is, in fact, an explanation of what he has demonstrated by example, namely by favouring neither the left nor the right foot as he entered the temple. Courageous as he is, he jumped in with both feet. Throughout the story he shows himself to be an admirable Enlightenment communicator by this resort to action in preference to words. Thus, when reasoned discussion gets him nowhere with Sétoc as he seeks to convince him of the superstitious nature of his religious worship, he lights some candles and throws himself at their 'feet' – with great success: 'Sétoc comprit le sens profond de cet apologue' (86). In persuading Almona that the rigours of suttee are, to say the least, supererogatory, it is clear that his eloquence has been much aided by the charms of his own person (just as Almona will later persuade the priests of the need to spare Zadig by displaying her supposedly inadequate body). With the father who wants to see which of his sons loves him the more, Zadig's ploy is again to let actions speak louder than words. In the griffin and basilisk episodes he persuades those in thrall to taboo and quackery by actions, in the first case proposed (not eating the griffin) and in the second case effected (playing ball). In both cases he persuades obliquely, not by confronting the prejudice or false belief directly, but by assimilating it and disarming it. In the same way Voltaire addresses the belief that virtue brings happiness and in the same way, through narrative example, he stealthily destroys the equation.

    In the two chapters of the 'Appendice' this method is given great prominence. Indeed the contrast with Jesrad's 'imported', metaphysical methods is made explicit: 'Je n'aime pas le surnaturel, dit Zadig; les gens et les livres à prodiges m'ont toujours déplu' (119). Where anyone can profess financial integrity and true love with fine words, these qualities reveal themselves reliably only in action; and Zadig's stratagems in these final chapters have all the hallmarks of a scientific experiment set up to demonstrate an empirical fact. Moreover, as in the case of Sétoc's stars, the lesson registers more firmly in the mind of the receiver for having to be inferred from the evidence by the receiver himself. The most useful lessons, like the most useful books, are those where the pupil-reader has to do half the work by putting two and two together.

Where the 'Appendice' may bring untidiness to the happy ending of traditional story-lines, it offers a fitting conclusion to the allegory of persuasion that is *Zadig*. The final chapter begins, in a manner which is becoming almost predictable, with a reference to Rollin's 'l'esprit et le cœur'. The pitfalls of verbal pedagogy are made explicit:

'l'esprit et le cœur!' . . . on n'entend que ces mots dans les conversations de Babylone;[17] on ne voit que des livres où il est question du cœur et de l'esprit composés par des gens qui n'ont ni de l'un ni de l'autre. (120)

Set against this bookish persuasion are the practical demonstrations of *Zadig*. And true to its own principles *Zadig* the book seeks to persuade by practical example. The nearest thing to a theoretical 'lesson' in *Zadig* is voiced by Jesrad: 'L'ermite soutint toujours qu'on ne connaissait pas les voies de la Providence, et que les hommes avaient tort de juger d'un tout dont ils n'apercevaient que la plus petite partie' (112). In its subtitle *Zadig* makes clear that providence is its subject, and in its narrative it subjects the reader to this very experience of partial vision. There are alluring vistas of pattern and significance, but we remain essentially none the wiser about any authorial grand design which might provide a satisfactory metaphysical answer to the problem of evil. Nevertheless all the possible evidence of human vice and virtue has been provided, and this time, unlike in *Le Monde comme il va*, the 'good side' is represented convincingly in action. In *Zadig* the counterpart of Babouc's statue is not so much Jesrad's Book of Destiny as the (fictionally invented) problematic and lacunary nature of the text itself. Indeed, not only is *Zadig* a partial text, it is also a translation. Where *Zadig*, 'tout instruit qu'il était dans plusieurs langues, ne put déchiffrer un seul caractère' in Jesrad's Book of Destiny (109), so too (as Sadi informs Sheraa) the original of *Zadig* was written in Old Chaldean 'que ni

---

[17] This allusion recalls the scathing reference to Babylonian conversation at the beginning of ch. 1 and so reinforces the framework technique to which the 'Appendice' contributes.

vous ni moi n'entendons' (56). It has been translated into Arabic for
the amusement of Ouloug-beg, just as the incomprehensible signs
of providence have been translated by Voltaire into the amusing
language of the *conte*.

   Zadig constantly gives the impression of telling only half the story,
as if we too were reading the left-hand side of a broken tablet. In
the story it is a parrot who restores the integrity of the tablet and
thus rescues Zadig from execution for treason. Does this perhaps
suggest a necessary connection between unthinking verbal imitation
and conformity to a dominant ideology, such that by contrast the
fragmentary and the linguistically innovative are to be seen as guar-
antees of an authentic independence of mind? For this is not the
only parrot in Voltaire's *contes*. At the end of *Le Blanc et le noir* (with
which *Zadig* has many Oriental and Manichean affinities) Topaze
fails in his attempt to demonstrate the nature of time to Rustan and
resorts to a parrot who will explain everything: 'vous en serez content; sa mémoire est fidèle, il conte simplement, sans chercher à
montrer de l'esprit à tout propos et sans faire des phrases. – Tant
mieux, dit Rustan, voilà comme j'aime les contes' (266–7). Unfortu-
nately, it turns out, the manuscript recording the story of this prelapsarian narrator has been well and truly lost.

   As readers of *Zadig*, too, we must tolerate the absence of any ideal
psittacine narrator who can reveal all. We must make do with an
incomplete translation. Where *Micromégas* shows that we do not
know the long and the short of it, *Zadig* demonstrates that we do
not know the half of it. Just as Astarté and Missouf are said to bear
a close resemblance to one another (81), so the two conceptions
of providence which they represent – benevolent logic or wanton
caprice – may not be easy to distinguish. Zadig may be admirable in
that 'en tout il préférait l'être au paraître' (66), but it may not always
be possible to tell which is which.

   But at least we know that *Zadig* is not just one of those 'contes
qui sont sans raison et qui ne signifient rien' (56) which are so
beloved of Ouloug's sultanas. It may resemble one of the *Thousand
and One Nights*, which in turn are likened to meandering conversations, but, as we know, *Zadig* 'dit plus qu'il ne semble dire'. It
resembles rather the private conversation which Sadi requests from
Sheraa: 'une minute pour avoir l'honneur de vous parler raison' (56).
In fact the final 1756 version of *Zadig* shows Sadi to be using the
conte as a means of seduction, for the new last chapter – 'Les Yeux

bleus' — concerns precisely a man's search for a woman he can trust.[18] Indeed so does the whole of *Zadig*. Sadi is sending this manuscript to Sheraa to please her but also to test her: 'Vous avez même un petit fonds de philosophie qui m'a fait croire que vous prendriez plus de goût qu'une autre à cet ouvrage d'un sage.' Will she be like the other sultanas who prefer the Oriental equivalent of Mills and Boon, or will she resemble the sultan himself who 'aimait mieux la lecture de *Zadig*'? 'Je me flatte que vous ne leur ressemblerez pas, et que vous serez un vrai Ouloug.' Indeed, will she note the similarity of the names Sadi and Zadig?

By employing 'le style de la raison' and by requesting the honour 'de [n]ous parler raison', Voltaire seduces us in both 'esprit' and 'cœur' and puts us to the test. He has no answer to the 'énigme' of providence, but he does have an answer for those who would propose an answer. Pope's *Essay on Man* ends on a confident note:

> That virtue only makes our bliss below;
> And all our knowledge is, ourselves to know.

Anyone who has read *Zadig* cannot but see the naïvety in such confidence. Virtue brings no bliss, and little do we know. What Voltaire wants is that we should share his scepticism. He cannot order us to do so, but he can inveigle us by narrative into an attitude of mind that mirrors his own. Doubt is what marks Zadig out for angelic enlightenment. If we will but abandon our blind faith in easy explanations and dare to doubt, then we may be enlightened by *Zadig*. It is up to us to break the taboo and say 'Mais . . .': thus will each reader show herself to be 'un vrai Ouloug'. Once again, where reason falls short, the fable provides. Moreover, perhaps the real secret is not only to read stories but to tell them: 'Arbogad buvait toujours, faisait des contes, répétait sans cesse qu'il était le plus heureux de tous les hommes, exhortant Zadig à se rendre aussi heureux que lui' (95). In the *Thousand and One Nights* story-telling is a matter of life and death: in *Zadig* it offers a path to happiness and human understanding more sure than that of reason or virtue. Perhaps the sultana Sheraa will realize that, in name at least, she is already half-way to becoming Schéhérazade.

---

[18] Cf. the feminist readings of Carol Sherman, in whose view Voltaire is always thinking of a female reader. See *Reading Voltaire's 'Contes': A Semiotics of Philosophical Narration* (Chapel Hill, NC, 1985), 14.

MEMNON OU LA SAGESSE HUMAINE

Written towards the end of 1748 and/or at the beginning of 1749, *Memnon ou la sagesse humaine* was published late in 1749. The name of the central character is, of course, a leftover from the first version of *Zadig*, while the story as a whole takes as its starting-point the same dubious assertion that virtue in the form of good behaviour ('sagesse') will bring happiness: 'Pour être très sage, et par consé-quent très heureux, il n'y a qu'à être sans passions' (125). It concludes that true 'sagesse' (wisdom) may lie elsewhere. Of all Voltaire's *contes* it is the most explicit example of the recurrent narrative scheme whereby a theoretical design for living is adopted a priori and then found wanting; and, as in *Micromégas*, this process is accompanied by the metamorphosis of the central character from a cipher into a sympathetic (human) being. For, commendable though Zadig may be, he is an idealized portrait of the 'sage' and, for all his suffering, it is impossible to see him as anything but exemplary and formulaic. Because he is perfect and shows no weakness, other than one single moment's loss of patience, he fails to move. From *Memnon* onwards Voltaire begins to depict the human condition in a manner which plays on the reader's sensibility and engages him or her more and more in the events portrayed. 'Man in the world' becomes 'people like us in the world'.

At the beginning of the story Memnon's 'system' is essentially the same as the programme of moderation set out ten years earlier in the *Discours en vers sur l'homme*. Presented, in an economical paradox, as 'le projet insensé d'être parfaitement sage', this programme con-sists in temperance and prudence, those two cardinal virtues which are less emphasized in *Zadig* than justice and fortitude. The delights of the fair sex, the bottle, the table, and good company are foresworn, and an independent financial future is assured by investment in gilt-edged government stock. After the plan, the reality — a transition which is effected by Voltaire with symbolism that is similarly econ-omical: 'Ayant ainsi fait son petit plan de sagesse dans sa chambre, Memnon mit la tête à la fenêtre' (126). The patronizing tone here adopted by the narrator is maintained in the unsympathetically brief, matter-of-fact, and mechanical way in which Memnon's system is systematically shown to founder. Our hero is doing his best, the narrator seems to imply, but really anyone could have told him how foolish he was being. The knowing puns ('examiner . . . ses affaires', 'la conseilla de si près'), the ironic repetition of 'le sage Memnon', and the appeal to a worldly readership ('Comme ils en étaient là, arrive l'oncle, ainsi qu'on peut bien le penser'), all serve to distance us from this expert in living. Proverbial wisdom is shown to be his downfall:

On le fait boire pour dissiper sa tristesse. Un peu de vin pris modérément est un remède pour l'âme et pour le corps. C'est ainsi que pense le sage Memnon; et il s'enivre. On lui propose de jouer après le repas. Un jeu réglé avec des amis est un passe-temps honnête. Il joue; on lui gagne tout ce qu'il a dans sa bourse, et quatre fois autant sur sa parole. (127)[19]

But the narrator's tone ceases to be unsympathetic, and such a response to Memnon's woes is displayed to disadvantage by the ladies at the court-house and the 'satrape' who speaks to him 'd'un air de hauteur, et ricanant amèrement' (128). While his system has been foundering, Memnon has been displaying some estimable and understandable human qualities: the desire to help someone in distress, the need for company, the reluctance to be a wet blanket, the hope for justice. In the latter part of the story, the boot, so to speak, is on the other foot. Now Memnon, a chastened realist, meets a superior prig who has his own system. This new Jesrad may come from a small star near Sirius but he plainly lacks the charm, not to mention the stature, of Micromégas. The nonsensical character of what he is about to pronounce is wittily adumbrated in the punning description of his appearance: 'Il avait six belles ailes, mais ni pieds, ni tête, ni queue, et ne ressemblait à rien' (128). Being all angel, and having not a leg to stand on, this 'bon génie' is a parody of the Christian ministry. Like some monk who follows his vows to the letter, this purveyor of heavenly truth has no need of women, no need to eat, no money (129). His sole occupation is to 'veiller . . . sur les autres globes qui nous sont confiés'. But, as Memnon points out in his new role as human humorist: 'C'est bien la peine . . . d'avoir un bon génie dans une famille, pour que de deux frères l'un soit borgne, l'autre aveugle' (129).

The angel's sermon is not entirely false, since he points out what the story has already demonstrated in practice: the impossibility of the 'projet d'être parfaitement sage'. He presents a vision of man's

[19] On the treatment of proverbial wisdom in *Memnon* see also Bennington, *Sententiousness and the Novel*, 26–8.

place in the scheme of things which obviously derives once more from Leibniz and Pope but travesties their Optimism in its arguments. Leibniz never maintained either that God actually created 'cent mille millions de monde' beyond this one (they were simply possible) nor that there exists one world where everything is perfect. The idea that 'tout se suit par degrés' is a version of the Great Chain of Being, which is then parodied in the hypothesis that the bottom of the chain is a globe 'où tout le monde est complètement fou'. Finally, Pope's 'tout est bien' (130), for all that the context is faithfully recorded ('en considérant l'arrangement de l'univers entier') appears ludicrous in the light of what has gone before: 'Ah! je ne croirai cela, répliqua le pauvre Memnon, que quand je ne serai plus borgne.' Here, at the end, the narrator's use of 'pauvre' is not patronizing but compassionate.

Memnon ou la sagesse humaine marks an important point in Voltaire's development as a *conteur*. There is a note of bitter and disabused pessimism now, which may well derive from the *conteur*'s personal circumstances. By the end of 1748 Voltaire cannot be said to have been having the most Leibnizian time of it: disfavour at court following temporary success, ill health, Mme du Châtelet's affair with Saint-Lambert, all combined to banish the comparative serenity which Voltaire had enjoyed during the first ten years of his life at Cirey (1734–44). The events of 1748 in particular seem to have marked a watershed, the ridge coming between the 1748 version of *Zadig* and *Memnon* (as well as the less Optimistic additions to *Zadig* in 1752/3). This was also the moment at which Voltaire appears finally to have renounced his faith in human free will and to have espoused the determinist views to which Frederick of Prussia had been trying to persuade him since the 1730s: 'Je ne vis point comme je voudrais vivre, mais quel est l'homme qui fait son destin? Nous sommes dans cette vie des marionnettes que Brioché mène et conduit sans qu'elles s'en doutent.'[20]

For René Pomeau this marks the beginning of Voltaire's career as a *conteur*.[21] Although more recent research has shown that his career began earlier, there is still an element of truth in Pomeau's claim. The immediate effect of this pessimism on Voltaire's stories is a new sympathy for humanity, and this sympathy finds eloquent

[20] D3601 (2 Jan. 1748, to Cideville).
[21] *La Religion de Voltaire*, 248.

expression in the *conte*. Indeed there is a kind of paradox at work here, and one which is similar to that which informs Diderot's *Jacques le fataliste*. As long as Voltaire took a libertarian view of the human condition, his characters were in fact essentially ciphers, products of the genre and/or philosophical debate in which they found themselves. Now that he has become more aware of human beings as powerless puppets, his representatives of humanity take on more of the attributes of everyday reality, and his plots more of the substance and muddle of human existence. Just as Jacques le fataliste is more 'real' than his master, so Memnon and the characters in *Candide* and *L'Ingénu* have considerably more flesh and blood than Zadig or the 'philosophes' in *Micromégas*.

As to Memnon, he is clearly a counterpart of Mesrour in *Le Crocheteur borgne*, but each is missing a different eye. Mesrour sees only the good side, and his dream, correspondingly, is one of escapist delight which brings no disenchantment in its wake. Memnon comes to see the bad side, and his dream affords no consolation or solution. Mesrour, however, is well able to look after himself, and his debonair devotion to 'eau-de-vie' may amuse but it is unlikely to pull at a reader's heartstrings. Moreover he poses no threat: he knows his place and is happy with it. He is exemplary in an implausible way. In *Memnon*, on the other hand, the angel's complacent belief that 'il faut que tout soit en sa place' (130) rings false: 'Eh mais! dit Memnon . . .'. Where is man's place in the world now? What is man's place in the universe? In Memnon's wry rejoinders to his 'bon génie' there is a dogged resilience which may affect the reader and persuade him or her of this character's essential humanity.

As to the metaphysical dimension, if the definitive post-1748 *Zadig* shows us that we do not know the half of it, then here we learn that we cannot see the half of it. Gone is the cheering universal vision projected on to a peripatetic Sirian; gone are the revelations of telescope and microscope. The more Voltaire observes the problem of evil and man's pursuit of happiness, the less he sees. Memnon's angel may be 'tout resplendissant de lumière' (128), but it is a light that blinds. To the comforting logic and order of Jesrad's Optimism Zadig offered up a 'Mais': Voltaire now dares to say 'même non'.

Lettre d'un turc was written at about the same time as *Memnon* and published in 1750. Like *Micromégas* and *Le Monde comme il va* it is another traveller's tale, but this time the narrative is in the first person. It is true that, in a certain sense, *Micromégas* is a first-person narrative since the narrator intervenes in the story from the outset, claiming to have met Micromégas on the latter's most recent visit to Earth, and later comments on his own activity as a narrator-cum-historian. But he is not a participant in the plot. *Le Monde comme il va* is subtitled 'Vision de Babouc écrite par lui-même' but, although Babouc is directly involved, the narrative is nevertheless firmly in the third person, perhaps to suggest the distance between Babouc and his dream self. The epistolary Turk, however, is Voltaire's first first-person eyewitness, thus anticipating Scarmentado and the first-person narrators in *L'Homme aux quarante écus*. For all that Voltaire the puppeteer/story-teller may identify with his major characters, and even depict his own self and experience in them, he usually prefers nevertheless to manipulate his marionnettes from a distance. In this respect, then, *Lettre d'un turc* is an exception.

On this occasion the voyage of reason is undertaken to visit a 'correspondant' — i.e. a corresponding member of a learned society. In the absence of any detail about this society one must infer that the Turk's grown-up pen-pal, Omri the Brahmin, is as much a member of the society of *philosophes* as the Muslim narrator. For the latter manifests the usual characteristics of Voltaire's enlightened travellers: 'je tâchai de m'instruire . . . j'écoutais beaucoup et remarquais tout' (131). The function of this voyage of reason is, as before, that of defamiliarization: here, of monastic life and the ethos of the 'honnête homme'. Visiting the Gavani pagoda to observe the fakirs, the Turk notes the behaviour of the contemplatives and then of the followers of the 'anciens gymnosophistes, qui menaient une vie active' (131). The former either count the vowels in a holy book or hang about in a trance; the latter go in for dancing on their hands or doing unmentionable things with nails. A French 'correspondant' could have written of endless masses or convulsive trances on the graves of Jansenist deacons. Strange ways, indeed, but as this Turkish man of the world tolerantly observes: 'au demeurant les meilleures gens du monde' (132).

The defamiliarizing focus of the story is concentrated on

one particular 'gymnosophiste', Bababec. With the abuse of the confessional not far from his mind, Voltaire shows Bababec sitting nude in his cell, chained, on a stool of nails 'qui lui entraient dans les fesses'. Him being a revealer of naked truth, 'Beaucoup de femmes venaient le consulter'; and Voltaire the Turk cannot resist a double pun when he remarks that 'on peut dire qu'il jouissait d'une très grande réputation' (132). In the ensuing conversation between Bababec and Omri, dubious Gallic humour gives way to rather simple fun at the expense of metempsychosis and the Brahmin heavens, which number thirty-five. The nub of the *conte*, however, lies in the comparison between a layman's life of virtue and that of a fakir, which, though ostensibly no less virtuous and no less practical, is as pointless as its seat is pointed.

Omri's rather solemn self-portrait suggests that *Memnon ou la Sagesse humaine* may not be Voltaire's last word on the subject of happiness and virtue at this time: 'Je tâche, dit Omri, d'être bon citoyen, bon mari, bon père, bon ami; je prête de l'argent sans intérêt aux riches dans l'occasion; j'en donne aux pauvres; j'entretiens la paix parmi mes voisins' (132). As in *Le Monde comme il va* this statement of the good has to be taken on trust; we are shown no evidence of this worthy life in action. But there is no suggestion that we should not believe Omri to be a splendid citizen in every way. For Bababec, of course, such virtue is not enough if Omri does not '[se mettre] quelquefois des clous dans le cul'. This fakir is nothing if not a fundamentalist, and in his view the nineteenth heaven is the very best Omri can hope for in the circumstances. What follows is obviously a condemnation of the arrogance and lack of practical value of the fakir's absurd mortification of the flesh. Worse, it conceals a lasciviousness which means that while Bababec tries the life of an 'honnête homme' for a fortnight, he returns to his previous existence for the sake of his sex life: 'les femmes ne venaient plus le consulter; il . . . reprit ses clous, pour avoir de la considération.'

The first of Voltaire's *contes* to focus centrally on religion, *Lettre d'un turc* is a slight story in which the obviousness of the anti-clerical message is matched by the low register of the wit. Effects of incongruity are at their most manifest, with the narrator's sneeze putting paid to a fakir vision of the 'lumière céleste' (132) and would-be entrants to the thirty-fifth heaven running about the place with their heads stuck up a pipe (132). The rarefied mysticism of Eastern religion is debunked by the frank evidence of man at his most corporeal, and one notes a new readiness to call a spade a spade, or at least a 'derrière' a 'cul'. The deadpan luridness of la Vieille in *Candide* is not far away.

The flavour of Enlightenment is pronounced in the implicit plea for religious toleration: the Turk and his Brahmin friend Omri get along famously and ecumenically in both ablution and diet, while co-religionists Omri and Bababec fall out because they interpret their common faith differently in respect of the after-life. One sees, too, the familiar preference for practicality over metaphysics: generous alms are worth a thousand nails up the backside. Above all there is a philosophy of action which, too, prepares for *Candide*. Omri has no patience with the unproductive Bababec: 'Je fais cent fois plus de cas d'un homme qui sème des légumes, ou qui plante des arbres, que de tous vos camarades qui regardent le bout de leur nez ou qui portent un bât par excès de noblesse d'âme' (133). Horticultural Candide will say much the same thing to Pangloss at the end of that story, although the Optimist's penchant for the fair sex, not to mention a dose of the clap, means that when he contemplates 'le bout de son nez', he will find it most regrettably 'rongé' (151).

By 1750 Voltaire's career as a *conteur* may be said to be fully under way. In particular it is now evident that the medium of story-telling is enabling him to approach the problem of evil from a number of different angles and to present a series of provisional 'solutions' which dispense with the metaphysical subtlety of a Leibniz and which each suggest a possible *modus vivendi*. *Le Monde comme il va* affirms that we must take the rough with the smooth but enjoy the smooth to the full. *Zadig* displays the merits of enlightened virtue battling against the odds and mutedly commends a dogged perseverance. Zadig's final statement is a sign that his curiosity, at least, has not been quenched: 'voyons à quoi me réserve ma triste destinée.'

The ideal world described by the 'bon génie' in *Memnon* is a bleak, inhuman place, which is unlikely to help him fulfil his stated aim: 'je viens pour te consoler' (129). The world of Zadig and Memnon is a world in which the passions may cause evil but are to be embraced for all that; and Voltaire is at one with Jesrad when the latter argues that the passions are 'les vents qui enflent les voiles du vaisseau . . .: elles le submergent quelquefois; mais sans elles il ne pourrait voguer' (112). But it is not always easy to weather the storm. Memnon's sarcastic rejection of providence is one possible response, and Scarmentado will be his heir. Omri's belief in humanity and culture is another.

What *Lettre d'un turc* shows above all, however, is that the storm is bad enough without adding the hot air of theological dispute. Man's natural desires are a sufficient threat to order and harmony without creating new sources of abuse and dissatisfaction. Jesrad states that 'Tout est dangereux ici-bas, et tout est nécessaire' (112). Why add to the dangers with the man-made follies of religious fanaticism and unnatural behaviour (chastity, abstinence, mortification of the flesh, torture, burning at the stake, etc.)? Such is the infamy of man in the world, and it must be extirpated. Voltaire's famous campaign to 'écraser l'infâme' began in earnest only when he established his 'safe house' at Ferney in 1759, but *Lettre d'un turc* shows that it is already beginning. For the moment, the infamy of Bababec ceases for a mere fortnight: later the effects will be more lasting.

7
Small Consolations
Songe de Platon, Histoire des voyages de Scarmentado, and Les Deux Consolés

Je viens pour te consoler.

(129)

Following the flurry of *contes* which Voltaire wrote or published between 1746 and 1751, there was an eight-year lull until the appearance of *Candide* in 1759. During this period only three new stories were published, all of them in the Cramer edition of Voltaire's *Oeuvres complètes* in 1756. *Songe de Platon*, as we have seen, has been thought to date back to 1738/9, but it now seems unlikely to have been written before 1752/3.[1] In several ways it is, of course, reminiscent of *Micromégas*. It is very much a *conte philosophique* in so far as it is specifically concerned with the works of Plato, especially the *Timaeus*, the *Phaedo*, and the *Symposium*. Like *Micromégas* it stresses the need for comparison and the importance of seeing things in context; and once again fun is poked at analogical reasoning (15).

But the tone of *Songe de Platon* is very different. In *Micromégas* the poor design of the earth is criticized by the Saturnian (27), but his fault-finding is intended to show the partiality of his judgement since he is taking the tidiness of his own planet as an absolute yardstick. In *Songe de Platon*, on the other hand, the criticisms are more extensive and more telling. Man has no saving graces now, least of all 'ce que vous appelez "la raison"' which is 'trop ridicule, et approche trop de la folie' (16). The metaphysical discussions in *Micromégas* show the extent of this 'folie', of course, but the compensation of man's ability to measure is absent from *Songe de Platon*. Now, too, disease is a major factor in the equation, and a new note is struck by

[1] See above, Ch. 5, n. 5.

the scathing account of how smallpox annually decimates the world's population, while 'la sœur de cette petite vérole' puts paid to the genital health of the remaining nine-tenths. Pangloss is near.

The Leibnizian theory of possible worlds is here traced back to its Platonic origins, but there is little persuasiveness in the depiction of Démogorgon, creator of the earth, doing his level best to mix good and evil to man's greatest advantage. It is small consolation to know that things are worse on Mars, and even smaller consolation that Earth and the other planets constitute no more than a 'coup d'essai', and that the Demiurge's construction workers will be back in 'quelques centaines de millions d'années' (17) to have another go at getting things right. Not that they ever will, of course: perfection, as Plato and Leibniz know, lies with God (17).

Gone, therefore, is the reassuring Newtonian vision of *Micromégas*. In that story a fundamentally sanguine vision of the human capacity to understand the universe is projected on to the citizen of a Sirian planet who journeys through space as easily as the new science is pushing forward the frontiers of knowledge. In *Songe de Platon*, on the other hand, the anthropomorphic account of Démogorgon depicts the gallant effort of an artist ('à peu près comme Phidias et Zeuxis': 15) who thinks he has managed a masterpiece only to be booed and hissed. For Voltaire any cosmological explanation of the problem of evil is now rather like one of his own failed tragedies. The mess that man is in seems like a bad dream — or one of Plato's. In his day, as in the days of the Old Testament, 'Les rêves . . . donnaient une grande réputation' (15). Now the best sort of dream takes the form, not of metaphysics or religiously interpreted visions, but of fiction, and a fiction that wakens. Our eyes have been opened to the inadequacy of the Platonic theory of creation: 'Et puis vous vous réveillâtes' (17). Voltaire's last word on the matter comes in the *Dictionnaire philosophique*: 'Cette fable théologique tombe en poussière par l'objection terrible qu'il n'est pas dans la nature d'un Dieu tout-puissant et tout sage de faire bâtir un monde par des architectes qui n'y entendent rien.'² But already in *Songe de Platon* he had destroyed the 'fable théologique' with his own fable of reason.

---

² *Dict. phil.*, 69 ('Bien (Tout est)').

HISTOIRE DES VOYAGES DE SCARMENTADO

If *Songe de Platon* is an anti-*Micromégas*, then the *Histoire des voyages de Scarmentado* is an anti-*Zadig*. While Zadig brings the wisdom of Solomon successfully to bear on schism and dispute, Scarmentado encounters religious controversy at every turn only to hasten on as soon as he can, leaving the disputants to their murderous devices. He has no Astarté to spur him on nor bearded angel to set him straight. He discovers that the world is full of religious sects for whom the faith is best served by cruelty to the infidel, and he finds ultimate happiness in the tolerance of his wife's own infidelity. Zadig may not know the half of it, but Scarmentado has seen it all.

Written in the immediate aftermath of Voltaire's unhappy departure from Frederick's court, this story has often been thought among the bleakest and most personally bitter of all Voltaire's *contes*. Scarmentado's *Histoire*, like Babouc's vision in *Le Monde comme il va*, is 'écrite par lui-même', but this time the writer also adopts the first-person voice to tell us directly the story of his life and how he has been 'scarmentado'.[3] Despite this personal immediacy, the circumstances of Voltaire's own experience may have had less to do with the bleakness of *Scarmentado*, however, than what he had learnt in the course of his research for the *Essai sur les mœurs*, which was published in the same year. One may imagine the historian reacting as the Ingénu will later: 'Il lut des histoires, elles l'attristèrent. Le monde lui parut trop méchant et trop misérable. En effet, l'histoire n'est que le tableau des crimes et des malheurs' (315). The problem of evil is not just a little local difficulty, therefore, but has now assumed wide historical and geographical dimensions. Where the cosmic vision of *Micromégas* and even *Songe de Platon* tended to minimize the presence of evil by presenting it within a wider perspective, now Voltaire's *contes* tend to maximize it by presenting it as an eternal and universal phenomenon beyond which it is impossible to see. Hence the fact that this is the first of Voltaire's *contes* to turn the voyage of reason into a global tour. Candia (Crete), Rome, France, England, Holland, Spain, Turkey, Persia, China, Macao, Delhi, Africa: such is the Cretan's itinerary before he returns home to live happily ever after in cuckolded bliss. Such, too, is the somewhat mechanical geographical device which will later be employed in

---

3   From the Spanish 'escarmentar': *v. intr.*: to be tutored by experience; *v. tr.*: to inflict an exemplary punishment.

several *contes* — notably *Candide*, of course, where the New World is added to the Old, but also in *La Princesse de Babylone* and *Les Lettres d'Amabed*.

In *Scarmentado* geographical expansion is complemented by a new reliance on historical fact, and the story begins specifically in 1600. Where previously Voltaire tended to rely on a fund of fictional stories for his material,[4] now he looks to the history of real events to supply the substance of his plots. Most importantly, where once he had sought to demystify the 'invraisemblance', say, of the imaginary journey (in *Micromégas*), by giving each of its stereotypical stages a basis in fact, now he reverses the process and makes the real look unreal. Man's inhumanity to man becomes the most unbelievable fable of all. Be it an exorcism in Rome, or tucking into a nice bit of roast maréchal d'Ancre in France; the Gunpowder Plot in England, or Calvinists beheading Calvinists in Holland; the Spanish Inquisition cracking down on godparents who have the audacity to marry each other, or Turkish Muslims alternately bent on circumcision and impalement; the 'monde comme il va' presents a weird and wonderful spectacle: and 'tis all true. Most of the events recorded in the story took place between 1605 and 1620.

Indeed *Scarmentado* begins by drawing attention to its own veracity. Again as one sees in *L'Ingénu* (317–18), Voltaire the historian was scornful of the way in which all races other than the Chinese attribute mythical origins to themselves. Here Scarmentado, who is the son of the governor, is celebrated by the local poets and said to descend from Minos, the son of Europa and Zeus (in the form of a bull) and later King of Crete. When Scarmentado's father is disgraced, the mythical lineage is amended accordingly and he is now said to descend from the bastard offspring of Minos' wife Pasiphae by an unknown lover. But by a nice irony, Scarmentado will prove heir to a bull only because he ends up wearing the horns of a cuckold. Reality is rather different from the insincere mythologizing of mediocre poets.

The story as a whole proceeds to move repeatedly from the fabulous to the real in the same manner, and, as in *Lettre d'un turc* and the example just quoted, the descent is from spurious myth, mysticism, or metaphysics to the bottom line of sex. Thus the

---

[4] *Zadig*, for example, is a compendium not only of virtue and vice but of anecdotes from other books. See Ascoli (ed.), *Zadig*, ii. *passim*.

15-year-old Scarmentado is despatched to Rome for his education: 'J'arrivai dans l'espérance d'apprendre toutes les vérités' (135). And what happens? 'Monsignor Profondo ... voulut m'apprendre les catégories d'Aristote, et fut sur le point de me mettre dans la catégorie de ses mignons' (135). The 'system' of Catholic upbringing is then superseded by the reality of prostitution (la signora Olimpia who 'vendait beaucoup de choses qu'on ne doit point vendre': 135) and the decidedly non-mystical 'bonnes grâces' of la signora Fatelo. The allegorical absurdity of the names conceals a very basic reality, as do those of the révérends pères Aconiti and Poignardini.

And so the process continues. Scarmentado reaches France during the reign of Louis le juste: but where is the justice in cannibalism (136)? The 'libertés de l'Eglise gallicane' actually mean the Saint Bartholomew's Day massacre of the Huguenots; etc., etc. It would be superfluous to point out all the instances of this technique whereby abstraction is first stated and then exploded. At issue particularly is the duplicity of language itself, thanks to which holiness and 'le bien de l'Eglise' mean being good at blowing up parliaments and burning people to death (136), and thanks to which also, for the Dutch politician, tolerance is a 'dogme abominable' (137). As he proceeds on his voyage of discovery, Scarmentado becomes an ironic sounding-board for these weasel-words. In Holland he has not the leisure to wait for 'ce temps funeste de la modération et de l'indulgence' (137); in Spain he notes that the Royal Family 'parut extrêmement édifiée' by the Inquisition (137) and its 'petite fête' (138), and he echoes the description of his imprisonment as a case of being 'mal logé' (138). His own use of language is innocent, indeed candid, and he speaks his mind about the huge throne of the Inquisitor. But these 'indiscrètes paroles' (137, 138) are what land him in trouble. Even when he resolves 'de ne plus dire mon avis sur les fêtes que je verrais' (138), he cannot suppress the subversion of his candour when he states a preference for mutton that is tender (139). Similarly, when he attempts, chameleon-like, to blend with the linguistic background by amorously chanting '*Alla, Illa, Alla*' (139), he discovers that mere parrot imitation is no solution either. Borrowing the language of the enemy without understanding it is just as dangerous as using your own words.

As if to symbolize his linguistic inadaptation he is now provided with an interpreter and, during the visit to China, this works so well that his ability to convey the truth about the Pope to a rational

if improbably titled monarch ('Sa Sacrée Majesté tartaro-chinoise')
provides 'l'aventure la moins funeste de ma vie' (140). But an
interpreter is not proof against the dangers of guilt by association,
and in India a young Frenchman's 'indiscrètes paroles' provoke a
hasty getaway. The interpreter it was who died: 'il fut exécuté en
place publique, et tous les courtisans avouèrent sans flatterie que sa
mort était très juste' (141). Finally the black pirate's 'discours si sage'
provides an object-lesson in bitter unadorned truth as the layers of
respectability covering slavery and colonial gold-digging are stripped
away. The world is revealed as a kind of linguistic con-trick such
that further travel is pointless and, as Flaubert's Bouvard and Pécuchet later realize, the only obvious sensible course of action is to go
back to where one started.

Voltaire's story, like the pirate's 'discours', is also an exercise in
demystification, not only of the language and ritual employed to
disguise barbarous inhumanity in the name of religion, but also of
the voyage of reason itself. The central figure in this *conte* is an
Enlightenment anti-hero, and his biography a kind of anti-
Bildungsroman. As will happen in *Candide*, the starting-point is illegitimacy (albeit stemming from his mythical origins) and paradise:
'J'étais dans un âge où tout cela me paraissait fort plaisant' (135).
The future too may promise paradise: in France ('Heureux le temps
où il ne fera que plaisanter': 136), and in Holland (the prospective
'temps [. . .] de la modération et de l'indulgence': 137). But in the
present the quest for knowledge ('Le désir de voyager me pressait
toujours': 138) is characterized by disillusion and an imperative need
to conceal such wisdom as may have been gained: 'Je ne disais mot;
les voyages m'avaient formé' (141). Scarmentado may be 'Instruit
par le passé' (141), but the fruits of instruction are but the wiliness
and cunning of the survivor. Travel, as for the modern tourist, is
now a case of ticking something off a list the better to appreciate
'Home, sweet home': 'Il me restait de voir l'Afrique, pour jouir de
toutes les douceurs de notre continent' (141).

The central character, if not quite a man without qualities, is
nevertheless a man with no name. He is simply a function of his
past. As Everyman he represents the human being as a blank page
upon which experience inscribes a series of minuses. The few
paltry plus points serve merely to highlight the negativity of the
rest. Thus, on leaving Rome without being much the wiser about
'toutes les vérités' for which he had come: 'Je partis très content

de l'architecture de Saint-Pierre' (136); when religious controversy proves problematical in Constantinople: 'Pour m'en consoler, je pris à loyer une fort belle Circassienne' (139); and an unscheduled ship's refit in Golconda brings a sightseer's bonus: 'J'eus la consolation de l'envisager [le grand Aureng-Zeb] le jour de la pompeuse cérémonie dans laquelle il reçut le présent céleste que lui envoyait le shérif de la Mecque' (140). Such are the small consolations along the route of Scarmentado's world tour, at the end of which he can nevertheless claim that 'J'avais vu tout ce qu'il y a de beau, de bon et d'admirable sur la terre' (142). Voltaire's indictment of man in the world is comprehensive and categoric. The voyage of reason is now a round trip during which the optimistic paradise at the time of departure has become, upon return, a world in which, like Candide, one wonders 'quel démon exerce partout son empire' (210). The problem of moral evil is now so acute that happiness is horn-shaped.

LES DEUX CONSOLÉS

And what good does it do to say so? Such is the question posed by *Les Deux Consolés*. At one level this brief story demonstrates in a rather laborious way that it is small consolation to an unhappy person to learn of others who have been just as unhappy and in similar ways. As his name suggests, Citophile loves to cite examples as parallels to a present situation; but, true to Voltairian form, his system of consolation breaks down upon the death of his only son. Time, not example, is the great healer; and at the end of the story Voltaire resorts, like Babouc, to a statue in order to make this lesson plain.

At a more reflexive level *Les Deux Consolés* also points to the inadequacy of story-telling as an antidote to misfortune. The cause of the anonymous lady's grief is not stated, but it has a 'juste sujet'. Citophile's soothing stories concern a number of 'belles princesses' whose plight is more or less wretched and more or less plausible, but the clear implication is their irrelevance to the lady's own 'malheurs'. From Henrietta Maria and Mary, Queen of Scots, to the princessly student of philosophy who is permanently lame after jumping out of the window, the examples are either known already ('Je sais toute cette histoire, répondit la dame': 143) or an irritating disturbance ('Pourquoi ne voulez-vous donc pas que je songe aux miens?': 144). Classical models like Hecuba or Niobe are no more consoling, just as the lady's considerately compiled list of 'tous les rois qui avaient perdu leurs enfants' is no help to Citophile. Each person's grief is unique: 'Ah! dit la dame, si j'avais vécu de leurs temps [of Hecuba and Niobe], ou de celui de tant de belles princesses, et si pour les consoler vous leur aviez conté mes malheurs, pensez-vous qu'elles vous eussent écouté?' (144).

What stories, then, should a *conteur* address to his fellow human beings which may serve to alleviate the misery of the human condition? Tales based on classical mythology will be as remote as the histories of kings and queens. Even if he were to depict the miseries of the common man, what good would that do? The *conteur* could decide, like Scarmentado, that it is better to say nothing: 'Gardons le silence' (138). Or he can try to engender the same effect as Time the great healer. Citophile and his lady meet again after three months: 'ils se revirent et furent étonnés de se retrouver d'une humeur très gaie' (144). Perhaps the biggest consolation is laughter — the laughter of *Candide*.

8

The Candid *Conte*

Candide ou l'optimisme

Oui . . . il est beau d'écrire ce qu'on pense;
c'est le privilège de l'homme.

(218)

Candide, as everyone knows, is the longest and funniest of Voltaire's stories: quite simply, the best of all possible *contes*. More has been written about this story than about any other work in the Voltairian canon. In book upon book, article after article, and edition without number, commentators have debated its art and meaning; and as André Magnan astutely observes: 'C'est en fait le type du livre *pré-lu*.'[1] It is, of course, a satire on Optimism or, as Jean Sareil prefers to put it: 'une charge féroce contre les théories leibnitzo-wolffo-popiennes.'[2] It is also: a satire on systems; a discussion of the problem of evil; a comparison of Utopia and reality; a pursuit of the secret of happiness; an education; and, above all, a comedy.

Candide marks a watershed in Voltaire's career as a *conteur*. Not only is it the culmination of his story-telling to date, it will also prove a hard act to follow. Several masterpieces in the genre are still to come: the *conte sensible* of *L'Ingénu*, the *conte-souper* of *L'Homme aux quarante écus*, and the *conte* about *contes* that is *Le Taureau blanc*. But never again will Voltaire quite manage the sustained verve, comprehensiveness, and intricacy of structure that one finds in *Candide*. Here a whole range of previously used ingredients are brought together in one magic recipe. The global voyage of reason; the innocent observer; the combination of real events with the implausibly novelettish; the catalogue of evil; the incongruous juxtaposition of the sacred and the profane; the school of experience; the rejection

[1] André Magnan, *Voltaire. 'Candide ou l'optimisme'* (Paris, 1987), 9.
[2] 'De *Zadig* à *Candide*, ou Permanence de la pensée de Voltaire', *Romanic Review*, 52 (1961), 273.

of metaphysics in favour of an ambiguous gospel of practicality; the lacunary text of a translation. Further, a willingness to call a spade a spade combines once more with erudite allusions to various 'graves auteurs', as Voltaire exposes the absurdity of human pretension and the reality of human drives, the madness of metaphysics and the fundamental importance of facts. *Candide* is the supreme fable of reason.

Such is the spontaneous and improvised tone of *Candide* that Voltaire was long thought to have dashed it off in a matter of days, but Ira O. Wade's discovery of the La Vallière manuscript of the story in 1956/7 revealed careful and more protracted composition. The *conte* was begun probably in the autumn of 1757 and completed by the summer of the following year. It appeared on or shortly before 22 February 1759,[3] the manner of its publication being even more artful than that of *Zadig*. The Cramers, Voltaire's Genevan publishers, produced an initial print run of 2,000 copies, twice the number ordered by Voltaire for *Zadig* and about the norm at that time for a book that was expected to sell well.[4] Unbound copies of the work in pocketbook duodecimo format were discreetly despatched from Geneva on 15 and 16 January: 1,000 copies to the publisher Robin in Paris, 200 to Marc-Michel Rey in Amsterdam, and others to London and what is now Belgium. Being unbound, the text was not only lighter to transport but also easier to smuggle past the authorities. The gatherings were subsequently bound at the relevant destination and released on a prearranged date. The object was to effect simultaneous publication of *Candide* in at least five major European centres before the censors could repress it — and, in those days before copyright, to ensure the sale of as many copies as possible before the edition could be pirated.

The Genevan authorities became aware of *Candide* on 23 February,[5] their Parisian counterparts a day later. Despite the Paris police's attempts to seize all copies of *Candide* and to smash the presses on

---

3 On the question of the date of publication see *Candide*, ed. René Pomeau, *CW*, xlviii. 53–62. Given that Voltaire always claimed that his birthday was 20 Feb. and not 21 Nov. (see Pomeau, *D'Arouet à Voltaire*, 18, 27), one wonders if he may not have chosen that day for one of his greatest coups.

4 e.g. *La Nouvelle Héloïse*, published by Rey. See Maurice Cranston, *The Noble Savage. Jean-Jacques Rousseau (1754–1762)* (London, 1991), 251.

5 The 'Compagnie des pasteurs' regarded *Candide* as containing 'des choses sales, inspirant l'inhumanité, contraires aux bonnes mœurs, et injurieuses à la Providence' (D.app. 173).

which further editions were being printed, some 6,000 copies in at least six editions were sold in Paris by 10 March. It has been estimated that by early March some 20,000 copies of the work had been sold throughout Europe.[6] The Establishment had failed to stem the tide, and the Vatican's placing of *Candide* on its Index of forbidden books on 24 May 1762 seems all the more vain and belated as a result.[7] *Candide* had become a bestseller — indeed, together with *La Nouvelle Héloïse, the* bestseller of the eighteenth century.

Why *Candide?* The less satisfactory answers to this perennial question have insisted too greatly on the misfortunes of Voltaire's own life as the spur to his onslaught on Optimism. The ephemeral success at Louis XV's court, the disappointments at Frederick's and the humiliating arrest at Frankfurt, the death of Mme du Châtelet, ill health, all are seen to have played their part. Yet by 1758 Voltaire had already been settled at Les Délices outside Geneva for some three years and had found relative contentment in the company of his niece Mme Denis, and indeed in gardening. He was now comparatively immune from interference by the French and Genevan authorities, and the vast spate of writing that poured from his pen in tract and letter testifies to the positive spirit in which he was addressing the business of living.

The other factor often cited as a catalyst in the creation of *Candide* is the Lisbon earthquake of 1755. While Voltaire, along with the rest of Europe, was profoundly shocked by this natural disaster, his reaction had nevertheless already been voiced in the *Poème sur le désastre de Lisbonne.* Certainly he was made to focus more intently on the problem of physical evil, which had played a very small part in his work before then: but, having got the *Poème sur le désastre de Lisbonne,* so to speak, off his chest, he soon reverted to his usual preoccupation with the problem of moral evil. As Haydn Mason has noted, the earthquake in *Candide* stands out within the corpus of Voltaire's *contes* precisely by being exceptional, and even here Voltaire is more concerned with human reaction to it than (as in the *Poème*) with the metaphysical implications.[8] More typical of Vol-

---

[6]   See *Candide,* ed. Pomeau, 53–64.

[7]   The first unexpurgated school edition of *Candide* in France dates from 1969! See Magnan, *Voltaire. 'Candide ou l'optimisme',* 114.

[8]   Haydn Mason, 'Voltaire's "Sermon" Against Optimism: The *Poème sur le désastre de Lisbonne',* in Giles Barber and C. P. Courtney (eds.), *Enlightenment Essays in Memory of Robert Shackleton* (Oxford, 1988).

taire's position is the attempt one sees later in the *Histoire de Jenni*
to minimize the problem of physical evil by attributing the scope of
its effects to human foolishness. As it might be, you cannot blame
God if people persist in living on the San Andreas Fault.[9] A letter
of 16 December 1755 shows where Voltaire stands even in the
immediate aftermath of the disaster:

Je plains, comme vous, les Portugais; mais les hommes se font encore plus
de mal sur leur petite taupinière que ne leur en fait la nature. Nos guerres
égorgent plus d'hommes que les tremblements de terre n'en engloutissent.
Si on n'avait à craindre dans ce monde que l'aventure de Lisbonne, on se
trouverait encore passablement bien.[10]

A SATIRE ON SYSTEMS

The main function of the earthquake in *Candide* is not so much to
impugn an omnipotent and beneficent God as to ridicule the systems
by which men seek to explain and govern their lives. In the light of
the suffering and destruction caused by the earthquake, Pangloss's
Leibnizian faith in 'le meilleur des mondes possibles' seems plainly
as ridiculous as the suggestion of the Coimbra dons that an Inquisition will surely prevent another. Leibniz's Optimism is, of course,
mercilessly satirized in *Candide*, as is the philosophy of Pope. Rape,
pillage, murder, massacre, butchery, religious intolerance and abuse,
torture, hanging, storm, shipwreck, earthquake, disease, cannibalism,
prostitution, political oppression and instability: all is well. With the
licence of satire, the systems of both Pope and Leibniz are travestied.
Neither of them argued that all is well. Both acknowledged the
reality of evil and, while Pope held that it was part of an overall plan
that was good, Leibniz did not believe that all evil necessarily led
directly to good. Certainly neither of them proposed, as Pangloss
does, that 'plus il y a de malheurs particuliers, et plus tout est bien'
(154).

What Voltaire takes against is the intellectual and practical lazi-
ness to which faith in such a system can lead. In part this is because
he sees Optimism as a form of fatalism, although in the preface to
Essais de théodicée Leibniz precisely warns against this conception of

---

[9] This was Rousseau's attitude in his 'Lettre sur la Providence' (*Œuvres complètes*,
eds. Gagnebin and Raymond, iv. 1061).
[10] D6629 (to Allamand).

'le destin à la turque':[11] 'On a besoin [writes Voltaire] d'un dieu qui parle au genre humain. L'optimisme est désespérant. C'est une philosophie cruelle sous un nom consolant.'[12] Accordingly he seeks to discredit Optimism in *Candide* not only by presenting its tenets in incongruous proximity with evidence which refutes these tenets (Pope and Leibniz would say 'appears to refute'), but also by repeating them as catch-phrases to suggest intellectual and moral automatism. 'La raison suffisante', 'les effets et les causes', 'le meilleur des mondes possibles', 'tout est bien': each recurs with the frequency of a 'Hail Mary' unwittingly muttered.

That Optimism is rejected *qua* system rather than merely *qua* Optimism is evident from the caricature of other systems within the *conte*. Martin's Manicheism seems more in line with the facts of experience as the story relates them, yet even he is shown to be prejudiced in the sense that he interprets the evidence exclusively in terms of an a priori model of interpretation. Thus Candide is deep in melancholy at the failure of Cacambo to return but, in a manner reminiscent of the heartless Pangloss, all Martin can offer by way of consolation is theory and demonstration: 'Martin ne cessait de lui prouver qu'il y avait peu de vertu et peu de bonheur sur la terre, excepté peut-être dans Eldorado, où personne ne pouvait aller' (211). The whole sub-plot of Cacambo's despatch to bring back Cunégonde is designed to provide evidence of Cacambo's goodness and loyalty with which to refute Martin's pessimistic forecast that Cacambo will do a bunk; and, as if to put any Manichean readers to retrospective shame, Voltaire closes the section describing this despatch with a clear signal: 'Cacambo partit dès le jour même: c'était un très bon homme que ce Cacambo' (194). When the narrator comments at the end on Martin's 'détestables principes' (230–1) – and with a directness of value-judgement which is rare in *Candide* – it is not so much the Manicheism which is detestable as the fact that Martin judges by such fixed 'principes'. Martin has rightly predicted that Candide's goodness in giving Giroflée and Paquette money would have a bad result, but the support this lends to his Manichean theory is even more regrettable than their wretchedness because it suggests that systems of this kind can be a reliable guide.

[11]   *Essais*, ed. Brunschwig, 30–3.
[12]   D6738 (to Elie Bertrand, 18 Feb. 1756). Cf. the first of the *Homélies prononcées à Londres en 1765* (1767): 'le parti de l'optimiste . . . n'est au fond que celui d'une fatalité désespérante' (*Mélanges*, 1123).

Other systems are equally suspect. The military system with its press-ganging infringement of civil liberty, its licensed murder (or 'boucherie héroïque'), and its cannibalism in time of siege; the Church system with its dietary proscriptions and its licensed roasting that differs only incidentally from the human kebabs of the Oreillons' barbecue; the caste system wherein heraldic quarterings matter more than love but which offers Italian princesses no protection against being raped and quartered; the system of metropolitan culture wherein laughter is a form of rage (203) and tears a sign of aesthetic vulgarity (202); and the system of deductive logic itself, which feeds on its own premises and chops with no less murderous intransigence than any Bulgar: 'Je suis toujours de mon premier sentiment, répondit Pangloss, car enfin je suis philosophe: il ne me convient pas de me dédire' (228).

The whole of *Candide* is devoted to the demystification of these spurious 'fables' of reason, and the *conte* operates on two main levels. First, at the explicit, exemplary level of Candide himself whose education demonstrates how, like the Homme aux quarante écus, the product of a system can become a human being. And second, at a more implicit, insidious level, thanks to which the reader is repeatedly subjected, as in the *Histoire des voyages de Scarmentado*, to a process of exposure, to a movement from the falsity of stereotype and the linguistic sign to the 'truth' of the evidence.

CANDIDE AS A 'CONTE DE FORMATION'

In *Zadig* Voltaire uses the structure of the Oriental tale as a model of the Providentialist view of history. Here in *Candide* he uses the structure of chivalric romance. The hero, in pursuit of his beloved, undergoes a series of ordeals by which he proves himself worthy of her (except, alas, that she is no longer quite so worthy of him). Needless to say, much of the comedy in *Candide* derives from the exaggerated, accumulated, and incongruous nature of these ordeals. This time there is no question of the Providentialist view being taken seriously. 'Tous les événements sont enchaînés dans le meilleur des mondes possibles', proclaims Pangloss to the bitter end (233): but both his sequence of events and his implied definition of happiness as consisting in the consumption of 'des cédrats confits et des pistaches' are absurd. 'Cela est bien dit', answers Candide. These are just fine words; what is needed is practical action. Indeed the very notion of 'enchaînement' is undermined by the episodic structure of the story which, far from suggesting a divine plan at work, puts one rather in mind of Frank Ward O'Malley's definition of life as 'just one damned thing after another'.

Given that Pangloss's Providentialism is ridiculed, along with the teleology of romance narrative, where therefore should either Candide or the reader look for order in this chaos? Despite its rejection of Providentialism *Candide* is actually a more positive work than *Zadig* in this respect. In the latter *conte* the final version removes the assurance of a happy ending and leaves Zadig still scratching his head. In *Candide*, however, we see that there is an order to events, the order of education. And we see, too, that this order operates at the two levels previously mentioned: of Candide and of the reader.

As far as Candide himself is concerned, things happen to him suddenly and surprisingly, without apparent rhyme or reason. Yet all the time he is turning these experiences to account so that his final comment that 'il faut cultiver notre jardin' grows necessarily out of his past experience. The episodic foolery of chivalric romance is counterbalanced by the characteristics of what would come to be known as the 'roman de formation', or *Bildungsroman*. For the reader, each new episode in the story may also seem contingently appended to the last, but, as will be seen presently, it becomes apparent that each narrative incident fits in to a carefully ordered 'argument' running through the *conte*. As it were: 'tous les événements sont enchaînés dans le meilleur des contes possibles.'

Like the nameless hero of the *Histoire des voyages de Scarmentado*, Candide is, as his name etymologically suggests, a piece of white paper on which experience comes to write itself. Like *Zadig*, the story divides approximately into two halves: the first (chs. 1–18) describing a series of prohibitions and escapes; the second (chs. 19–30) the hero's ambition to be reunited with Cunégonde. Four mentors accompany him through equal stages of the journey: Pangloss (chs. 1–6); la Vieille (chs. 7–13); Cacambo (chs. 14–19); and Martin (chs. 20–25). In the last five chapters Candide is his own man. Candide's education consists essentially in the repeated discovery of the discrepancy between Pangloss's system and the facts of life: not only of his own, but of Cunégonde's (as he hears it recounted in ch. 8) and la Vieille's (chs. 11 and 12). By chapter 13 he questions Pangloss's philosophy explicitly:

C'est bien dommage, disait Candide, que le sage Pangloss ait été pendu contre la coutume dans un auto-da-fé; il nous dirait des choses admirables sur le mal physique et sur le mal moral qui couvrent la terre et la mer, et je me sentirais assez de force pour oser lui faire respectueusement quelques objections. (173)

On reaching Eldorado in chapter 18, he is in no doubt that Pangloss was wrong, at least about Thunder-ten-tronckh:

Ceci est bien différent de la Westphalie et du château de monsieur le baron: si notre ami Pangloss avait vu Eldorado, il n'aurait plus dit que le château de Thunder-ten-tronckh était ce qu'il y avait de mieux sur la terre; il est certain qu'il faut voyager. (188)

He finally renounces Optimism in chapter 19 when he sees the effects of slavery in Surinam:

O Pangloss! s'écria Candide, tu n'avais pas deviné cette abomination; c'en est fait, il faudra qu'à la fin je renonce à ton optimisme. — Qu'est-ce qu'opti-misme? disait Cacambo. — Hélas! dit Candide, c'est la rage de soutenir que tout est bien quand on est mal (193);

and on hearing the applicants for the job as his companion, he is confirmed in his new outlook:

Il songeait à Pangloss à chaque aventure qu'on lui contait. Ce Pangloss, disait-il, serait bien embarrassé à démontrer son système. Je voudrais qu'il fût ici. Certainement, si tout va bien, c'est dans Eldorado, et non pas dans le reste de la terre. (196)

Thereafter Candide seeks to think more independently, and his new readiness for flexibility is apparent in his choice of Martin as the successful applicant. The other short-listed applicants are no less miserable than Martin, and thus no less eligible under the terms of the competition to be considered 'le plus dégoûté de son état et le plus malheureux de la province' (195). But Martin is likely to be the most entertaining; and, as when Zadig at Balzora unites religious disputants in the opinion that they cannot be of one opinion, there is pleasing irony here as the unsuccessful grumblers grumble that Candide has committed 'une grande injustice' (196). Candide is thus now ready to bend the rules and to expect less simple solutions to problems.

Soon, on the voyage back to the Old World, Candide comes to realize that truth may be unobtainable in the abstract, and that conversation, like story-telling, may offer more consolation than any system: 'Ils [Candide and Martin] disputèrent quinze jours de suite, et au bout de quinze jours ils étaient aussi avancés que le premier. Mais enfin ils parlaient, ils se communiquaient des idées, ils se consolaient' (198). Here, in embryo, is the lesson of *L'Homme aux quarante écus*: namely, that conversation and the amiable exchange of inconclusive thoughts may be the essence of 'sagesse'.

As yet, however, Candide is unable to judge safely for himself. He is still deceived by appearances, be it the attempt at fraud by the abbé from Périgueux (ch. 22), or the 'happiness' of Paquette and Giroflée (ch. 24) and Pococuranté (ch. 25). But any temptation to accept Martin's alternative system of Manicheism is removed by the reappearance of Cacambo (ch. 26). Indeed the temptation to espouse any system is finally removed by two examples of the sterility of intransigence: first, as already mentioned, that of Pangloss, imprisoned within his metaphysical logic (228) and unable to develop along with the other 'gardeners' at the end; and second, in chapter 29, the young Baron's snobbish refusal to allow his sister to marry an illegitimate commoner like Candide. The Baron will never change: and so he is condemned once more to the mindless repeated action of a galley-slave.

In the final chapter of the *conte*, Candide learns three things: that opting out is no solution to the problems of living; that the metaphysical dimension of the problem of evil is best ignored; and that work is the secret to happiness. The first lesson is prompted by la Vieille's rhetorical outburst, which is in accordance with her general philosophy that life is for the living:

Je voudrais savoir lequel est le pire, ou d'être violée cent fois par des pirates nègres, d'avoir une fesse coupée, de passer par les baguettes chez les Bulgares, d'être fouetté et pendu dans un auto-da-fé, d'être disséqué, de ramer en galère, d'éprouver enfin toutes les misères par lesquelles nous avons tous passé, ou bien de rester ici à ne rien faire? (230)

The second is expounded by the dervish, whose reputation as 'le meilleur philosophe de la Turquie' may lead one to suspect him both as a philosopher and as an Oriental fatalist:

Mais, mon Révérend Père, dit Candide, il y a horriblement de mal sur la terre. — Qu'importe, dit le derviche, qu'il y ait du mal ou du bien? Quand Sa Hautesse envoie un vaisseau en Égypte, s'embarrasse-t-il si les souris qui sont dans le vaisseau sont à leur aise ou non? (231)

The third comes from the 'bon vieillard' who takes no interest in politics: 'Je n'ai que vingt arpents, répondit le Turc; je les cultive avec mes enfants; le travail éloigne de nous trois grands maux: l'ennui, le vice, et le besoin' (232). Finally, the essence of the 'bon vieillard's' lesson is summarized by Martin: 'Travaillons sans raisonner, dit Martin; c'est le seul moyen de rendre la vie supportable' (233). But even this is an abstraction, a sweeping, systematic statement. Candide's manner of expression is less dogmatically exclusive, more practical, more environmentally sound: 'il faut cultiver notre jardin.'

It is education, then, the process of enlightenment, which gives shape to experience, and not only for Candide. Cunégonde learns that there are finer castles than that of Thunder-ten-tronckh (162); and la Vieille learns from being digitally explored by pirates that travel broadens the mind (168). Indeed her mind has been so broadened, and she has learnt so frequently not to trust to appearances, that she seems almost unwilling to blame the monk for robbing them in the inn at Badajoz when he is most blatantly the culprit: 'Dieu me garde de faire un jugement téméraire!' (165). Worrying whether you have a leg to stand on (or a buttock to sit on) breeds futile, incapacitating caution.

GARDENS

At the end of *Candide*, therefore, retrospect should suggest not the absurd chain of events described by Pangloss but the Lockian 'steps by which the mind attains several truths'. Movement through time means movement towards increased knowledge and wisdom. It remains to be seen whether the lessons learnt by Candide in the final chapter can be regarded as at all conclusive. For the moment, however, it is important to note how the replacement of providence by the order of education is accompanied at the narrative level by the underpinning of the entertaining spoofs of chivalric romance and the picaresque novel with a symbolic order of a more serious kind. Candide's voyage of reason is represented as a journey from one Garden of Eden to another via Eldorado, or from falsity to reality via the ideal.

The castle of Thunder-ten-tronckh is, of course, a fool's paradise. It is characterized by pretension of various kinds: architectural, genealogical, intellectual, and even horticultural. The seeds of the Fall are sown in the 'petit bois qu'on appelait "parc"' (146), where

Cunégonde observes Pangloss's 'leçon de physique expérimentale' (during which, one later infers, he contracts syphilis). Armed with the apple of her new sexual knowledge, this Westphalian Eve seduces her Adam; and he is duly cast out into a wintry landscape where 'il se coucha sans souper' (147). Voltaire's vision of Hell, it would seem, is a world without supper.

The farm outside Constantinople is a pragmatist's paradise: not some abstract garden of 'good works' as Pangloss theologically and uselessly suggests (232–3), nor a garden like Pococuranté's which you simply install at vast expense and then want to replace; but a garden of human beings in which the talent of each is a plant to be nurtured so that society as a whole benefits while the individual finds fulfilment. In this paradise male chauvinism still prevails, as the women make pastry, sew, and do the laundry, but Teutonic snobbery and Jesuit arrogance at least have been banished. The philosophically inflexible Pangloss is presumably retained on the grounds that every paradise needs a fool. Candide's talent, of course, turns out to be that of moral leadership.[13]

This journey from falsity to reality leads, at the very centre of *Candide*, via the authentic Garden of Eden of Eldorado. Here there is true merit — architectural, social, intellectual, and even agricultural, if not horticultural: 'Le pays était cultivé pour le plaisir comme pour le besoin; partout l'utile était agréable' (184). Deism is the only religion; there is a liberal monarchy; commerce is encouraged by the funding of free restaurants for tradesmen and waggoners; intellectual freedom is permitted; the spirit of scientific enquiry is fostered; the arts are encouraged; public buildings are praised (even, one assumes, by the royal family); women can join the Guards; and the King's wit survives being translated. Eldorados, it seems, do not date.

Nor does human nature change. Sex and vanity are the instruments of the Fall as Candide and Cacambo leave Eldorado in pursuit of their sweethearts and in order to show off their riches and surpass the wealth of all the world's monarchs put together. Experience will tell that neither ambition was worth the sacrifice: Cunégonde has become ugly and shrewish, and kings are either deposed and turned into carnivalesque lookalikes, or else they meet a bad end in the

---

[13] *Pace* Roy Wolper who argues that Candide learns nothing and remains 'a dunce' to the end. See his 'Candide, Gull in the Garden?', *Eighteenth-Century Studies*, 3 (1969).

manner of those whom Pangloss so eruditely lists (232). It would
have been better not to leave, and this is the lesson they should have
learnt in Eldorado. Travel may broaden the mind, but wanderlust
may blow it. The Incas who once lived there 'en sortirent très impru-
demment pour aller subjuguer une partie du monde' (187) rather as
Candide and Cacambo want to go off and lord it. But, says the King:
'quand on est passablement quelque part, il faut y rester' (190).
While it might be said that Eldorado is physically a remarkably
difficult place to leave anyway, and that Eldoradan observance of
time-honoured oaths is much facilitated by its towering mountains,
the King's approach is evidently the right way to think of the matter,
not negatively like Martin who 'était fermement persuadé qu'on est
également mal partout' (230).[14]

'CONCLUSION'

Thus, at the level of narrative order, a symbolic progression under-
pins the spoof of chivalric romance, and, like the process of 'education', brings the reader to a 'Conclusion'. The last chapter of
Candide asserts closure in its very title and implies that we are about
to discover 'le bout des choses', much as *Micromégas* promises to
reveal this to the earthlings with his 'beau livre de philosophie'
(37). But just as *Micromégas. Histoire philosophique* ends by drawing a
philosophical blank and just as *Zadig ou la destinée* returns an open
verdict on the nature of providence, so too *Candide ou l'optimisme*
comes to no clear-cut conclusion about optimism. About Optimism,
yes: as a philosophical system, Optimism is discredited, not so much
(and certainly not only) because its tenets are shown to be implausible in the light of the evidence, but essentially because it is a system.
As such it is as inhuman and as dangerous as all the other systems
which are ruthlessly satirized in the story. Thus, in manifestly parallel episodes, Candide offers succour to his syphilitic old tutor in time
of need (152), while the Optimist lets his pupil faint with pain and
exhaustion rather than give best in arguing about the causes of the
earthquake: 'Comment, probable? répliqua le philosophe; je soutiens
que la chose est démontrée' (156).

---

[14] For further discussion of the gardens in *Candide* and useful bibliographical
references to other treatments of the subject, see Patrick Henry, 'Sacred and Profane
Gardens in *Candide*', *SVEC* 176 (1979).

Yet the picture of the human condition presented in *Candide* is not unrelievedly bleak, and there may be some grounds for optimism. First, human beings may be admirable for their will to survive. As la Vieille says:

je voulus cent fois me tuer, mais j'aimais encore la vie. Cette faiblesse ridicule est peut-être un de nos penchants les plus funestes: car y a-t-il rien de plus sot que de vouloir porter continuellement un fardeau qu'on veut toujours jeter par terre? d'avoir son être en horreur, et de tenir à son être? enfin de caresser le serpent qui nous dévore, jusqu'à ce qu'il nous ait mangé le cœur? (172)

And indeed the reader of *Candide* is made particularly conscious of human resilience and the will to live by the comic frequency with which characters thought to be dead (Pangloss, the young Baron, etc.) 'miraculously' return to life.

Second, human beings may be admirable for this very awareness of their ridiculousness, indeed for their capacity to laugh at adversity. Perhaps, even, there is some value in adversity. After all, Pococuranté is the man who has everything and, precisely, is bored. He seeks to improve his garden by having a bigger and better one, but without personal effort. He never travels: people visit him (and without difficulty, unlike Eldorado). Indeed, unlike most of the characters in *Candide*, he has no story to tell. Perhaps some measure of deprivation, some evil, is actually beneficial, because it lends purpose and contrast to life. Perhaps Pope and Leibniz are not entirely wrong; and, according to this line of argument, purpose would lie in developing one's own individual talents, apparently self-centredly (away from Constantinople) but ultimately to the benefit of society. Presumably Cunégonde does not scoff all her pastries herself.[15]

But in the end there is only the semblance of a solution to the problem of evil in *Candide*. The dervish's view reflects the dismissive arrogance of a big name in the world of philosophy. One appreciates that he may be loath to discuss pre-established harmony with Pangloss, but his whole attitude implies a shutting not only of his door

---

[15]   A useful survey of this question is provided by David Langdon, 'On the Meanings of the Conclusion of *Candide*', *SVEC* 238 (1985). Langdon tries 'to reconcile the interpretations of those critics for whom the end of the *conte* expresses Voltaire's personal resignation, in the years following his abrupt departure from the court of Frederick II, to withdrawal from public affairs into the limited world of his Genevan retreat and those who, like Lanson, see instead a general summons to combat evil by cooperative endeavour, in so far as it is possible for man to do so' (432).

but also of his mind to the question of theodicy. The 'bon vieillard's' advocacy of work leaves much out of account. Industry may prevent boredom, vice, and need, but what about intellectual and emotional fulfilment?[16] How does, or did, he get on with the mother of his lovely children? Like the dervish, he shuts his mind, and no doubt his eyes too—in his case, to the political chaos around him. The regular to and fro of 'bateaux chargés d'effendis, de bachas, de cadis, qu'on envoyait en exil', not to mention the occasional cargo of 'têtes proprement empaillés qu'on allait présenter à la Sublime Porte' (230), causes him no concern. But the inhabitants of the 'métairie' cannot look out of their symbolic window without being aware of an imperfect and threatening world that needs to be set to rights. Martin echoes the dervish by saying we should stop philosophizing, but an enquiring mind is one of the more desirable human attributes. It would seem, indeed, to be the saving grace of Pangloss, who is described in the last chapter as 'aussi curieux que raisonneur' (232). Which leaves la Vieille's view that it is better to be buttockless than bored. Candide rejects Martin's Pascalian version of this option ('que l'homme était né pour vivre dans les convulsions de l'inquiétude, ou dans la léthargie de l'ennui') and comments non-committally: 'C'est une grande question' (230). So it is—and one that receives no answer. And what of the other questions raised by *Candide*? What, indeed, of romance?

To the random chaos of existence *Candide* brings not the order of Jesrad's Leibnizian Providentialism but the literary order of a symbolic journey from a false, Germanic Eden to a state of rather muted Turkish delight. But the story offers only an illusion of closure: the final, famous aphorism fails to hide much uncertainty and gives on to as much of a white page as *Micromégas* or the dots which follow Zadig's 'Mais'. *Candide* is ostensibly translated from the German of one Doctor Ralph, but consists also of the addenda found in his pocket when he died at the battle of Minden. Were all the addenda found? Perhaps the final page was lost. Where reason fails, the fable provides—if nothing else, an excuse for the absence of an answer.

---

[16] Bottiglia argues that intellectual work is not ruled out by the ending of *Candide*. See *Voltaire's 'Candide'*, 113–14.

CANDOUR

Yet the fable of *Candide* does provide a kind of solution, but in the form of a mental attitude rather than a set of answers to the riddles of living. Peter France has suggested that this attitude is one of comic detachment,[17] but a more fundamental habit of mind is being inculcated by *Candide*. What one finds at every turn in the story is the same process of exposure which is at work in *Scarmentado*, a laying bare of the reality beneath the masks of pretension and hypocrisy. The central character is notable for his transparency: 'Sa physionomie annonçait son âme' (145); yet in the world which he inhabits the face of things is more usually a façade. Pangloss is 'all tongue' since he would prefer to talk than to garden, but he is also the one-eyed representative of a world in which the unglamorous realities of life are universally disguised by a sophistical use of language. Just as Candide observes the world about him in open-eyed simplicity (and with 'le jugement assez droit, avec l'esprit le plus simple'), so too *Candide* calls the bluff of language.

Voltaire's more oblique method of doing this is the pun. The young Baron 'paraissait en tout digne de son père' (146): worthiness is clearly relative. Pangloss 'prouvait admirablement...': the wonder is that anyone should believe him. The Baroness weighs in at three hundred and fifty pounds: hence the 'très grande considération' in which, so to speak, she is held. Dignity, admiration, respect: all so much bunkum. Paquette is 'docile' (146) as she 'learns' from Pangloss; the lesson in turn fills Cunégonde with the 'désir d'être savante'. Enlightenment itself is but a question of sex, and science the knowing art of the bedroom. *Candide* is full of such puns which expose language's claim to univocal status. Never trust the gloss which is put on a situation: consider the evidence.

More directly, Voltaire exposes the language of reason itself: there is no more slippery word in *Candide* than 'car'.[18] His first step in ridiculing the Leibnizian penchant for cause and effect is to reverse

---

[17]   See Peter France, 'The Literature of Persuasion', in John Cruickshank (ed.), *French Literature and its Background*, 6 vols. (Oxford, 1968–70), iii. 72. Cf. D15499 (2 Mar. 1769, to Gaillard): 'Heureux les philosophes qui peuvent rire et même faire rire! Si on n'avait pas ce palliatif contre les misères, les sottises atroces et même les horreurs dont on est quelquefois environné, où en serait on?'

[18]   See Pierre Haffter, 'L'Usage satirique des causales dans les contes de Voltaire', *SVEC* 53 (1967) for statistical information; and Gerald Prince, 'Candid Explanations', *Saggi e ricerche di letteratura francese*, 22 (1983) for a perceptive analysis of this question.

them. Thus the Baron is a great lord 'car son château avait une porte et des fenêtres' (145), whereas the latter follows from the former. Here the narrator is mimicking the false logic of Pangloss's lesson about noses being designed for spectacles and legs for breeches; which lesson is accepted by Candide 'car il trouvait Mlle Cunégonde extrêmement belle' (146). No less slippery is the term 'par conséquent': Pangloss is 'le plus grand philosophe de la province, et par conséquent de toute la terre'.

Panglossian non-sequiturs are the fig leaf of naked presumption and self-importance, and as such they are directly comparable with the other ways in which the inhabitants of Thunder-ten-tronckh seek linguistically to redefine reality for their own vanity. The Baron becomes a great nobleman simply by calling things by different names. His 'petit bois', as already noted, becomes a ' "parc" ': 'les chiens de ses basse-cours', 'ses palefreniers', and 'le vicaire du village' become respectively 'une meute', 'ses piqueurs', and 'son grand aumônier'. Finally, though not entitled, he causes himself to be addressed as 'monseigneur'. In short, 'il faisait des contes' (145): he is a fabulist of the wrong sort, a purveyor of mendacious fictions.[19]

Similar linguistic duplicity characterizes the account of Pangloss's romp in the bushes with Paquette. Not only is this episode of alfresco fornication transformed into a travesty of enlightenment (the famous 'leçon de physique expérimentale'), but also the facts of sexual stimulation are veiled in the language of logic and the metaphysics of Optimism: 'elle vit clairement la raison suffisante du docteur, les effets et les causes.' By a supreme irony Optimism now becomes an accurate explanation of 'le monde comme il va' since, as the rest of *Candide* will show, human sexual organs are the single most important cause of evil. In this parody of chivalric romance the principal motive force is not 'love', but sexual desire. Candide himself, innocent and good, simply fancies Cunégonde: there is no question of admiring her moral qualities or writing any sonnets to her (cf. 167). Cunégonde is introduced into the story as a sexual comestible: 'haute en couleur, fraîche, grasse, appétissante' (146). Candide's Eve is the apple of his eye. Once 'fallen', Cunégonde spends the rest of the story in bed (as her name would doubtless suggest): with her Bulgar

---

[19] Michel Gilot makes the point that in *Candide* 'faire des contes' is pejoratively contrasted with 'raconter son histoire' and 'écouter l'histoire de . . .'. See his 'Fonctions de la parole dans *Candide*', *Littératures*, 9–10 (1984).

captain whom she admires for his 'peau blanche et douce' (161) and despite his limited intellectual range ('d'ailleurs peu d'esprit, peu de philosophie'); with Don Issacar and the Grand Inquisitor, though she pretends to have resisted them (cf. 162 and 174); and with Don Fernando d'Ibaraa, etc. Sexual appetite is again literalized when the lovers are temporarily reunited in Portugal and Cunégonde remarks: 'Vous devez avoir une faim dévorante; j'ai grand appétit; commençons par souper' (163). But when Candide finally makes an honest woman of her, the apple is no longer quite so delicious: 'sa belle Cunégonde rembrunie, les yeux éraillés, la gorge sèche, les joues ridées, les bras rouges et écaillés' (228). To the very end she is a physical object.

But at least she has not got the clap. 'L'amour', that great motive force in Western literature, is in *Candide* little more than a source of disease. Once again Voltaire uses the notion of 'la raison suffisante' to clever ironic purpose:

[Candide] s'enquit de la cause et de l'effet, et de la raison suffisante qui avait mis Pangloss dans un si piteux état. 'Hélas! dit l'autre, c'est l'amour; l'amour, le consolateur du genre humain, le conservateur de l'univers, l'âme de tous les êtres sensibles, le tendre amour. — Hélas! dit Candide, je l'ai connu, cet amour, ce souverain des cœurs, cette âme de notre âme; il ne m'a jamais valu qu'un baiser et vingt coups de pied au cul. Comment cette belle cause a-t-elle pu produire en vous un effet si abominable?' (153)

Pangloss's answer, famously, is his genealogy of syphilis; and when Pangloss adds that while some nationalities have yet to contract the disease: 'il y a une raison suffisante pour qu'ils la connaissent à leur tour', once again 'raison suffisante' is a synonym for sex. The history of the world turns out to be one long 'histoire de cul', and the 'enchaînement' of providence a series of diseased couplings. Indeed the beginning of this saga of genital acts offers a brief parodic re-enactment of the original Genesis: 'j'ai goûté dans ses bras [Paquette's] les délices du paradis, qui ont produit ces tourments d'enfer dont vous me voyez dévoré' (153). As Candide seems to realize: 'n'est-ce pas le diable qui en fut la souche?'

Here the notion of original sin has been stripped of its theological niceties and presented in lurid factuality. This particular thread is taken up once more in Paquette's story (ch. 24) and then again at the end of *Candide* when we learn that, having used up the money which Candide gave them: 'Paquette continuait son métier partout, et n'y gagnait plus rien' (231). Syphilitic promiscuity is the only life she knows. In this the one difference between Paquette and her former mistress is the latter's immunity from disease. The cant involved in the distinction between a prostitute and a kept woman is never explicitly denounced in the story, but it is evidence of the assurance with which Voltaire relies on narrative and implicit situational parallelisms in *Candide* that the point makes itself.

Sex appears in many different guises in *Candide*, from the strenuously heterosexual to the homosexual and the bestial (ch. 16). Its ubiquity is veiled by euphemism and custom but, candidly viewed, it emerges as the 'raison suffisante' of a quasi-providential narrative order. Not only Candide and Cunégonde are driven by their physical desire for one another. La Vieille's story hinges, first, on the possessive jealousy of her intended husband's ex-mistress (who poisons his chocolate, thus giving the lie to Pangloss's belief that it is worth putting up with syphilis because without it 'nous n'aurions ni le chocolat ni la cochenille': 153); and, second, on the concubinary pluralism of pirates and agas. Pococuranté's pluralism, on the other hand, is part of his particular problem of having too much of a good thing (215). For the ladies the sight of naked flesh adds interest to an *auto-da-fé* (162), and it lands both Pangloss and the Baron in the galleys (ch. 28). In Paris actresses pretend to be queens but earn their keep in less royal style, while a madame in a brothel calls herself a 'marquise'.

Not only love is demythified in this way. War, justice, power, are all exposed as areas of linguistic sham. To be a military man is ostensibly to be a hero. But the word 'héros' is gradually stripped of its glory by incongruous usage (148–9), and the alternative 'stipendiaires' (153) seems more apt. Money, that other 'raison suffisante' in *Candide*, is at the root of war — though sex, in the form of rape, is clearly also one of the rewards of 'heroism'. War clothes itself in the language of liberal justice: 'liberté', 'juridiquement' (149), 'les lois du droit public' (150); but the reality is being flayed or burned alive.

In the case of sex the euphemism of pedagogic terminology is replaced by the 'candid' rhythm of the narrative, as calmly reciprocated courtship gives way to feverish foreplay:

Cunégonde et Candide se trouvèrent derrière un paravent; Cunégonde laissa tomber son mouchoir, Candide le ramassa, elle lui prit innocemment la main, le jeune homme baisa innocemment la main de la jeune demoiselle avec une vivacité, une sensibilité, une grâce toute particulière; leurs bouches se rencontrèrent, leurs yeux s'enflammèrent, leurs genoux tremblèrent, leurs mains s'égarèrent. (147)

The lovers' unity of purpose is conveyed linguistically by the repetition of identical clause structures; and their embrace is conveyed in the move from separate nouns to the insistent use of the aptly possessive pronoun. Anatomical zones are placed in telling order; and the final sequence of verbs summarizes the whole drama of sexual encounter: to meet, to warm, to thrill, to stray. This is a candid picture of 'l'amour, le tendre amour'. Similarly with war. Not for Voltaire 'cette répétition continuelle de combats qui se ressemblent tous' which makes Homer so boring (216); but a piece of writing which figures in its very structures the incoherence and inhumanity of military slaughter:

Ici des vieillards criblés de coups regardaient mourir leurs femmes égorgées, qui tenaient leurs enfants à leurs mamelles sanglantes; là des filles éventrées après avoir assouvi les besoins naturels de quelques héros rendaient les derniers soupirs; d'autres, à demi brûlées, criaient qu'on achevât de leur donner la mort. Des cervelles étaient répandues sur la terre à côté de bras et de jambes coupés. (150)

Once more there is a powerful insistence on parts of the body and a revealing absence of any reference to psychological states. But where previously the effect was to stress the sheer physicality of Candide and Cunégonde's attraction to one another, now the result is a striking picture of the dehumanizing nature of war — from the point of view both of the 'heroic' assailant answering a call of nature and of the victim reduced to a piece of mutilated flesh. One notes how the repeated use of plurals conveys the indiscriminate, depersonalizing effect of war; how the past participles suggest the stunned aftermath of shocking assault; the banal repetition of the subject–verb–object sequence and the pathetic inadequacy of 'étaient' as a final verb, with the brains and severed limbs lying beside each other rather as the people themselves are scattered in immobile poses; and the nightmare illogic of old men gazing at 'leurs femmes' and 'leurs enfants'. Where, indeed, have all the *young* men gone?

LITERATURE AND HUMANITY

Such is the candour of *Candide* in its presentation of sexual desire and military aggression; and it advertises itself as a new approach to the presentation of humanity in literature. For Candide's visit to Pococuranté's library towards the end of *Candide*, during which his host makes disparaging references not only to Homer[20] but also to several other writers of antiquity and to 'ce barbare' Milton, makes explicit what is implicit in Voltaire's story-telling technique in the first three chapters of *Candide*: namely, that he is taking issue with the way in which the realities of love and war are customarily concealed by language and 'great' literature, and that he himself is endeavouring to offer a 'candid' portrait of these phenomena in his own words. As with the treatment of war, much of the subject-matter discussed by Candide and Pococuranté is that which also occurs in *Candide*, and so the Venetian nobleman's commentary becomes a kind of guide to what the author of *Candide* regards as estimable and desirable by his ideal reader. Who needs Milton's *Paradise Lost* and its 'long commentaire du premier chapitre de la Genèse en dix livres de vers durs' (218) when they can read the first few pages of *Candide* or Pangloss's history of syphilis? Horace is excessive in both the sublimity and the grotesqueness of his imagery, though his epigrams are quite memorable. No more memorable, however, than 'il faut cultiver notre jardin' or even 'mangeons du jésuite' (182). Like Pococuranté one is daily already subject to sufficient oratory for Cicero's to be redundant; and, with a nice touch of Voltairian self-mockery, Pococuranté adds: 'je me serais mieux accommodé de ses œuvres philosophiques; mais, quand j'ai vu qu'il doutait de tout, j'ai conclu que j'en savais autant que lui, et que je n'avais besoin de personne pour être ignorant' (217).[21]

When Virgil is taken to task for the stereotypical nature of his characterization ('son pieux Enée, et le fort Cloanthe', etc.: 216–17), one might think that *Candide* is guilty of the same fault as the *Aeneid*, for it seems that Voltaire's characters are similarly flat. The Virgilian epithet may have been incorporated into their names — Candide, Pangloss, Cunégonde, Cacambo, la Vieille, Vanderdendur, the marquise de Parolignac, les Bulgares — but the predictability of

[20]   Where such disparagement is explicitly linked with candour: 'Tous les gens sincères m'ont avoué que le livre leur tombait des mains, mais qu'il fallait toujours l'avoir dans sa bibliothèque, comme un monument de l'antiquité, et comme ces médailles rouillées qui ne peuvent être de commerce' (216).
[21]   Cf. the ironic self-reference following the meeting with the six kings in Venice: 'Mais, dit Candide, voilà une aventure bien peu vraisemblable que nous avons eue à Venise. On n'avait jamais vu ni ouï conter que six rois détrônés soupassent ensemble au cabaret' (223).

which Pococuranté complains may perhaps seem none the less marked. Yet in fact Voltaire's handling of his characters constitutes another display of candour, in this case by demonstrating how human reality may belie or exceed the type. For continually the characters in *Candide* do or say surprising things which run counter to the expectations which their name, class, nationality, or literary ancestor may lead us to entertain, thus forcing us to recognize them as real people who are not easily categorized, as human beings not ciphers.

Candide's education is the most obvious example of this capacity to alter in the course of the story. Pangloss's pupil may begin as a simple allegory for innocence, but he evolves into a more rounded figure. Indeed, by the end of the story, he actually ceases to be candid when he conceals his reluctance to marry Cunégonde (just as the Ingénu later ceases to be ingenuous (337) and the Homme aux quar-ante écus becomes M. André). When he abandons Optimism (193) and thus resigns as its representative, his moods and beliefs fluctuate wildly and betray only too human inconsistency (like Zadig in the middle of that story). After being robbed by Vanderdendur and fined by a Dutch magistrate: 'La méchanceté des hommes se présentait à son esprit dans toute sa laideur; il ne se nourrissait que d'idées tristes' (195); yet not long afterwards: 'quand il songeait à ce qui lui restait dans ses poches, et quand il parlait de Cunégonde, surtout à la fin du repas, il penchait alors pour le système de Pangloss' (196–7; cf. also the end of ch. 23 and the beginning of ch. 24). Maturity comes when he is shown to be able to feel both positive and negative at once:

Candide, partagé entre la joie et la douleur, charmé d'avoir revu son agent fidèle, étonné de le voir esclave, plein de l'idée de retrouver sa maîtresse, le cœur agité, l'esprit bouleversé, se mit à table avec Martin, qui voyait de sang-froid toutes ces aventures. (220)

By contrast, Martin's 'sang-froid', which is much emphasized at this juncture in the story, looks as inhuman and indeed cold-blooded as the inflexibility with which he places his interpretative grid of Manicheism upon the confusing results of human passions (his 'détestables principes').

Other characters are shown 'escaping' from their prescribed roles in a similar manner. We find Cunégonde, despite her noble lineage and her literary function as the beautiful princess, washing shirts and cooking for the Bulgar captain or drying dishes and hanging out tea-towels. Pangloss's womanizing shows that even Leibnizian philosophers are part of the human condition, and there is something surprisingly open-eyed about his confession that he is professionally debarred from changing his mind. La Vieille it is, despite being a caricature of the caution that comes with age and experience, who paradoxically serves as the mouthpiece of the energetic and essentially youthful philosophy that life is for the living and must be experienced to the full. Moreover she is brought to literary life as a brilliant example of the stoic understatement characteristic of the high-born for whom 'noblesse oblige'. Her story is studded with self-deprecating apologies for the ordinariness of her most extraordinary catalogue of woes: 'ce sont des choses si communes qu'elles ne valent pas la peine qu'on en parle' (168); 'Des scènes pareilles se passaient, comme on sait, dans l'étendue de plus de trois cents lieues . . .' (169). Her capacity to take things in her stride is as comic as the succinctness of her expression, particularly in repulsing the unwelcome if ill-equipped advances of the insistent *castrato*: 'Je l'instruisis en peu de mots des horreurs que j'avais essuyées, et je retombai en faiblesse' (170). Given her style, therefore, she seems all the more human for the bathetic filial exasperation in her declining to relate 'combien il est dur pour une jeune princesse d'être menée esclave à Maroc avec sa mère' (168).

Touches like this save Voltaire's characters from being mere types or mouthpieces. One of the more obvious spokesmen in *Candide* is Jacques the Anabaptist. A counterpart of Martin later in the story, and of M. Vanderdendur the Dutch merchant who tricks Candide and then, like Jacques, goes to a watery death, he is both a representative of human goodness and, in this 'pire des mondes possibles', too good to last. He, too, is humanized by incongruous exasperation, in his case with the difficulty a creditor faces in recovering his money from a bankrupt once the receivers have gone in (154). Charitably he absolves the Almighty of responsibility for this state of affairs, but clearly this generous man is well aware of the value of the florins he bestows on the poor. Moreover, while his virtue is real enough, the source of his wealth is far from 'candid' since it derives from the sale of 'étoffes de Perse qu'on fabrique en Hollande' (151). A venial deception, of course, but one that belongs in the pretentious world of Thunder-ten-tronckh.

As to Cacambo, he is much more than the faithful Achates. True to the usual style of eighteenth-century depictions of master–servant relations, he is in many ways a better man than his master. He shares Candide's straightforwardness and decency, and these qualities are reflected in the unsophisticated style which the narrator adopts to communicate them: 'Il ... aimait fort son maître, parce que son maître était un fort bon homme' (175); 'c'était un très bon homme que ce Cacambo' (194). Yet his zest for living ('C'est un très grand plaisir de voir et de faire des choses nouvelles') and his optimism ('quand on n'a pas son compte dans un monde, on le trouve dans un autre': 176) are combined with an earthy realism, be it about the capacity of women to fend for themselves in adversity (175) or the political system of the Jesuits in Paraguay: 'Los Padres y ont tout, et les peuples rien; c'est le chef-d'œuvre de la raison et de la justice' (176). Thus, while he has Candide's ability to see 'le caca en beau', he is no dupe; and his resourcefulness, his extensive *curriculum vitae* (175) and wealth of experience ('Cacambo, qui en avait vu bien d'autres, ne perdit point la tête': 179), and his ability to speak several languages make him an early representative of the ideal of humanity which is arrived at in the final chapter of the story.

It may seem rather optimistic to apply the term 'ideal' to the motley crew of gardeners with which *Candide* ends, but membership of this community seems to derive from a set of values which the story has been constantly proclaiming. One such value is internationalism. Nationalities in *Candide* are notable for their bad points: German snobbery and gluttony (178–9), Spanish arrogance and fanaticism, English melancholy and cruelty (ch. 23), Italian vanity and exaggeration (in La Vieille's assessment of her youthful charms). The Dutch are money-grubbing slave-drivers, and the least loathsome of the French is a surgeon with an amorous eye to the main chance (172). But the Germans are clearly the worst, for they are also given to metaphysics and excessive sentimentality (177); so that the movement from a highly nationalistic, Westphalian Thunder-ten-tronckh to an international community on the borders of Europe and Asia is as much of a step forward as the translation of the German of Dr Ralph into the language of reason.

National and racial stereotypes are an easy source of comedy in *Candide* — the very mention of Turkey seems to require reference to both bathing (226) and towels (228) — and sometimes the reader may wonder if such stereotypes are not being reinforced in a rather unenlightened way. This is particularly so in the case of the relentless anti-Semitism which is manifest in the depiction of Don Issacar (163) or the Jewish financiers by whom Candide is 'tant friponné' (230).[22] But Voltaire generally is using national stereotype as a way of indicting the spineless acquiescence of human beings in the 'fables' of power which govern them. People are dehumanized by the writer if, as it were, they have already shown historical evidence of disqualifying themselves from membership of the human race. Thus in the Admiral Byng episode attention is called to the fact that so many 'atrabilaires' Britons turned out to watch rather than to protest. Accordingly the land of Newton and Locke is dismissed in a page. Likewise with the *auto-da-fé* in Lisbon, where absurd cruelty provides a spectacle (with refreshments) for passive and unthinking collaborators in the fictions of authority. Prussian responsibility for the million deaths of the Seven Years War is not without its relevance in the depiction of the Bulgars, or Cunégonde's brother, or even Pangloss.

Of the eight people who make up the final community, four are German, two Italian, one (Martin) is presumably Dutch, and the other (Cacambo) is a quarter Spanish and a quadroon. Yet, with the exception of Pangloss, they have all lost such national characteristics as they ever exemplified and are now simply human beings. They have been knocked about by life: at least three have syphilis, two are severely mutilated, and a further two (Cunégonde and Paquette) are looking distinctly raddled. All the noble pretensions with which the story began have gone: two of those present (Candide and la Vieille), and possibly three (Cacambo), are illegitimate by birth, and all eight are now what they are by virtue of their own attributes as human beings.

Here is a new form of characterization to set against the predictable heroes of epic. And here too is a new form of literature to contrast with the sterile lucubrations of the Establishment. Like the guided tour of Pococuranté's library at the end, the earlier visit to the Paris theatre and the subsequent literary discussion which takes place in the unlikely setting of the marquise de Parolignac's 'salon'

---

[22] Anti-Semitism is a marked trait in all Voltaire's works and a rare blind spot in his enlightenment. On this question see Arthur Hertzberg, *The French Enlightenment and the Jews. The Origins of Modern Anti-Semitism* (New York, 1968; repr. 1990), 280–313. Hertzberg concludes: 'The vital link, the man who skipped over the Christian centuries and provided a new, international, secular anti-Jewish rhetoric in the name of European culture rather than religion, was Voltaire' (313).

both allow explicit statement of the ills of the 'uncandid' use of language and literature. Candide finds his first play moving, but the genuineness of his non-verbal reaction is proscribed by the critic, who legislates for taste on the basis of Cartesian metaphysics and the verbal barrage of 'vingt brochures' (202). The euphemism whereby 'les honneurs de la sépulture' in fact means the right 'de pourrir avec tous les gueux du quartier dans un vilain cimetière' (202) is symptomatic of a metropolis dominated by the duplicity of language. Whether it is a supper-party, a work of theology, or the latest tragedy, the hallmarks of Parisian discourse are artificiality, plagiarism, vanity, bad judgement, and lack of wit (204–5). 'On ne sait point parler aux hommes' (205): such is the verdict on the moderns as it was on the ancients. It is no accident that in Paris Candide should be the dupe of a forged letter.

Candide is, like Candide, a bastard work: as Voltaire's brain-child it is the offspring of a 'bon et honnête gentilhomme du voisinage', but it goes unrecognized by a mother who insists inhumanely on the noble device. Art in *Candide*, like Candide's mother's snobbery, is deeply suspect. For Pococuranté the paintings of Raphael are worthless because they fail to deliver 'une imitation vraie de la nature elle-même' (215); opera is a monstrous hybrid of bad drama and silly songs; and music is an excuse for the tedious display of virtuosity (216). Blasé the Venetian nobleman may be, but his judgements are reminiscent of those of the 'homme savant et de goût' in Paris, and they constitute, within the context of *Candide*, a catalogue of the ills which *Candide* itself seeks to avoid.

Music in any form is particularly suspect throughout the story, and there is an implicit parallel between the use of language to obfuscate the truth and the use of music to conceal the horrors of war and religious fanaticism. Thus the account of the battle between the Bulgares and the Abares reveals the barbarity beneath the beauty: 'Rien n'était si beau, si leste, si brillant, si bien ordonné que les deux armées. Les trompettes, les fifres, les hautbois, les tambours, les canons, formaient une harmonie telle qu'il n'y en eut jamais en enfer' (149). The description of the *auto-da-fé* displays a similar contrast, this time with the added 'false' beauty of oratory: '[Candide et Pangloss] marchèrent en procession . . . et entendirent un sermon très pathétique, suivi d'une belle musique en faux-bourdon. Candide fut fessé en cadence, pendant qu'on chantait' (158). Perhaps the most extreme example of the inhumanity of art is the sacrifice of a man's virility on the off-chance that he may end up with a pretty voice. La Vieille's handsome castrato is one of the lucky ones: he at least sang in a princess's chapel choir. The others died or went off to govern the Papal States. Castration in the name of the muse epitomizes the whole range of unnatural and barbarous inhumanity which *Candide* seeks to attack.

Its own response to the aesthetics of the academy is the *conte*, this apparently artless, oral medium employed by mankind everywhere and since time immemorial. Throughout *Candide* people are forever telling stories to each other: Pangloss (twice), Cunégonde, la Vieille, the Baron, his son (twice), Paquette, Giroflée, all become narrators at one time or another. Story-telling is a natural, human activity which abolishes the barriers of hierarchy. Everyone has their story to tell, as Candide discovers both on the ship to South America and when he wishes to return. In the first case la Vieille, no mean *conteur* herself, challenges Cunégonde:

Enfin, mademoiselle, j'ai de l'expérience, je connais le monde; donnez-vous un plaisir, engagez chaque passager à vous conter son histoire; et s'il s'en trouve un seul qui n'ait souvent maudit sa vie, qui ne se soit souvent dit à lui-même qu'il était le plus malheureux des hommes, jetez-moi dans la mer la tête la première. (173)

Later, when Candide advertises for a travelling-companion who will be 'le plus dégoûté de son état et le plus malheureux de la province', the response is overwhelming: 'Il se présenta une foule de prétendants qu'une flotte n'aurait pu contenir' (195). Had Candide the time, each could have been relied on to 'raconter . . . son histoire'. Story-telling is thus a universal activity, and the story itself always the same: it is the story of man's inhumanity to man.

Candide is that universal story: hence its resemblance to a myth. One of the principal aims of *Candide* is to debunk nonsensical fictions which authors seek to pass off as real. But its alternative to these fictions is not some form of greater 'realism'. It does not seek to pretend that its characters are real live flesh-and-blood men and women living in the world we ourselves inhabit. It does not seek to lull us with the illusions of descriptive detail or psychological analysis. On the contrary, *Candide* prefers to 'narguer la vraisemblance'.[23]

---

[23] René Pomeau, 'De *Candide* à *Jacques le fataliste*', in *Enlightenment Studies in Honour of Lester G. Crocker* (Oxford, 1979), 250.

This is a world outside real time. Season and climate are absent, except in brief symbolic moments. Even if some of the events in *Candide* are historically attested, all of them are extraordinary and implausible in their concatenation; while the characters, for all the human touches which they exhibit, remain actors in the narrator's mental drama. But this unreality is a candid unreality, a transparent lie through which the truth of the human condition reveals itself. *Candide* may be called a myth, or fable, of reason in the sense that it presents, in enlarged and simplified form, the story of man employing his intelligence to look reality full in the face and being prepared to live honestly with what he sees. Honestly and, in the last analysis, optimistically. Even Martin acknowledges this: 'C'est toujours bien fait d'espérer' (219).[24] Like Pandora's box, and like the *Poème sur le désastre de Lisbonne*, Candide contains an ultimate message of hope. 'Il faut cultiver notre jardin': there is a future, there is a moral imperative, and *we* can do something about it. As a fable of reason, *Candide* is also a fable of the Fall in that it describes the passage from a faith in total explanations to a knowing acceptance of uncertainty. And it is a fallen fable in that it is a piece of story-telling which is aware of just how untrue stories can be. It opens with the candour of a children's fairy-story: and it ends with the candour of enlightenment. *Candide* tells it like it is — freely, openly, man to man, and man to woman. Truth, not artifice, is beauty: 'il est beau d'écrire ce qu'on pense; c'est le privilège de l'homme' (218).

---

[24] Cf. 196: 'Candide avait un grand avantage sur Martin, c'est qu'il espérait toujours revoir Mlle Cunégonde, et que Martin n'avait rien à espérer.'

III
Literature and Enlightenment

La philosophie est enfin venue, elle a dit:
'Ne parlez en public que pour dire des vérités
neuves et utiles, avec l'éloquence du sentiment
et de la raison.'

(459)

9
Education and 'Merry Hissing'

Histoire d'un bon brahmin, Pot-pourri, Le Blanc et le noir,
Jeannot et Colin, Petite digression, and *Aventure indienne.*

Il y a là de quoi parler beaucoup.

(237)

The theme of education which is central to *Candide* remains a dominant concern of Voltaire's in the stories which he wrote and published during the following decade. Born on the threshold of 'ce
siècle qui est l'aurore de la raison',[1] he may be thought to have spent
his whole life endeavouring to make others see reason; but the issue
of enlightenment through education was an especially live one at
this particular moment. With the acquisition of Les Délices and
then Ferney, Voltaire had placed himself both geographically and
domestically in a position where he could write and publish more
freely and thus further the *philosophes'* cause even more vigorously
than before. As he was launching his campaign against 'l'infâme', the
Jesuits, who had been responsible for so much of French education,
were being relieved of their functions (on 1 Apr. 1762): all 124 Jesuit
collèges were obliged to close.

Already since 1750 a 'great debate' had been taking place concerning the future of education in France, notably as to whether it should
be under the control of the Church or the State.[2] D'Alembert's
article 'Collège' for the *Encyclopédie* in 1753 had attacked the Jesuits'
teaching methods, and one of the most powerful cases for a state
system was argued in the *Essai d'éducation nationale* published in 1763
by Louis-René de La Chalotais (1701–85), an influential member
of the Parlement at Rennes and an implacable opponent of the
Jesuits. La Chalotais sought to replace the Jesuit curriculum based

---

[1] *Le Philosophe ignorant,* 94.
[2] See Roland Mortier, 'Les "Philosophes" français et l'éducation publique', in
his *Clartés et ombres du siècle des lumières. Etudes sur le XVIIIᵉ siècle littéraire* (Geneva,
1969).

on a study of the classics, rhetoric, and traditional metaphysics with one consisting of modern philosophy, science, history, and literature.[3] More radically still, and within two months of the ban on the Society of Jesus, Rousseau had stated his own educational theory in *Emile*, which was immediately censured by the Sorbonne and condemned by the Paris Parlement, not least because of the deist *Profession de foi du vicaire savoyard* which it contained.

Not to be pedagogically outdone, it would seem, Voltaire published the first version of his *Dictionnaire philosophique* in 1764 and *Le Philosophe ignorant* in 1766. The former was designed to be a handy reference book for budding free-thinkers looking for a lead from the Master in their discussions of central metaphysical, moral, and theological questions. Accordingly it was condemned by the Paris Parlement on 19 March 1765. *Le Philosophe ignorant* was intended more as a summary of 'all / Ye know on earth, and all ye need to know' about Western and Oriental philosophy, which, given Voltaire's continuing attitude to metaphysics, accounts for the brevity of the work. Much of the survey is presented as a whirlwind voyage of reason around the world (if not in eighty days, then in 'cinquante-neuf doutes')[4], a thinking man's Grand Tour to replace the 'centaine de cours de philosophie où l'on m'explique des choses dont personne ne peut avoir la moindre notion'.[5] The main lesson learned, and loudly proclaimed in the latter sections of the work, is that all mankind shares the same notions of right and wrong. Where Rousseau saw feeling as the most reliable guide to virtue, Voltaire sees this universal sense of justice as 'un développement de la raison donnée de Dieu'.[6] Moral education is what counts, and it is best effected by listening to reason:

Je répète encore qu'au lieu de ces idées innées chimériques, Dieu nous a donné une raison qui se fortifie avec l'âge, et qui nous apprend à tous, quand nous sommes attentifs, sans passion, sans préjugé, qu'il y a un Dieu, et qu'il faut être juste.[7]

---

[3] A curriculum of which Voltaire approved and from which the Ingénu will benefit, while in *Jeannot et Colin* Jeannot's foolish advisers reject it. See Voltaire's letters to La Chalotais, D11051 (28 Feb. 1763) and D11273 (22 June 1763).

[4] See Grimm *et al.*, *Correspondance littéraire, philosophique et critique*, 16 vols. (Paris, 1877–82), vii. 51.

[5] *Le Philosophe ignorant*, 67.

[6] Ibid. 80. Subsequently, however, he alters the emphasis and talks of acquiring 'l'idée de la justice . . . par le sentiment et la raison', concluding even that 'La société n'est fondée que sur ces notions qu'on n'arrachera jamais de notre cœur' (84).

[7] Ibid. 81.

Le Philosophe ignorant thus shows particularly clearly the enduring relevance of Voltaire's famous remark to Frederick of Prussia in October 1737: 'Je ramène toujours, autant que je peux, ma métaphysique à la morale.'[8]

Of particular interest from the point of view of Voltaire's career as a *conteur*, *Le Philosophe ignorant* demonstrates what rôle the *conte* has to play in this moral education. For the whole work pivots on a reversal of the value attributed to the word 'fable'. Thus the greater part of Voltaire's alternative 'cours de philosophie' is taken up with disparaging previous philosophies or philosophers as fictions or purveyors of fiction: be it 'fables' (Hesiod, the Phoenicians, the Chaldeans); 'romans' (Manicheism, Descartes, Spinoza); 'allégories puériles' (Zoroaster); a 'château enchanté' (Spinoza); 'un monde si imaginaire' (Descartes); 'rêves' (Malebranche, Stoicism, Platonism, Leibnizianism); or simply 'folie' (Pascal).[9] But the work ends with a eulogy of Aesop, whose fables are pronounced both profound and true:

A quoi tendent ces fables aussi profondes qu'ingénues, ces apologues qui semblent visiblement écrits dans un temps où l'on ne doutait pas que les bêtes n'eussent un langage? Elles ont enseigné presque tout notre hémisphère. Ce ne sont point des recueils de sentences fastidieuses qui lassent plus qu'elles n'éclairent: c'est la vérité elle-même avec le charme de la fable . . . Que nous apprennent toutes ces fables? Qu'il faut être juste.[10]

The Aesopian fable is uncomplicated; it prefers beguiling narrative to tedious *sententiae*, and it encourages a spirit of justice and toleration. Its naïvety may no longer be possible, or desirable; but in his own *contes philosophiques* the merits of Aesop continue to constitute Voltaire's ideal.

HISTOIRE D'UN BON BRAHMIN

Between *Candide* and *L'Ingénu* Voltaire published six minor *contes*. The first of these, the *Histoire d'un bon brahmin*, was composed in 1759 and published in 1761. Voltaire referred to it as a 'parabole',[11] but the role of narrative is limited, and the work resembles rather a philosophical dialogue devoted to the question whether blissful

---

[8] D1376 (*c.*15 Oct. 1737).
[9] *Le Philosophe ignorant* 56; 61, 48, 66; 86; 64; 47; 60, 71; 68.
[10] Ibid. 90.
[11] D8533 (13 Oct. 1759, to Mme du Deffand).

ignorance is to be preferred to an intelligent but painful awareness of the limits of human understanding. In some respects the story is reminiscent of *Lettre d'un turc* in that it consists of the first-person narrative of a traveller to India who meets a representative of an Eastern religion. But the narrator is even less individualized than the Turk; the element of defamiliarizing satire is absent; and the device of a voyage of reason whereby the mind explores and discovers beyond itself is now almost defunct. It is true that the narrator professes himself deeply struck by the Brahmin's preference for intellectual awareness over contented mindlessness, and that he learns something about himself as a consequence: 'je m'examinai moi-même et je vis qu'en effet je n'aurais pas voulu être heureux à condition d'être imbécile' (237); but one wonders if anything other than the threat of the censor required this lesson to be learnt from Oriental travel.

The *Histoire d'un bon brahmin* is essentially an inner Voltairian dialogue about the incompatibility of happiness and intellectual enquiry. The good Brahmin is largely a self-portrait of one who, like Gordon in *L'Ingénu*, has studied for forty years but is none the wiser. The unsolved riddles are reminiscent of both *Micromégas* and *Zadig*: what is time? what is matter? how do we think? how do we move? why do we exist? And why is there evil? One might have thought that the ramifications of this last question had by now been exhausted by Voltaire the story-teller, and indeed there is a weary inadequacy about the Brahmin's reply:

Je suis aussi en peine que ceux qui me font cette question. Je leur dis quelquefois que tout est le mieux du monde; mais ceux qui ont la gravelle, ceux qui ont été ruinés et mutilés à la guerre n'en croient rien, ni moi non plus. (236)

It has been suggested that the portrait of the Brahmin constitutes a comic pastiche of Pascal.[12] The Brahmin's anguish at his own ignorance is summed up in his concluding statement: 'je ne sais ni d'où je viens, ni ce que je suis, ni où j'irai, ni ce que je deviendrai' (236); and clearly this is a direct echo of the *Pensées*:

Je ne sais qui m'a mis au monde, ni ce que c'est que le monde, ni que moi-même; je suis dans une ignorance terrible de toutes choses; je ne sais ce que c'est que mon corps, que mes sens, que mon âme et cette partie

---

[12] *RC*, 894, n. 2.

même de moi qui pense ce que je dis, qui fait réflexion sur tout et sur elle-même, et ne se connaît non plus que le reste . . . Comme je ne sais d'où je viens, aussi je ne sais où je vais . . .[13]

But these words are attributed by Pascal to a sceptic who makes a virtue of doubt; and he comments after the sceptic's speech: 'Qui souhaiterait d'avoir pour ami un homme qui discourt de cette manière? . . . En vérité, il est glorieux à la religion d'avoir pour ennemis des hommes si déraisonnables.'

For Voltaire the Brahmin is 'bon' because he is honest and, like Zadig, dares to doubt. One should therefore take at face value the narrator's compassionate concern for the Brahmin: 'L'état de ce bon homme me fit une vraie peine: personne n'était ni plus raisonnable ni de meilleure foi que lui' (236). Accordingly one may better appreciate the important new note which is struck by this *conte*, the note of 'sensibilité': 'Je conçus que plus il avait de lumières dans son entendement et de sensibilité dans son cœur, plus il était malheureux.' This might have been written by a French Romantic *c*.1830: at the very least it prepares for the important parallel treatment of 'l'esprit et le cœur' in *L'Ingénu*.

The problem of evil is now part of the greater problem of man's ignorance of the eternal verities, and of how he should live an enlightened life in the midst of such darkness. Once again, as in Pococuranté's library and later with the Homme aux quarante écus, the lessons of antiquity are rejected: 'Je lis nos anciens livres, et ils redoublent mes ténèbres' (236). Selfish epicureanism and extravagant metaphysics are also dismissed as unsatisfactory. Perhaps in the end happiness can only be achieved by the kind of simple, unquestioning religious faith demonstrated by the old woman who, like Flaubert's Félicité in *Un cœur simple*, is an 'automate' (236). But whereas Félicité has a poignant authenticity to set against the tawdry rationality of her Rouennais milieu, Voltaire's old woman is representative of an unacceptable denial of reason. None of the 'fallen' *philosophes* consulted by the narrator hankers after prelapsarian innocence or is prepared to 'accepter le marché de devenir imbécile pour devenir content' (237).[14] And yet, and yet: 'enfin de quoi s'agit-il? d'être

---

[13] L. 427.
[14] In this respect, therefore, the *Histoire d'un bon brahmin* is a reply to Rousseau's *Discours sur l'inégalité* and its apparently favourable depiction of the happiness of a brutish, non-thinking state.

heureux' (237). Zadig learnt that virtue does not bring happiness, and now the lesson is that reason, that supreme value of the eighteenth century, does not bring happiness either. One must choose to be unhappy.

The question at issue in this slight tale is a crucial one in terms of eighteenth-century thinking,[15] and it ends by stating an irresolvable paradox: 'préférer la raison à la félicité, c'est être très insensé' (237). Both the Brahmin and the narrator recognize that it is in the nature of such paradoxes that they spawn verbiage. The former is professionally required to provide an answer and can but play for time: 'il faut répondre; je n'ai rien de bon à dire; je parle beaucoup, et je demeure confus et honteux de moi-même après avoir parlé' (236). The narrator ends the story with a similar observation: 'Comment donc cette contradiction peut-elle s'expliquer? Comme toutes les autres. Il y a là de quoi parler beaucoup.' The very brevity of this particular short story is thus established as a sign of its own authenticity. When it comes to the 'big' questions, therefore, once again the fable may serve in Mallarméan fashion to 'authentiquer le silence'.[16]

POT-POURRI

Pot-pourri, as its title suggests, poses something of a challenge to the critic's powers of recuperation. Many editors of Voltaire's *contes* have simply omitted it, ostensibly on generic grounds, while for the editors of the Pléiade edition, who rightly include it, the work ranks as 'le plus audacieux, et certainement le plus énigmatique' of Voltaire's *contes*. They remark wistfully that 'Le moins qu'on puisse dire de cette composition, c'est qu'elle est obscure' (900). The difficulty of this particular *conte* can be exaggerated, since its constituent rotting parts all contribute quite unmistakably to a heady anti-Christian aroma. Nevertheless, both in its attack on 'l'infâme' and in its formal structure, *Pot-pourri* may certainly be considered one of Voltaire's most daring *contes*.

It was begun during the summer of 1761, by which time Voltaire had decided to come out more openly in opposition to the Christian Church. Largely complete by July of the following year, it was

[15]   See Mauzi, *L'Idée du bonheur*, 99–100, and ch. 12.
[16]   From 'Le Mystère dans les lettres', in Mallarmé, *Œuvres complètes*, ed. Henri Mondor and G. Jean-Aubry (Paris, 1945), 387.

revised in 1764 and published early in 1765. Returning to the idea which informs the portrait of the happy woman in the *Histoire d'un bon brahmin*, namely that belief in revealed religion represents a form of automatism, Voltaire now 'translates' the story of the New Testament into a spurious history of the famous puppeteer Brioché. Brioché is Joseph, Polichinelle his son. The latter sets up a troupe of puppeteers who manage to steal customers even from the quacks of Orvieto, that capital of quackery. Subsequently, in the absence of Polichinelle, the troupe seek to sell nostrums themselves and fall in with le sieur Bienfait (St Paul), a gifted puppet-maker. His ambitions are wealth and renown, and indeed his puppet-theatre proves a great success once established in Italy, especially when a resurrected Polichinelle is billed to dance with Mme Gigogne (the Old Woman Who Lived in a Shoe). But one of his employees sets up in opposition, and soon the world of the puppet-theatre is notable for its 'grandes querelles' (250).

This bold satire on the history of the Christian Church is conveyed in sections 1, 3, 7, 9, and 11 of the fifteen short sections into which *Pot-pourri* is divided. The narrator claims to be reading this history in the notebooks of a certain Merry Hissing; and the first of the intervening sections is represented as the intrusion of the contemporary world upon his reading. Subsequent intervening sections are not explicitly motivated, but at least one of them provides a displaced continuation of the Christian story, while the remainder present evidence of, and constitute an implicit commentary on, the consequences of the 'grandes querelles' with which the pseudo-history of puppetry ended. Thus in section 2 the narrator witnesses the confiscation of drugs from Jesuit apothecaries and debates the feud between the Jesuits and the Jansenists with his neighbour M. Husson. In section 4 an apparently unconnected account of Dumarsais's attack on the venality of high state offices raises the implicit point made by Dumarsais[17] that more talented incumbents could be appointed if the posts were opened to wider competition. The parallel with an impoverished Polichinelle trying to make his way in life (sect. 3) turns the founder of Christianity into a thwarted careerist.

Sect. 5 appears to break the sequence of alternating sections which had led one to anticipate a return to the history of Brioché. Instead we are given the story of a chevalier Roginante from Ferrara who

[17] See *RC*, 934, n. 11.

visits Amsterdam to purchase a collection of Flemish masters. Where one might have expected some allegorical account of the Resurrection (given that sect. 7 continues with a travesty of the Acts of the Apostles),[18] we find ourselves in the company of one who sounds as if he has sprung from the pages of Ariosto. But the paintings which he buys are, respectively, a portrait of Christ, a painting of the Holy Family, and a landscape. Each painting represents, therefore, how the climax of the Christian story has since been interpreted: (1) by the Dutch Christian who believes in the divinity of Christ; (2) by the Socinian who denies this divinity but believes nevertheless that the Christ child 'fut la créature la plus parfaite que Dieu ait mise sur la terre' (242); and (3) by the Jew whose race holds 'cette famille en exécration' and for whom, therefore, Christ does not figure on the religious horizon. Rather than offer a puppeteering account of the final moments in the Christian story, the wary polemicist thus smuggles them in beneath the double veil of fictional story and visual art.

The lack of unanimity in the interpretation of the Passion leads on to an illustration of the sectarian division which has followed in its wake. In section 6 this illustration focuses on the fanaticism of M. de Boucacous, 'Languedocien très chaud et huguenot très zélé' (243), and combines examples of religious intolerance with discussion of religious art, a combination which is repeated in section 8 in the consideration of Corneille's *Polyeucte*. The references to works of art are now no longer a screen for impiety but rather a commentary on the fictive character of the Christian story, and indeed of all established religions. The central image of *Pot-pourri* is of a church manipulating its puppet-priests and bamboozling a popular, undiscriminating audience: 'les hommes ont toujours aimé les marionnettes' (240). In section 10 this equation of theology and charlatanry is extended to cover the Jewish faith and the world of Islam; and the well-travelled M. Husson concludes: 'Le petit peuple, d'un bout du monde à l'autre, croit fermement les choses les plus absurdes' (249). Religion is the opiate of the people, and (in sect. 9) the Reformation simply 'retrancha plus de cinquante ingrédients qui entraient dans l'orviétan, composa le sien de cinq ou six drogues, et,

---

[18]   The Crucifixion is passed over lightly at the end of sect. 3 with the hypothesis that Polichinelle 'fut avalé par un crapaud' (241), which is repeated in sect. 7 (246).

le vendant beaucoup meilleur marché, ... enleva une infinité de pratiques à Bienfait [i.e. the Catholic Church]'.

The remaining sections of *Pot-pourri* bring the history of the Christian Church up to date by portraying the Vatican as bent on extorting money from the faithful (sect. 13); by showing the lavish consumption of this wealth by the Cistercians at the expense of the impoverished and potentially useful 'curé de campagne' (sect. 15); and by listing injustices perpetrated by the Jansenists (sect. 15). The latter list brings the story full circle by reminding the reader of the demise of the Jesuits at the beginning and of M. Husson's sage prediction: 'vous n'y gagnerez rien: vous serez accablé par la faction des jansénistes ... Songez que les fanatiques sont plus dangereux que les fripons' (240). M. Husson is clearly a better prophet than Nostradamus (cf. 246).

Interspersed with this concluding 'alternative' survey of the contemporary ecclesiastical scene is a running debate on the gullibility of man (sects. 10 and 12) and the undesirable economic consequences of religious faith. How can any nation cultivate its garden when it has so many saints' days (sect. 14)? Alsace is here the negative counterpart of the Stock Exchange in Amsterdam (sect. 5) where, as with the London Stock Exchange described in the *Lettres philosophiques*, religious differences are temporarily set aside in the pursuit of financial gain. In Porentru, as in Roginante's Ferrara, religion is bad for business and thus ultimately detrimental to the poor by virtue of the obstacles it places in the path of greater prosperity.

As to the debate on human gullibility, this follows on from the comparison of Christ to Punch and theology to an opiate. In *Pot-pourri* the preaching of religion is presented as essentially a fairground performance. It is a con-trick of which the intrinsic fraudulence is further concealed (as was evident in *Candide*) by the suspect beautification of art, be it painting, or music (244–5), or Cornelian tragedy. Being an anti-Christian work, *Pot-pourri* sides rather with the 'pagans': with 'l'*Œdipe* des Grecs' (248); with the pagan plays of Racine who is a better artist, 'profanement parlant', than David the psalmist (245); with Ovid, whose '*Métamorphoses* ... sont, par la malice du démon, bien mieux écrites, et plus agréables que les cantiques juifs' (245); and with La Fontaine. 'Comment', the narrator asks M. Husson, 'dans l'histoire d'un peuple, trouve-t-on à la fois la Saint-Barthélemy et les *Contes* de La Fontaine, etc.?' (250). The implication here is that the most likely antidote to religious oppression is the simplicity and wisdom of the *conte*, a model which the narrator of *Pot-pourri* seeks in a post-classical way to follow.

Indeed M. Husson is his tutor in narrative. M. Husson's answer to the narrator's question is simple: 'Le genre humain est capable de tout.' When the narrator urges him to set down his thoughts in 'un beau livre qui développât toutes ces contradictions' (250), M. Husson's response is reminiscent of Babouc's resort to a statue in *Le Monde comme il va*: 'Ce livre est tout fait, dit-il; vous n'avez qu'à regarder une girouette; elle tourne tantôt au doux souffle du zéphyr, tantôt au vent violent du nord: voilà l'homme.' As the following section (sect. 13) demonstrates, the written word is open to wilful misinterpretation. Either, like the Bible, it is cited as an authority but without containing the evidence required (the Sorbonne theologian cannot find biblical justification for France paying monetary tribute to the Vatican); or, in the absence of an 'auteur canonique', a dubious piece of written evidence is misread to suit the convenience of the reader (the casuistical Jesuit's assertion that Babylon 'means' Rome). In fact, as later in *L'Homme aux quarante écus*, weighty tomes are symbols of oppression: 'Je m'étonne que, dans l'énorme quantité de livres dont les auteurs ont gouverné l'Etat depuis vingt ans, aucun n'ait pensé à réformer ces abus' (251).

The debate between the narrator and M. Husson, on the other hand, is a model of how 'truth' should be communicated and received. M. Husson is 'une bonne tête' but also 'une tête de fer qu'on ne fait jamais changer de sentiment' (240). 'Je tâchai de l'adoucir', says the narrator, both here and later in the story: 'M. Husson est un rude homme. J'ai fait ce que j'ai pu pour l'adoucir; mais je n'ai pu en venir à bout. Il a persisté dans son avis, et moi dans le mien' (248). The narrator is no less of a free-thinker than his neighbour, and no less stubborn. But then, at the end of section 10 and in the light of a good point made by the narrator, M. Husson's iron conviction bends: 'J'y rêverai, me dit-il; cette idée me paraît bonne.' In parallel fashion the narrator's faith in the possibility of setting down an explanation of moral evil categorically in a book is weakened by M. Husson's use of the example of the weathercock. The 'truth', even for a 'philosophe' freed from the yoke of superstition, cannot be stated univocally.

Hence, perhaps, the enigmatic final section of *Pot-pourri*, in which the narrator travels through Burgundy with 'M. Evrard que vous connaissez tous'. We all know him because he is the type of simple-minded person who takes us literally when we are being ironic. He is, in Voltairian terms, an otherwise commendable figure: he is a passionate opponent of Cistercian excess and an eloquent victim of Jansenist injustice. But he has something of the fanatic about him, an urgency for change which rides roughshod over the complexities of human life. 'Vous allez trop loin, et trop vite', warns the narrator: 'ce que vous dites arrivera certainement dans deux ou trois cents ans; ayez patience' (253). And what might now be called this totalitarian tendency in M. Evrard is reflected in his language, which betrays the absurd extravagance which the narrator had earlier ridiculed in the Psalms: 'je suis las de tous les abus que je vois: il me semble que je marche dans les déserts de la Lybie, où notre sang est sucé par des insectes quand les lions ne nous dévorent pas' (253). Moreover he is a windbag: 'M. Evrard me conta des aventures de de cette espèce pendant deux heures entières' (253–4).

Just as the cosmopolitan M. Husson had earlier taught the narrator the lesson of the universality of moral evil (249), now the narrator tries to pass on the same message to M. Evrard in order to reconcile him to the shortcomings of the human condition and in effect to render him more tolerant: 'Mon cher monsieur Evrard, j'en ai essuyé plus que vous; les hommes sont ainsi faits d'un bout du monde à l'autre: nous nous imaginons que les abus ne règnent que chez nous' (254). Having illustrated his point with an allusion to La Fontaine's two cuckolds Astolphe and Joconde, the narrator then attempts to counter with sarcasm the philosophy of 'if you can't beat 'em, join 'em'. But, alas, 'M. Evrard me crut': 'c'est à présent l'homme de France qui vole le roi, l'Etat et les particuliers de la manière la plus dégagée et la plus noble, qui fait la meilleure chère, et qui juge le plus fièrement d'une pièce nouvelle.' M. Evrard has gone over to the other side and, worst of all, become an arbiter of taste.

But the principal lesson of *Pot-pourri* is that 'When in Rome . . .' is, in more senses than one, absolutely not the answer to the problem of moral evil. M. Evrard has misunderstood the narrator, and so serves as an object lesson to the reader. We must be alive to the ironies of *Pot-pourri* and ready to read, not only between the lines but also between the sections. The fragmentary nature of this *conte* is Voltaire's textual equivalent of the shifting signals of M. Husson's weathercock. In fact one may be tempted to think that *Pot-pourri* is the story of how its narrator came to write it; how, having read the work of Merry Hissing and indeed had some difficulty in recuperating it ('N'ayant rien entendu au précédent chapitre de Merry Hissing, je me transportai chez mon ami M. Husson': 247), and having been misinterpreted by his first 'pupil' because his irony was ill-tuned, he then creates a fiction of multiple layers which forces the reader out of his passive, puppet-like acceptance of the written word and obliges him, once more, to put two and two together. As Voltaire wrote to Damilaville:

Je crois que la meilleure manière de tomber sur l'infâme est ... de faire voir combien on nous a trompé en tout; de montrer combien ce qu'on croit ancien est moderne; combien ce qu'on nous a donné pour respectable est ridicule; de laisser le lecteur tirer lui-même les conséquences.[19]

The reader is obliged to unpack these Chinese boxes and to 'translate' the allegories: only a M. Evrard will think that this story is really about puppets, and only a M. Evrard will think that *Pot-pourri* is a hotchpotch of unconnected anecdotes. Despite the complex structure Voltaire has a plain story to tell, unlike those Christian purveyors of 'galimatias' and 'orviétan' (246), and once more it is the tale of a metamorphosis. The fiction of Christianity has been replaced by the authentic provisionality of philosophical debate: Mme Gigogne has been superseded by the *conte gigogne*. Unlike the Jesuit apothecaries at the beginning, *Pot-pourri* offers no drug to dull the mind but rather a highly original and formally daring concoction which turns ecclesiastical rot into the sweet scent of enlightenment.

LE BLANC ET LE NOIR AND JEANNOT ET COLIN

Voltaire's next two *contes*, *Le Blanc et le noir* and *Jeannot et Colin*, both appeared in April 1764 in a volume entitled *Contes de Guillaume Vadé*. The fairground milieu of *Pot-pourri* is evoked once more by the implied reference to Jean-Joseph Vadé (1720–57), the author of scabrous verse and popular comic opera.[20] But no Guillaume Vadé is known to history, nor Catherine Vadé, the supposed writer of the

---

[19]   D11978 (9 July 1764).
[20]   For an informative account of Vadé see Robert M. Isherwood, *Farce and Fantasy. Popular Entertainment in Eighteenth-Century Paris* (New York and Oxford, 1986), 116–19. Vadé was famous for introducing the so-called 'style poissard' or 'poissarderie' to the Opéra-Comique, which itself, in terms of literary register, stood half-way between the Classicism of the Théâtre Français (Comédie Française) and the popular culture of the fairground. By identifying with Vadé, Voltaire would seem to be trying to 'écraser l'infâme' of literary, as well as religious, intolerance.

preface to this anthology of her late cousin's work. As well as *Le Blanc et le noir* and *Jeannot et Colin*, the volume contains seven *contes en vers* of a libertine kind, including *Ce qui plaît aux dames*; and in the preface Catherine Vadé refers to these as 'les contes à dormir debout' with which Guillaume used to entertain his family (which also numbers his brother, the equally fictional Antoine Vadé, and Jérôme Carré, 'son cousin issu de germain').[21] As well as being distinctly anti-Catholic in its comments on church burial and the significance of baptismal names, this preface prepares for the risqué and, as it were, downmarket nature of some of the *contes* which follow by insisting on their oral quality and by debunking literary pretension, in particular the notion of bequeathing one's great works to posterity. The predominant tone is one of irreverence, and Catherine's final hope that 'messieurs les Parisiens, pour qui Vadé et Carré ont toujours travaillé, me pardonneront ma préface'[22] indicates whose pretension and reverence are in question.

Both *Le Blanc et le noir* and *Jeannot et Colin*, therefore, need to be read within the context of anti-Establishment, anti-metropolitan, and indeed anti-Jansenist sentiments. The *Contes de Guillaume Vadé* also includes the *Discours aux Welches*, in which Voltaire warns against the scourge of earnestness and solemnity: 'J'apprends qu'il s'élève parmi vous une secte de gens durs qui se disent solides, d'esprits sombres qui prétendent au jugement parce qu'ils sont dépourvus d'imagination, d'hommes lettrés ennemis des lettres, qui veulent proscrire la belle antiquité et la fable.'[23] The *Contes de Guillaume Vadé* are thus anti-Jansenist in their insistence on the virtues of both popular and ancient culture (in which the Jansenists would have found evidence of pagan immorality) and in their recurrent insistence on education of a resolutely unorthodox kind.

Both stories are parodies of prevailing literary clichés, respectively the *conte oriental* and the *conte moral*; and in each case the main target is the simplistic didacticism for which these fashionable genres had been made to serve as vehicles. In this they resemble many of the accompanying *contes en vers*, where La Fontaine's favoured genre becomes the medium for some playful depictions of the joys of

---

[21] Mol., x. 5.
[22] Mol., x. 8.
[23] *Mélanges*, 700.

sex to purported pedagogical purpose.[24] In these *contes en vers* the earnestness of instructive literature is shown to be a hypocritical cover for more salacious readerly desires. Thus, as in *Pot-pourri*, the Voltaire of the *Contes de Guillaume Vadé* sides openly with the 'pagans' and denounces the complacent, false enlightenment purveyed by second-rate moralizers who imply that they have an answer for everything. True enlightenment is a more difficult business, and *L'Origine des métiers*, the last of the *contes en vers*, ends with a reminder of human ignorance: '. . . et bien peu de nous / Sont descendus du dieu de la lumière.'

Le Blanc et le noir is ostensibly written by Antoine Vadé, to whose works Catherine refers in her preface as 'quelques belles dissertations'. In the 'Avertissement' to the *Supplément du Discours aux Welches* Antoine, the supposed author of the *Discours* itself, is described as being 'grave, profond, et sérieux . . . ; il n'aimait à s'occuper que de choses utiles. La gloire de la nation et le bien public l'intéressaient par-dessus tout; il s'affligeait des abus qui empêchent l'un et l'autre, et plus encore de ce que ceux qui voulaient les réformer ne commençaient pas par se réformer eux-mêmes.'[25] Guillaume, on the other hand, the 'author' of the *contes en vers*, is described as being 'gai, plaisant, et léger'. The Vadé brothers, therefore, may represent a tension in Voltaire between the urbane entertainer and the committed polemicist.

Le Blanc et le noir marks a return to the world of the *Thousand and One Nights* which Voltaire had sent up in *Le Crocheteur borgne* and *Zadig*. Again, as in *Le Crocheteur borgne* (and *Songe de Platon*), the story turns out to be the account of a dream. But now Voltaire apes the devices of the Oriental tale not to poke fun at Oriental licentiousness nor (principally) to debate the issue of fatalism but to demonstrate how narrative has been deceitfully used to foster the illusion that moral questions are susceptible of easy solutions. As its title suggests, *Le Blanc et le noir* considers whether these questions can be seen in black and white terms. As its title may also suggest, it considers whether the doctrine of Manicheism provides a clear-cut answer to the problem of evil.

---

[24] e.g. esp. *Gertrude ou l'éducation d'une fille*, but also *Ce qui plaît aux dames* and *L'Education d'un prince*.
[25] *Mélanges*, 702.

On the face of it the allegory of *Le Blanc et le noir* is straightforward. Rustan seeks happiness (in the agreeable shape of the Princess of Kashmir) and is subject to the conflicting advice and designs of Topaze and Ebène, his two geniuses, the one good and the other evil. The reader is lulled into a false sense of interpretative security by the steady, alternating rhythm of the narrative as the forces of good and evil protect and endanger Rustan under constantly changing guises. Indeed the predictability and seemingly unsurprising nature of events is signalled in the opening sentence with its affiliation of the story to a familiar oral tradition: 'Tout le monde, dans la province de Candahar, connaît l'aventure du jeune Rustan.' Any apparent strangeness is immediately and easily dispelled: 'Il était fils unique d'un mirza du pays: c'est comme qui dirait marquis parmi nous, ou baron chez les Allemands.' The exotic is not disturbing but entertainingly quaint: 'On devait marier le jeune Rustan à une demoiselle, ou mirzasse de sa sorte.' The principal story-line – of a young man forgoing the chance of a good marriage for love of a foreign beauty – is reassuringly commonplace, not to say bourgeois. Even the stark paradoxes of the oracles seem unproblematic: 'Si tu vas à l'orient, tu seras à l'occident'; 'Si tu possèdes, tu ne posséderas pas; si tu es vainqueur, tu ne vaincras pas; si tu es Rustan, tu ne le seras pas' (256–7). In the world of the *conte oriental* one is used to inscrutable assertions that black is white, and white is black.

But this is the point. Manicheism is a 'fable' of reason on a par with the absurdity of the *Thousand and One Nights*. An alert reader may have been warned in the third paragraph of the story that Rustan's world is not our world: the diamond is engraved 'par un art . . . qui s'est perdu depuis', and the javelin unerringly strikes its target: 'ce qui n'est pas une chose bien extraordinaire parmi nous, mais qui l'était à Cachemire.' However, it is not until Rustan's final showdown with his two geniuses that we realize the full inadequacy of this Oriental answer to the problem of evil. *Le Blanc et le noir* bears many similarities to *Zadig*, not least the way in which an inquiring hero seeks ultimate enlightenment from wing-sprouting mortals. But, as Haydn Mason has noted,[26] *Le Blanc et le noir* is more pessimistic than *Zadig*: Rustan is fatally wounded, as is his beloved, and the questions posed by the hero at the end are both more testing and also less satisfactorily answered than those previously put to the angel Jesrad. Topaze's response is essentially the same as Jesrad's: 'Hélas! c'était ta destinée' (264); but Rustan manages rather more than a 'Mais . . .':

Si c'est la destinée qui fait tout, dit le mourant, à quoi un génie est-il bon?[27]

The paradoxes of Manicheism are probed: how can a good genius fail? is one single Creator responsible for both the good and the evil geniuses? Is this Creator good or bad? But these paradoxes prove less susceptible of the glib interpretation to which Ebène subjects the pronouncements of the oracles. Ebène himself displays his evil in answering with dogmatism and intransigence: 'Possible ou non possible . . . la chose est comme je te le dis' (264). Topaze, on the other hand, shows his goodness in an honest admission of ignorance. Replying to Rustan's final word in the matter: 'Il y a quelque chose là-dessous que je ne comprends pas', he can but concede: 'Ni moi non plus, dit le pauvre bon génie' (265).

As Mason has argued, Voltaire ultimately refuses to accept the Manichean position because it conflicts with his own visceral belief in a harmonious universe, a realm of order in which permanent strife between two warring principles is inconceivable.[28] Here in *Le Blanc et le noir* he contents himself with pointing out some of the logical difficulties inherent in Manicheism and demeaning the philosophical thesis by equating it with Oriental fable. But he goes further by using this equation to question the efficacy of conventional literary didacticism. For when Rustan, ever-inquisitive seeker after enlightenment that he is, wonders why and how he could have had such a weird dream in the first place, Topaze's hypothesis meets with a summary response: 'Dieu a voulu que cette file d'idées vous ait passé par la tête, pour vous donner apparemment quelque instruction dont vous ferez votre profit. — Tu te moques de moi, reprit Rustan' (265–6).

With a literal-mindedness which anticipates that of the Ingénu, Rustan objects that all the events of which he has supposedly dreamt cannot have been squeezed into the single hour during which he was asleep. Once more, therefore, like *Zadig* and the *Histoire d'un bon*

---

[27] The wordplay here on 'bon génie' is reminiscent of the puns on 'ascendant', etc. in ch. 18 of *Zadig*, and continues in Topaze's subsequent remark to the waking Rustan that 'vous vous portez à merveille' (265).

[28] 'Voltaire and Manichean Dualism', 1159–60. Cf. *Le Philosophe ignorant*, 61.

brahmin, a Voltairian *conte* ends by raising the mystery of time. Topaze's analogy between Rustan dreaming and Rustan being able to read Zoroaster's abridged history of the Persians in the space of an hour at once suggests a further analogy between Rustan dreaming and us reading *Le Blanc et le noir* and points to interesting considerations about the psychology of reading. Do we regard Voltaire's tale in the same light as a god-sent dream imparting a moral lesson? Does the suspension of disbelief which occurs in both dream and the reading of fiction also entail the suspension of our reason? Perhaps fiction can only pose the problems rather than solve them? For just as Rustan's hope that he will discover the answer to the problem of evil in death is frustrated by his waking from a dream, so our hope of learning about the mystery of time from the parrot is frustrated by the absence of the parrot's story from Antoine Vadé's papers.

Given Topaze's inability to communicate his essentially horological vision of time to Rustan, the parrot was to be the ideal narrator. Antediluvian, and thus comparable with the prelapsarian phoenix of *La Princesse de Babylone*, he represents the antithesis of the inauthentic 'littérateurs' whom Voltaire has in his sights: 'sa mémoire est fidèle, il conte simplement, sans chercher à montrer de l'esprit à tout propos et sans faire des phrases. — Tant mieux, dit Rustan, voilà comme j'aime les contes' (266–7). But the parrot's ideal story has been lost: naïve and truthful narrative can longer be achieved and has been replaced by the laboured, if well-intentioned metaphors of the pedagogical Topaze. As Voltaire writes (in anti-Jansenist vein) at the end of *Ce qui plaît aux dames* (which comes before *Le Blanc et le noir* in the *Contes de Guillaume Vadé*):

> On a banni les démons et les fées;
> Sous la raison les grâces étouffées
> Livrent nos cœurs à l'insipidité;
> Le raisonner tristement s'accrédite;
> On court, hélas! après la vérité:
> Ah! croyez-moi, l'erreur a son mérite.

For Voltaire, once again, a blank page is the only honest answer to a metaphysical question and the only authentic way to finish a *conte*. As at the end of the *Histoire d'un bon brahmin*, silence speaks volumes: 'le blanc' of the unsaid may be more eloquent than 'le noir' of inky disquisition.

Jeannot et Colin is also concerned with the relationship between literature and instruction; and, like *Pot-pourri* and *Le Blanc et le noir*, it juxtaposes popular culture with urbane sophistication to ambiguous ends. Essentially the story is a deft satire on the simplistic ideology and techniques of the *conte moral*. Voltaire's friend and protégé Marmontel had published several of his own *contes moraux* in the *Mercure de France* during the 1750s, and a collected edition published in 1761 had been a bestseller. But Marmontel was neither the first nor the only writer to use the subtitle *conte moral*, and indeed some of his stories are not particularly 'moraux'.[29] A large body of such stories existed, and it is against the shallow conformism of such works that Voltaire is writing in *Jeannot et Colin*.

But the irony has frequently been lost on readers of this story. Anxious to include the great name of the otherwise rather unsuitable Voltaire on the syllabus, arbiters of French secondary education for over a century and a half have taken the story at face value and presented it as an exemplary tale, particularly for those bent upon a career as an artisan.[30] Many respectable critics have also seen the story as a harmless little tale propounding a simple moral lesson about the virtue of friendship and have looked no further than the last sentence for its central message: 'le bonheur n'est pas dans la vanité.'[31]

Not only is it wildly improbable that Voltaire, albeit at the age of 72 and for some, therefore, on the very threshold of anecdotage, should forsake irony and turn his hand to homespun wisdom, the text itself repeatedly displays a disparity between the hollowness of earnest commonplace and the facts of life. As Benjamin Constant's *Adolphe* later put it: 'Les sots font de leur morale une masse compacte et indivisible, pour qu'elle se mêle le moins possible avec leurs actions, et les laisse libres dans tous les détails.'[32] For Voltaire the *conte moral* fosters morality as a system which governs through parroted generalities, whereas true enlightenment involves continuous reappraisal in the light of new and unique circumstances. This dis-

---

[29] See Christiane Mervaud, '*Jeannot et Colin*: Illustration et subversion du conte moral', *Revue d'histoire littéraire de la France*, 85 (1985), 602. This perceptive account of the story refines and takes further the controversial approach of Roy S. Wolper in 'The Toppling of Jeannot', *SVEC* 183 (1980).
[30] See Mervaud, 'Illustration et subversion du conte moral', 597.
[31] See Wolper, 'The Toppling of Jeannot', 69–70, for examples.
[32] *Adolphe*, ch. 1, end of para. 6.

crepancy between adage and actuality is highlighted in the fourth
paragraph of *Jeannot et Colin*, particularly in a series of well-chosen
puns. Thus the paragraph begins: 'Les lecteurs qui aiment à s'instruire
doivent savoir que . . .', which implies that the author is providing a
moral lesson in a traditional fashion. But on further reading it becomes
apparent that the 'instruction' on offer is more practical than moral,
namely how to succeed as a parvenu. 'Vous demandez comment on
fait ces grandes fortunes? C'est parce qu'on est heureux.' The passing
suggestion that happiness, and perhaps even an easy conscience, may
be the key to success is at once superseded by the alternative sense of
'heureux' as 'fortunate'. The idea of 'happy chance' is elaborated in a
cliché ('la fortune, qui élève et qui abaisse les hommes à son gré'), but
the ups and downs of life turn out somewhat literally (and perhaps in
imitation of Vadé's 'poissarderie') to be the sexual attractiveness of
Jcannot's father to the wife of a dealer in medical supplies (and Jeannot's mother to the dealer). Sleeping one's way to one's first million is
at once glossed with a further cliché: 'Dès qu'on est dans le fil de l'eau,
il n'y a qu'à se laisser aller'; and the smug voice of the 'nouveau riche'
is then perfectly reproduced by the mocking narrator: 'Les gredins
qui du rivage vous regardent voguer à pleines voiles, ouvrent des yeux
étonnés; ils ne savent comment vous avez pu parvenir; ils vous envient
au hasard, et font contre vous des brochures que vous ne lisez point.'

As Christiane Mervaud has shown, Voltaire's story contains many
of the obvious traits of the *conte moral*: the clear-cut and repeated
antithesis between good and evil, the final victory of good over evil,
the enduring qualities of the representative of the good leading to
the return of the errant mortal to the fold of the virtuous, the lessons
of moderation and practical utility, etc.[33] At the same time Voltaire
has given some of these topoi an ironic twist: success is achieved not
only through the wife's adultery, but also through the husband's
(and with a symmetry that mocks the conventional binary structures
of the *conte moral*); the rich widow abandons Jeannot, not *vice versa*.
For Voltaire the easy opposition of 'goodies' and 'baddies' in second-
rate fiction is as misleading as the Manicheism dualism ridiculed in
Le Blanc et le noir. The 'monde comme il va' is still as difficult to
assess morally as Babouc previously found it on his visit to Persepolis,

[33] 'Illustration et subversion du conte moral', 601–9: 'Cette absence d'inquiétude,
ce recours à une sagesse médiocre, ce refus du tragique, du mal, de la souffrance qui
n'est bonne à rien, apparentent *Jeannot et Colin* au conte moral' (609). On the question
of 'sagesse médiocre', see Mauzi, *L'Idée du bonheur*, 175–9.

and Voltaire is once more in search of a narrative equivalent of Babouc's allegorical statue. Here he finds it in combining the clichés of the *conte moral* with a satire on Parisian education.

The milieu which has made the instructive *conte moral* fashionable is portrayed as one in which education is the inculcation of the art of show, or 'les moyens de plaire' (271). Latin, geography, astronomy, history, and geometry are rejected in favour of heraldry and dance. But when Jeannot's father goes bust, his son's bubble bursts too; and Jeannot's only resource, according to his advisers, is either to become a tutor or to write novels (275). Or both perhaps: for such has been his vacuous apprenticeship, we may infer, that the *conte moral* itself is about all Jeannot might now be capable of producing.

At this point the logic of the *conte moral* offers an alternative, thanks to the miraculous intervention of the worthy Colin. A return to rustic Auvergne, marriage to Colin's equally worthy sister, and learning the trade in 'ustensiles nécessaires aux grands et aux petits' (276): such are the instruments of Jeannot's redemption. Snobbery and vain parental ambition had torn him from his childhood paradise: 'un habit de velours à trois couleurs' (269) and a mirror had been his equivalent of Eve's apple. Now the bourgeois work ethic, filial devotion, serene conjugality, and contented provinciality will see to it that he lives happily ever after.

It might seem, therefore, that the moral of *Jeannot et Colin* is comparable with that of *Candide*: 'il faut cultiver notre jardin', albeit in the Auvergne. But it is evident that Voltaire is now, in some of the stories which follow *Candide*, not only indulging in more 'Merry Hissing' (here at the glossy superficiality of metropolitan life) but also exploring the ramifications of his famous aphorism further. How should one cultivate one's garden? How and what should one learn (and teach) in cultivating the mental garden? To what extent should the natural be aided and transformed by such cultivation? What is culture, or 'civilization'? These questions are central to *L'Ingénu* and *La Princesse de Babylone*, but here in *Jeannot et Colin* we begin to see what is at stake. Because, as Roy Wolper has rightly pointed out, the ending of the story scarcely presents an ideal: '[Jeannot's] final retreat to Auvergne represents a narrowing of the human potential . . . Notwithstanding stupidities, vanities and bruising indifferences, Paris nourishes the values and modes of the narrator.'[34] For Wolper

---

[34] 'The Toppling of Jeannot', 71.

the real lesson of *Jeannot et Colin* lies in the medium of the Voltairian *conte* itself: 'Through vicious satire and brilliant language, the narrator . . . vindicates intellectuality and artistic achievement and, therefore, justifies the merit of an education garnered in a city like Paris; the *conte*'s success is the narrator's (and the reader's) ultimate proof.'[35]

Vivienne Mylne has doubted the wisdom of Wolper's interpretation and takes the robust view that 'the not-very-bright Jeannot will best fulfil *his* potential in the provincial peace to which Voltaire despatches him'.[36] While one may warm to her common sense and doubt Jeannot's chances of ever becoming a witty Parisian *conteur*, nevertheless the fact remains that the garden which is presented for cultivation at the end of *Jeannot et Colin* leaves much to be desired (as indeed did that at the end of *Candide*). This becomes clear if we look forward to *L'Ingénu*, which was published in the following year. For here the provinces, in the shape of Lower Brittany, are evidently the realm of superstition and prejudice. To leave them for Paris is to run the risk of imprisonment and sexual exploitation; but, despite their experiences, all the main characters (except Mlle de Saint-Yves, that is) end up wanting to live there: 'on s'arrangeait pour vivre tous ensemble dans Paris, on faisait des projets de fortune et d'agrandissement, on se livrait à toutes ces espérances que la moindre lueur de félicité fait naître si aisément' (340). There is irony here, of course, both in the naïvety of their enthusiasm and in the fact that the lure of the metropolis should be sufficient so rapidly to banish all memory of its ills. Moreover the Ingénu has his doubts, mostly because of his inklings about the real reason for his release from the Bastille. But he himself will find some kind of fulfilment in Paris at the end of the story and, as will be discussed presently, the overall import of *L'Ingénu* suggests that the capital, and the high cultural level which its inhabitants periodically attain, represents a desirable form of human development to set against the deep conservatism of Lower Brittany. The Ingénu is fortunate in that he has been spared the mind-warping effects of a French education, but he still needs the stimulus of French culture and civilization to be turned from a brute into a man: nature needs to be nurtured.

The end of *Candide* leaves many questions about enlightenment

---

[35] Ibid. 82.
[36] 'Wolper's View of Voltaire's Tales', *SVEC* 212 (1982), 326.

unanswered, and it is not until *L'Ingénu* that Voltaire tackles them head on. Here in *Jeannot et Colin*, however, one can see the beginnings of the debate which is illustrated by the life of Hercule de Kerkabon. In some respects Jeannot's origins are ideal: he is the son of 'un brave laboureur des environs, qui cultivait la terre' and he goes to school in Issoire 'ville fameuse dans tout l'univers par son collège' (269). If anyone can cultivate a garden and improve his mind, then Jeannot can. And indeed it is the 'brave laboureur' turned marquis who has the right ideas about his son's education when they reach Paris (270–1). But Jeannot's development is interrupted by the forces of ignorance: the tutor 'qui était un homme du bel air, et qui ne savait rien' (270) and the successful author who turns out to be a 'gracieux ignorant' (271). In view of the utilitarian morality which informs most *contes moraux*, it is with some Voltairian glee that the fallacious reasons given for Jeannot's not learning Latin, geography, astronomy, history, or geometry all stem from the possible practical application of the branch of study in question. The time-honoured accusation that academic study is less profitable, less 'useful', than vocational training receives its just satirical deserts:

'Joue-t-on, s'il vous plaît, la comédie et l'opéra en latin? Plaide-t-on en latin quand on a un procès? Fait-on l'amour en latin?' Monsieur [Jeannot's father], ébloui de ces raisons, passa condamnation, et il fut conclu que le jeune marquis ne perdrait point son temps à connaître Cicéron, Horace et Virgile. (271)

The supposed utilitarian ideal presented at the end of *Jeannot et Colin* involves Jeannot learning to work in a 'bonne manufacture de fer étamé et de cuivre' producing the aforementioned 'ustensiles nécessaires aux grands et aux petits' (276). Unlike Latin, are these instruments then vital to the art of love-making, or only in the Auvergne?

In rejecting the study of history the private tutor comments that 'on étouffe l'esprit des enfants sous un amas de connaissances inutiles' (272). Again this is a time-honoured excuse for not teaching (or learning) anything, but the repeated and unironic assertion of a similar idea in *L'Ingénu* (294, 325) suggests that it is central to Voltaire's evolving conception of the ideal education. If education is given over to the instillation of prejudice, superstition, and myth (for example, as Voltaire would see it, theology or Cartesian physics), then such 'connaissances' are indeed 'inutiles'. But nature abhors a vacuum; and, with pleasant irony, by the time they have all decided what Jeannot should learn, namely to dance, nature has declared herself: 'La nature, qui fait tout, lui avait donné un talent qui se développa bientôt avec un succès prodigieux, c'était de chanter agréablement des vaudevilles' (273). A rather unlikely natural talent, this quickly brings his non-education to fruition: 'il acquit l'art de parler sans s'entendre, et se perfectionna dans l'habitude de n'être propre à rien' (273–4). This latter-day 'bourgeois gentilhomme' has made it, only to be ruined. Jeannot's subsequent return to Issoire at the end of the story is then a case of making the best of a bad lot. He has missed out on the education provided by a supposedly world-famous college, and he has fallen into the wrong pedagogical hands in Paris. Would, like the Ingénu, that he had been put in prison (as his father is): then he might have had the opportunity to study the things that matter.

Such a reading of *Jeannot et Colin* may seem unduly reliant on the comparison with *L'Ingénu*. Other than the urbanity of the narrator (whose exemplary status is perhaps overstated by Wolper) there is no explicit evidence of the desirability of the kind of education which Jeannot's advisers reject, merely some evidence of the undesirability of having no education at all. But the proposed reading may be reinforced by a brief consideration of the implicit allusions to Rousseau which stud the text, in particular those to the *Discours sur l'inégalité* (1755) and *Émile* (1762).

Voltaire had little time for the *Discours sur l'inégalité*. He had already satirized aspects of it in *Candide* and would do so again in *L'Ingénu*. The author of *Le Mondain* rejected Rousseau's thesis about the corruption of society and the natural goodness of man and wilfully traduced it in his famous sallies: 'On n'a jamais tant employé d'esprit à vouloir nous rendre Bêtes. Il prend envie de marcher à quatre pattes quand on lit votre ouvrage.'[37] As to *Émile*, Voltaire regarded it simply as a 'roman absurde qu'on ne peut lire'.[38] He made an exception of the *Profession de foi du vicaire savoyard*, which he clearly admired, although he refused to let this affect his by now extremely dim view of its author: 'c'est bien dommage qu'il ait fait le vicaire savoyard. La conversation de ce vicaire méritait d'être écrite par un honnête homme.'[39]

[37] D6451 (30 Aug. 1755, to Rousseau).
[38] D11975 (6 July 1764, to Damilaville).
[39] D12914 (2 Oct. 1765, to the comte and comtesse d'Argental).

However, as the *Sentiment des citoyens* (1764) and the *Lettre au docteur Pansophe* (1766) demonstrate, Voltaire's relations with Rousseau had reached a definite low point in the mid-1760s. There is consequently every reason to suppose that in *Jeannot et Colin*, as in *Candide* and the *Histoire d'un bon brahmin*, and later in *L'Ingénu*, one of Voltaire's satirical targets is Jean-Jacques. This would account, for example, for the way in which Jeannot's redemption by Colin is described at the end of that story: 'La bonté d'âme de Colin développa dans le cœur de Jeannot le germe du bon naturel, que le monde n'avait pas encore étouffé. Il sentit qu'il ne pouvait abandonner son père et sa mère' (276). The reference to natural goodness and Jeannot's reliance on sentiment for guidance as to where his filial duty lies both recall central Rousseauist notions. In Rousseau's terms the kind of education which Jeannot receives in Paris is the very epitome of all that he finds wrong with modern so-called 'civilization': its artificiality and reliance on show. Here we may be reminded also of the *Discours sur l'inégalité* in which, in this supposedly hypothetical history of man, Rousseau attributes the end of man's golden age to the discovery of song and dance.[40] Moreover there is evident Voltairian malice in the fact that Jeannot should turn out to have a *natural* talent for song and dance and that this talent should be susceptible of *development* (273), since for Rousseau these arts of display are unnatural and artificially contrived. Equally malicious is the fact that Jeannot's escape from Parisian ruin and return to Issoire (if not nature) should involve becoming a metal-worker, since it is precisely metallurgy and agriculture which Rousseau singles out in the *Discours sur l'inégalité* as the prime causes of the alienation of labour and consequent inequality among men.[41] In *Emile*, of course, part of Emile's ideal education had been to learn to be not a metal-worker but a 'menuisier'.[42]

If one bears in mind also Rousseau's disapproval of novels and the theatre, and his belief that such literature is morally acceptable only

[40] *Œuvres complètes*, eds. Gagnebin and Raymond, iii. 169–70.
[41] Ibid. iii. 171.
[42] Voltaire ridicules this in his *Notes sur la lettre de Voltaire à M. Hume* and comments: 'Ce n'est point ainsi, ce me semble, que s'exprimait le grand Fénelon, et ce n'est point ainsi que Mentor élevait son Télémaque. M. Jean-Jacques veut que son élève soit ignorant jusqu'à l'âge de quinze ans, et qu'il sache raboter au lieu d'apprendre la géométrie, l'histoire, la tactique et les belles-lettres' (*Mélanges*, 869). This provides further evidence that Voltaire regards Jeannot as having missed a golden educational opportunity in Paris.

if heavily didactic, it becomes quite evident that Voltaire's one and only *conte moral* is rather a sophisticated dig at Jean-Jacques. For Rousseau 'civilization' is evidence of the abuse of man's natural, God-given reason, a perverse deviation from natural virtue and humanity: for Voltaire it may indeed mean the kind of speciousness to be found all too often in Paris, but at its best it means the fulfilment of human reason and potentially the context most conducive to human happiness, the true, 'enlightened' happiness which Jeannot might have had.

PETITE DIGRESSION AND AVENTURE INDIENNE

The first edition of *Le Philosophe ignorant* (1766) includes two *contes* which were subsequently published separately and have since come to be treated as independent works: *Petite digression*[43] and *Aventure indienne*. The first of these, later entitled *Les Aveugles juges des couleurs* in the posthumous Kehl edition of Voltaire's complete works, may have originated as early as 1738[44] and probably relates closely to Voltaire's erstwhile campaign against the blind anti-Newtonian refusal to abandon Cartesian physics. On the other hand, it seems reasonable to consider the story at this point, rather than as Voltaire's third *conte*, since presumably it was its context within the *Le Philosophe ignorant* which led Voltaire to publish it at all. Jacqueline Hellegouarc'h expresses surprise that Voltaire should have waited so long to let this *conte* appear, but this begs the question both of the date of the final version and of the import of the story.

For Mme Hellegouarc'h *Petite digression* simply 'ajoute un bref contrepoint' to *Le Philosophe ignorant*,[45] and indeed it is true that the depiction of a 'dictateur' telling the blind what they should and should not believe recalls the intolerance and intellectual oppression against which the 'philosophe ignorant' is arguing by deriding metaphysics and championing scepticism and the need for justice. But while the original plot and imagery of *Petite digression* may date back to the 1730s, there are several aspects to the story which recall more

---

[43] In the table of contents the full title is given as *Petite digression sur les Quinze-Vingts*.

[44] See Jacqueline Hellegouarc'h, '*Les Aveugles juges des couleurs*: interprétation et essai de datation', *SVEC* 215 (1982). See also Vaillot, *Avec Madame Du Châtelet*, 86–7.

[45] 'Interprétation et essai de datation', 95.

recent Voltairian works, particularly *Le Blanc et le noir* and *Pot-pourri*. Thus the dictator's successive decrees that the blind are dressed in white, then in red (while they themselves, of course, have no empirical means of discovering what colour they are wearing), is reminiscent both of the title of *Le Blanc et le noir* and of that story's reflection on the need not to see things in absolute terms.

More importantly, *Petite digression* may well be another veiled, if considerably abbreviated, history of the Christian Church like *Pot-pourri*. In the beginning was peace and harmony, but along comes 'un de leurs professeurs', perhaps St Paul, who 'prétendit avoir des notions claires sur le sens de la vue': 'il se fit écouter, il intrigua, il forma des enthousiastes; enfin on le reconnut pour le chef de la communauté' (279). Whereas sieur Bienfait, the St Paul of *Pot-pourri*, 'devint si riche qu'il se mit à la tête de la troupe' (246), this 'premier dictateur' in *Petite digression* reverses the process and uses power to secure wealth: '[il] se forma d'abord un petit conseil, avec lequel il se rendit le maître de toutes les aumônes.' In papal style he upbraids his blind followers for doubting 'l'infaillibilité de leur maître'; and the result, as at the end of section 11 of *Pot-pourri*, is schism: 'Cette querelle forma deux partis.'

'Aumônes', 'infaillibilité', 'querelle': these fleeting but eloquent pointers to an anti-clerical allegory in *Petite digression* are difficult to ignore. The power of this particular *conte*, short though it is, lies nevertheless in its applicability to any number of historical or possible future situations in which peaceful human coexistence is disrupted by dogmatism. As in so many of Voltaire's *contes*, the underlying structure is one of paradise lost and paradise regained. The inhabitants of the hospice of the Quinze-Vingts may be deprived of one of their five senses, just as mankind in general is subject to the perplexing mystery of Creation, but the refined use of their remaining senses permits of a happiness that accepts its own limitations: 'Ils raisonnèrent parfaitement sur les quatre sens, c'est-à-dire qu'ils en connurent tout ce qu'il est permis d'en savoir; et ils vécurent paisibles et fortunés autant que des Quinze-Vingts peuvent l'être' (279). The fall from grace is caused by the 'dictateur': 'Il se mit à juger souverainement des couleurs, et tout fut perdu.' Where once the blind 'étaient tous égaux ... et leurs petites affaires se décidaient à la pluralité des voix', this Rousseauist vision of democracy is shattered by the rise to power of a 'professeur' (an educator, therefore), who looks remarkably like a Voltairian travesty of the 'législateur' in Rousseau's *Du contrat social* (1762). But paradise is ultimately regained by means of that very provisionality which is the hallmark of Voltaire's open-ended *contes*: 'la concorde ne fut rétablie que lorsqu'il fut permis à tous les Quinze-Vingts de suspendre leur jugement sur la couleur de leurs habits' (280).

True to its own message this particular *conte* leaves open the question whether the lesson being preached by its non-dictatorial author will in fact be learned: 'Un sourd, en lisant cette petite histoire, avoua que les aveugles avaient eu tort de juger des couleurs; mais il resta ferme dans l'opinion qu'il n'appartient qu'aux sourds de juger de la musique' (280). One cannot legislate against the enduring blindness of human prejudice and human error — least of all, Voltaire may be saying, against those of a philosopher-musician like Rousseau.

The end of *Aventure indienne* resembles that of *Petite digression* in that a vision of tolerance is replaced by a rather bitter, worldly-wise recognition that such a vision may be either illusory or purely temporary. This story tells of how Pythagoras, on a visit to India (no doubt to broaden his mind), discovers the horrors of the food chain and saves two Hindus from the pyre. It begins, like *Le Blanc et le noir* and later *La Princesse de Babylone*, by evoking the idyllic world of Indian fable. 'Comme tout le monde sait': once more we are in the familiar, comforting realm of folk tradition. Pythagore's education consists in learning 'à l'école des gymnosophistes, le langage des bêtes et celui des plantes': not for him, therefore, the nonsense Jeannot learns, but initiation into that primordial world described by the phoenix in *La Princesse de Babylone* (363–4) where man and beast once conversed for their mutual enlightenment. Fables are stories in which animals speak, but here, in Voltaire's fallen fable, what the animals (and plants) have to say quickly dispels the naïve and quaint charm of an apologue. Pythagore uncovers a world of pain and cruelty which is a scarcely concealed allegory of contemporary France in which the young chevalier de La Barre had just been executed (in July 1766) for no more than youthful impiety. Pythagore's India is the world of the Calas affair and the *Traité sur la tolérance* (1763), and vegetarianism has become a metaphor for religious toleration.

Coming originally almost at the end of *Le Philosophe ignorant*, and directly after the portrayal of totalitarian dictatorship in *Petite digression*, *Aventure indienne* is a 'translated' ('traduite par l'ignorant') account of how one man has sought to put into practice the programme of militant enlightenment outlined in the final section of *Le Philosophe ignorant*, entitled 'Commencement de la raison'. Faced with the renascent Hydra of fanaticism and religious persecution, how should one proceed?

quiconque recherchera la vérité risquera d'être persécuté. Faut-il rester oisif dans les ténèbres? Ou faut-il allumer un flambeau auquel l'envie et la calomnie rallumeront leurs torches? Pour moi, je crois que la vérité ne doit pas plus se cacher devant ces monstres, que l'on ne doit s'abstenir de prendre de la nourriture dans la crainte d'être empoisonné.

Voltaire himself had succeeded in having Calas's name posthumously cleared in 1765 for the alleged murder of his son in 1762, and, having afforded refuge to the Sirvens, was seeking to help them similarly. These Protestant victims of Jansenist injustice in the Parlements, as well as the Catholic chevalier de La Barre (and reader of Voltaire's own *Dictionnaire philosophique*) are transposed into the figures of the two Indians about to be burned in *Aventure indienne*. The flames of the pyre prove less strong than the 'flambeau' of enlightenment, and Voltaire seems to regard his own success (in the case of Calas at least) as no less implausible than the world of Indian fable: '[Pythagore] fit pourtant entendre raison aux juges, et même aux dévotes; et c'est ce qui n'est arrivé que cette seule fois' (283). The flames of persecution have not been permanently extinguished, however, and the final paragraph of *Aventure indienne* suggests that, in seeking to crush the monster of 'l'infâme', Voltaire was constantly aware that the ironies of providence might well make him its next victim: 'Ensuite [Pythagore] alla prêcher la tolérance à Crotone; mais un intolérant mit le feu à sa maison: il fut brûlé, lui qui avait tiré deux Indous des flammes. *Sauve qui peut!*'[46]

It is characteristic of Voltaire that he should conclude a work as abstract as *Le Philosophe ignorant* by relating its message to the practical world, albeit in this 'translated' way. The courageous decision to meet the Hydra face to face is the more impressive for the reminder in *Aventure indienne* of its author's own attempts to do so, and the end of the story shows a *philosophe* self-deprecatingly aware of the limits of his own achievements as an educator. As he wrote to James

---

[46] Cf. D10580 (11 July 1762, to La Chalotais): 'La société humaine me paraît ressembler à un grand naufrage. *Sauve qui peut* est la devise des pauvres diables comme moi.'

Marriott on 28 March 1766: 'Je ne crois pas que je parvienne jamais à faire établir de mon vivant une tolérance entière en France, mais j'en aurai du moins jeté les premiers fondements.'[47] For all his self-doubt he continued to try, not only in his campaigns on behalf of the victims of religious and political oppression but also in the *conte*. In his next one, *L'Ingénu*, Rousseau and 'l'infâme' are once more central to his syllabus.

[47]   D13224.

10

Hearts and Minds

L'Ingénu

La lecture agrandit l'âme.

(317)

L'Ingénu was another bestseller. Begun in the late autumn of 1766[1] and written mainly in the following spring and early summer, it was published in Geneva by the Cramers probably in the last week or so of July 1767. A Parisian edition appeared with 'permission tacite' on 3 September, and some three and a half thousand copies were sold within four or five days. Permission to publish was withdrawn on 17 September; but by the end of the year the *conte* had nevertheless appeared in at least nine editions. It was the subject of countless imitations, 'sequels' by other writers, and theatrical adaptations. By 1785 the work itself had gone through no less than thirty-nine editions.

Reasons for the popularity of *L'Ingénu* are not hard to find, such is the powerful cocktail of comic satire and righteous indignation which it presents. Drawing on the tradition of the 'noble savage', playing on the fashion for the sentimental novel, echoing the current debate about education, mindful of the recent expulsion of the Jesuits and the growing power of the Jansenist-dominated Parlements, and conscious of increasing provincial resistance to Parisian authority, Voltaire produced a *conte* which must have touched just about every possible nerve in his increasingly wide readership. But whereas the eponymous hero professes to owe his nickname to the fact that 'je dis toujours naïvement ce que je pense' (288), the tale itself has left most readers in a quandary as to what its author was actually trying to say. Was he just having fun at the expense of a number of sacred cows, or is there some more profound lesson?

[1] Perhaps even in 1764. See Haydn Mason, 'The Unity of Voltaire's *L'Ingénu*', in W. H. Barber *et al.* (eds.), *The Age of Enlightenment* (Edinburgh and London, 1967), 101, n. 15.

The dual nature of the work has proved particularly problematic, and various attempts have been made to come to terms with the way in which the *conte philosophique* of the first part (approximately chs. 1–12) relates to what is perceived as the *roman sensible* of the second (ch. 13 to the end). Critics have been loath to see artistic failure in this apparent disjunction of register; but this is chronologically the last of Voltaire's *contes* to escape the prevalent view that the septuagenarian story-teller began to lose his touch. Indeed Jean Starobinski actually calls *L'Ingénu* 'le dernier récit de Voltaire'.[2]

'HISTOIRE VÉRITABLE'

Before examining the ambiguity of *L'Ingénu* further, it may be helpful to look at some of the ingredients of Voltaire's cocktail more closely. The story is subtitled 'Histoire véritable tirée des manuscrits du P. Quesnel'. As the leading Jansenist after the death of Arnauld, Père Quesnel (1634–1719) is in one respect an appropriate choice of putative author since *L'Ingénu* paints such an unflattering portrait of the Jesuits. But he is also, of course, wildly incongruous, since a rather risqué *conte* about circumcision, adult baptism in the nude, marriage 'à la Huron', and fornication as the most efficient means to justice is about the last thing the austere Jansenist might have written. Indeed what he did write was the *Réflexions morales sur le Nouveau Testament* (1671), of which one hundred and one propositions were subsequently condemned by Clement XI in the Papal Bull *Unigenitus* in 1713. Since this Bull became a focus of the struggle between Jesuit and Jansenist, Crown and Parlements, the fictional attribution of *L'Ingénu* to Quesnel places the *conte* at the very heart of the political and religious turmoil of the day. Moreover, in the Ingénu's reading of the New Testament and in its debate on the nature of virtue, the story constitutes Voltaire's own 'réflexions morales sur le Nouveau Testament'. But where Quesnel had produced schism, Voltaire's aim is tolerance. 'Ingénu', meaning frank and free from deception, originally meant 'free-born'.[3] To translate

---

[2] See 'Le fusil à deux coups de Voltaire', *Revue de métaphysique et de morale*, 71 (1966); reprinted in *Le Remède dans le mal*, 145. For a survey of the main critical reactions see John S. Clouston, *Voltaire's Binary Masterpiece. 'L'Ingénu' Reconsidered* (Berne, Frankfurt am Main, and New York, 1986).
[3] This etymology is helpfully stressed by Priscilla P. Clark in '*L'Ingénu*: The Uses and Limitations of Naïveté', *French Studies*, 27 (1973).

the title of Voltaire's *conte* as 'Born Free' would doubtless be to lionize its hero unduly: but its author seeks also to liberate his reader from the prison of theological dispute and set him or her on the path to free thought. *L'Ingénu* is thus a celebration of 'le bien le plus précieux des hommes, la liberté' (314).

As to its being an 'histoire véritable', Voltaire is at one level guying the ease with which this tag was affixed to the most implausible of tales.[4] Partly to this end also, presumably, he begins *L'Ingénu* with the quaintest of legendary accounts of how the 'prieuré de la Montagne' came to be founded. But another reason for this folkloric opening is a tongue-in-cheek imitation of the kind of historiography which, later in the story, the Ingénu himself so scathingly and punningly attacks:

Une chose me frappe surtout dans cette ancienne histoire de la Chine, c'est que presque tout y est vraisemblable et naturel. Je l'admire en ce qu'il n'y a rien de merveilleux. Pourquoi toutes les autres nations se sont-elles donné des origines fabuleuses? (317)

'Tout y est vraisemblable et naturel'. One is reminded of Voltaire's own notorious comment on *L'Ingénu* itself: '*L'Ingénu* vaut mieux que *Candide*, en ce qu'il est infiniment plus vraisemblable.'[5] *L'Ingénu*, too, is a 'history', and one in which Voltaire seeks to go beyond the fabulous in his presentation of the truth but without espousing the false 'realism' of the *conte moral* or the sentimental novel. As the Ingénu writes, famously, at the end of his essay on ancient history: 'Ah! s'il nous faut des fables, que ces fables soient du moins l'emblème de la vérité! J'aime les fables des philosophes, je ris de celles des enfants, et je hais celles des imposteurs' (318).

Before considering the ways in which *L'Ingénu* is a reply to the impostors, it is important to note just how much of an 'histoire véritable' this *conte* actually is. Both the *Histoire des voyages de Scarmentado* and *Candide* are notable for the way in which Voltaire goes beyond *Zadig* in basing his illustration of the problem of evil on real events. But in these *contes*, as in *Pot-pourri*, the historical evidence is presented through a mist of fantasy. *L'Ingénu* not only dispels this

---

[4]   For the use of the tag in 18th-cent. fiction see M. J. Rustin, 'L' "Histoire véritable" dans la littérature romanesque du XVIIIᵉ siècle français', *CAIEF* 18 (1966).

[5]   D14279 (July 1767, to Gabriel Cramer). Haydn Mason rightly cautions against attributing too much significance to this statement of preference in 'The Unity of Voltaire's *L'Ingénu*', 96.

mist but is also the most historically based of all Voltaire's *contes*. Accordingly, the first two paragraphs of the story dealing with Saint Dunstan are followed by a third which begins with resounding precision: 'En l'année 1689, le 15 juillet au soir.' *L'Ingénu* is thus set four years after the Revocation of the Edict of Nantes, which had put an end to such tolerance as the Protestant, or Huguenot, minority had enjoyed in France since the promulgation of the original edict in 1598. Complementing the chronological accuracy with which the story of the Ingénu begins, many of the characters whom he and Mlle de Saint-Yves subsequently encounter are historical figures: notably Saint-Pouange and the commis Alexandre, but also (by letter or hearsay) Frère Vadbled, the marquis de Louvois, and the King himself. This is the world of Jesuit dominance, with Père François de La Chaise, the King's confessor (from 1675 to 1709), enjoying the power to persecute Huguenot and Jansenist alike. This is the world of the infamous *lettres de cachet*, those orders signed by the King and countersigned by a minister (and even by bishops or lesser governmental and ecclesiastical officials) for the imprisonment without trial of anyone who had incurred official, and often not so official, displeasure.

But in the France of 1767 *lettres de cachet* were no less widely used as an instrument of repression and persecution. By a clever twist the authentic seventeenth-century setting of *L'Ingénu* is also a veiled portrait of contemporary France. For Jesuit, read Jansenist.[6] As M. Husson had already suggested in *Pot-pourri*, the departure of the Jesuits and the new ascendancy of the Jansenists was not necessarily something to be welcomed: 'Songez que les fanatiques sont plus dangereux que les fripons' (240). In fact, despite their expulsion, the Jesuits were still a potent force in French politics. But clearly one of the lessons of *L'Ingénu* is that, when it comes to religious persecution: 'plus ça change, plus c'est la même chose.' With some historical licence Voltaire shows the Jesuits abusing their power in 1689 and both the Huguenots in Saumur and the Jansenists (represented by Gordon) as the victims of their oppression. In contemporary France, following *inter alia* the Calas, Sirven, and La Barre cases, Voltaire is only too aware of the religious prejudice warping the judgements pronounced by the Jansenist-dominated Parlements.

---

[6] A thesis first proposed by Francis Pruner in his *Recherches sur la création romanesque dans 'L'Ingénu' de Voltaire* (*Archives des Lettres Modernes* (no. 30); Paris, 1960).

Saint-Pouange has his modern counterpart in Louis de Saint-Florentin (1705–1777), Louis XV's minister who was responsible for Protestant affairs and the administration of *lettres de cachet*; and the Ingénu's period as an incarcerated autodidact may suggest La Chalotais, the advocate of a new kind of education who ends up in the Bastille.

Not only La Chalotais but the whole episode of the Breton Parlement's refusal in 1764 to levy new taxes may also partly account for the setting of *L'Ingénu*. While Lower Brittany was simply synonymous with provincial dullness, it is no accident that the cream of local society who come to supper at the Priory should include 'le bailli, le receveur des tailles et leurs femmes' (287) since magistrates and tax-collecting were now what Brittany was most famous for. Moreover, given Voltaire's opposition to the growing power of the Parlements, it is not surprising that the 'bailli' should be so mercilessly ridiculed along with his 'grand nigaud de fils' (294), nor that of all the main characters in the story they alone should not evolve and mature as a result of their experiences. Add to this the *verbatim* reference to the Bélisaire affair (318) and the fact that the Ingénu's portrait of the ideal Minister of War is a description of the duc de Choiseul, Louis XV's most powerful minister at this time, and it is evident that in its historical aim *L'Ingénu* is as well primed in its eighteenth-century as in its seventeenth-century barrel. Its target is 'l'infâme', 'l'infâme' of all ages, the intolerance and fanaticism born of religion and fed by internecine dispute.

ROUSSEAU

Another target is once more Rousseau, whose works epitomized for Voltaire the 'fables des imposteurs' which the Ingénu decries. In *Candide* Pangloss is a caricature not only of Leibniz but also of the author of the *Discours sur l'inégalité*, whom Voltaire later dubbed 'le docteur Pansophe'. Pangloss preaches the natural goodness of primitive man (151), equality in a state of nature (179), and the injustice of unequally distributed wealth (165). Together with the metaphysician's somewhat lubricious sexuality, not to mention the young Oreillon ladies who enjoy having their bottoms nibbled by monkeys (180),[7] these articles of faith serve to evoke another of

---

[7]   Voltaire lards this incident with Rousseau's key terms: 'Candide fut touché de pitié' (180–1); 'je ne m'attendais pas à tant de bonté d'âme' (181).

the 'systems' which *Candide* sets out to undermine. Moreover it is generally accepted that Voltaire added the section on Candide's visit to the marquise de Parolignac in 1761 as a 're-write' of Saint-Preux's visit to the brothel in Rousseau's *La Nouvelle Héloïse*.[8] And in *Jeannot et Colin*, as we have seen, both the *Discours* and *Emile* are very much to the forefront of its author's mind.

In *L'Ingénu* the entire Rousseau *œuvre* to date seems to be in the firing line. The tradition of the 'noble savage', of course, did not begin with the *Discours sur l'inégalité*: it can be traced back at least as far as Gabriel Sagard Théodat's *Grand Voyage au pays des Hurons* ... *avec un dictionnaire de la langue huronne* (1632), a copy of which, donated by the author, is consulted by the Prior to establish the Ingénu's bona fides (289). Subsequently the author of a history of Canada (1636), Sagard Théodat was a Recollect missionary, the Recollects being a reformed Franciscan order who sought detachment from the created and recollection in God. They found much to admire in the life of the Hurons, a small tribe who had become the allies of the French and were later almost wiped out by the Iroquois. From the beginning, therefore, the 'noble savage' was a useful 'fable', a convenient representative of dignified humanity in its original, untainted form with which to highlight the corruption and hidebound artificiality of the Old World.

The tradition of the 'noble savage' is thus closely akin to the Utopian travel literature of the seventeenth and eighteenth centuries which Voltaire had already travestied in *Micromégas* and *Candide*. As with the Sirian, here in *L'Ingénu* the alien visits rather than being visited; but his 'voyage of reason', profoundly educative though it will turn out to be, is now not so much a gentleman's Grand Tour as the journey of an orphaned tourist: 'de mon naturel j'aime passionnément à voir du pays' (288). He has a native curiosity which contrasts with the indolent stupor of Rousseau's natural man in the *Discours sur l'inégalité*. At the same time he has some (supposed) attributes of the savage which it suited Rousseau to overlook such as impetuousness and a taste for 'firewater'. But at least he is not a cannibal, though his story about the slaying of the Algonquin serves as a timely reminder of this further un-Rousseauistic aspect of life in the wild (as indeed does the death of Abacaba, devoured by a bear: 290). Not for nothing had Voltaire conversed with the four savages

---

8 *Romans et contes*, ed. Pomeau, 321.

brought to the Court at Fontainebleau in 1725 and enquired of one
female savage on what she fed her menfolk.[9] As ever, Voltaire looks
to the facts and takes to task one who, as Rousseau undeniably does
in the *Discours*, blurs the distinction between historical evidence and
allegorical hypothesis.[10] The facts tell him what the Ingénu concludes in his essay: that Canadians, having no sense of time or history, represent 'l'état naturel de l'homme', whereas 'L'espèce de ce
continent-ci me paraît supérieure à celle de l'autre. Elle a augmenté
son être depuis plusieurs siècles par les arts et par les connaissances'
(317). So much, in Voltaire's view, for the argument of Rousseau's
first two *Discours*.

   As in the case of *Jeannot et Colin*, *Emile* also looms large in the
background of *L'Ingénu*. Not only do all the elaborate images of
organic growth (notably at the beginning of ch. 12) recall the first
page of *Emile*, but the education of a young man is also accompanied
by that of a young woman.[11] The Ingénu's syllabus in the Bastille
excludes ancient history in favour of modern history, whereas Rousseau had proscribed the latter in favour of the former:[12] and the
education takes place in a setting which seems designed to pastiche
the famous sentence from the beginning of *Du contrat social*: 'je suis
né libre comme l'air', objects the Ingénu, 'Nous voici tous deux dans
les fers' (326). Whereas Rousseau insists that Emile must grow up
in the countryside so that he can learn from nature and be spared
the corruptions of the city, the Ingénu has to rely solely on books and
seems to thrive in conditions approximating to those of an English
boarding-school.

   Further, the whole question of the freedom of the individual and
the need for laws is debated, if cursorily, by the Ingénu and the abbé
de Saint-Yves (303); and Voltaire plainly takes the side of Hobbes
against Rousseau. For Hobbes, Voltaire, and the abbé de Saint-Yves
the state of nature, governed by natural 'law', is a world of 'brigand-

---

   9   *Dict. phil.*, 41 ('Anthropophages').
   10   See *Œuvres complètes*, eds. Gagnebin and Raymond, iii. 123, 171.
   11   Despite the importance which Lower Bretons appear to attach to baptism,
Mlle de Saint-Yves has no Christian name. The ironic parallel with *Emile* and the
Ingénu's baptism as Hercule would seem to offer the imaginative reader a choice
between Sophie and Omphale.
   12   *Œuvres complètes*, eds. Gagnebin and Raymond, iv. 528–9. But the Ingénu's
comment that 'l'histoire n'est que le tableau des crimes et des malheurs' (315)
coincides with Rousseau's that 'l'histoire . . . calomnie sans cesse le genre humain'
(iv. 527).

age naturel'; 'les conventions faites entre les hommes' are therefore indispensable. Rousseau would agree that such 'conventions' are needed but only because the natural virtue obtaining in the state of nature has been corrupted, requiring the reform of man's 'état social' in such a way that this will simulate the ideal conditions which prevailed during the golden age. For Voltaire, and Hobbes, nature is something to be controlled rather than simulated, and the abbé de Saint-Yves's speech makes clear that the 'savage' is no different from anyone else in this respect:

Il y a, dit-il, je l'avoue, beaucoup d'inconstants et de fripons parmi nous, et il y en aurait autant chez les Hurons s'ils étaient rassemblés dans une grande ville; mais aussi il y a des âmes sages, honnêtes, éclairées, et ce sont ces hommes-là qui ont fait les lois. Plus on est homme de bien, plus on doit s'y soumettre; on donne l'exemple aux vicieux, qui respectent un frein que la vertu s'est donné elle-même.

These references to inconstancy and virtue take on an ironic edge in the light of subsequent events, and indeed prepare for the implicit debate which is to come concerning just what an 'âme sage, honnête, éclairée' may or may not regard as morally acceptable. The story of Mlle de Saint-Yves herself, of course, is not without relevance to that other work of Rousseau's which Voltaire had already lambasted at length: *Julie ou la nouvelle Héloïse* (1761),[13] the length, plot, and high moral tone of which he found all particularly dreadful. As René Pomeau has suggested, the death of Mlle de Saint-Yves in *L'Ingénu* is an attempt to 're-write' the end of *La Nouvelle Héloïse*,[14] substituting a franker, less ennobling version of brutal reality, an 'histoire véritable', for alleged Rousseauistic cant.

Julie's departure from this world is, like that of Richardson's Clarissa Harlowe, too protracted to be quoted in full, but brief extracts may give some idea of the sentiments and style of writing which *L'Ingénu* is, so to speak, written against:

Ainsi se passèrent les entretiens de cette journée, où la sécurité, l'espérance, le repos de l'âme, brillèrent plus que jamais dans celle de Julie, et lui donnaient d'avance, au jugement du ministre, la paix des bienheureux dont elle allait augmenter le nombre. Jamais elle ne fut plus tendre, plus vraie, plus caressante, plus aimable, en un mot plus elle-même. Si quelquefois elle

---

[13] In the four *Lettres à M. de Voltaire* (by Voltaire but supposedly written to him by the marquis de Ximénès) published in Feb. 1761. See *Mélanges*, 395–409.
[14] *Romans et contes*, 321.

contraignait les plaintes que la souffrance aurait dû lui arracher, ce n'était point pour jouer l'intrépidité stoïque, c'était de peur de navrer ceux qui étaient autour d'elle; et quand les horreurs de la mort faisaient quelque instant pâtir la nature, elle ne cachait point ses frayeurs, elle se laissait consoler. Sitôt qu'elle était remise, elle consolait les autres . . . elle plaisait plus, elle était plus aimable qu'en santé même; et le dernier jour de sa vie en fut aussi le plus charmant.[15]

Compare the last moments of Mlle de Saint-Yves:

La belle et infortunée Saint-Yves sentait déjà sa fin approcher; elle était dans le calme, mais dans ce calme affreux de la nature affaissée qui n'a plus la force de combattre . . . Elle ne se parait pas d'une vaine fermeté; elle ne concevait pas cette misérable gloire de faire dire à quelques voisins: 'Elle est morte avec courage.' Qui peut perdre à vingt ans son amant, sa vie, et ce qu'on appelle l'*honneur*, sans regrets et sans déchirements? Elle sentait toute l'horreur de son état, et le faisait sentir par ces mots et par ces regards mourants qui parlent avec tant d'empire. Enfin elle pleurait comme les autres dans les moments où elle eut la force de pleurer. (344–5)

The physical cause of her apparent serenity, the reality of her regrets, the lack of vanity, all serve as counterpoint to the grand manner of Rousseau's account; and the moment of death itself, rather than being lingered over as in Rousseau and made the subject of a quasi-Christian resurrection, is replaced by a demythification of the very notion of a noble death:

Que d'autres cherchent à louer les morts fastueuses de ceux qui entrent dans la destruction avec insensibilité: c'est le sort de tous les animaux. Nous ne mourons comme eux avec indifférence que quand l'âge ou la maladie nous rend semblables à eux par la stupidité de nos organes. Quiconque fait une grande perte a de grands regrets; s'il les étouffe, c'est qu'il porte la vanité jusque dans les bras de la mort. (345)

For Voltaire, Rousseau's heroine is simply not human, and to present her as if she were is a dangerous lie on a par with the various 'systems' which all his *contes* seek to undermine. Sectarian divisions are bad enough, but actually to invent an alternative gospel in which virtue is natural, civilization automatically corrupt, and Julie the new Christ represents the antithesis of what Voltaire understood by enlightenment:

L'Ingénu . . . plaignit les hommes qui, non contents de tant de discorde

---

[15] *Œuvres complètes*, eds. Gagnebin and Raymond, ii. 729–30.

que leurs intérêts allument, se font de nouveaux maux pour des intérêts chimériques, et pour des absurdités inintelligibles . . . les convives écoutaient avec émotion et s'éclairaient d'une lumière nouvelle. (338–9)

In Voltaire's view, moral evil is endemic in the human condition, and man's virtue lies in coming to terms with it as best he may:

On parla de la longueur de nos infortunes et de la brièveté de la vie. On remarqua que chaque profession a un vice et un danger qui lui sont attachés, et que, depuis le prince jusqu'au dernier des mendiants, tout semble accuser la nature. Comment se trouve-t-il tant d'hommes qui, pour si peu d'argent, se font les persécuteurs, les satellites, les bourreaux des autres hommes? Avec quelle indifférence inhumaine un homme en place signe la destruction d'une famille, et avec quelle joie plus barbare des mercenaires l'exécutent! (339)

If this interpretation of the anti-Rousseau emphases in *L'Ingénu* is correct, it may be that its hero turns out to be more virtuous in the end than the woman who has died for him. It all depends on what lessons one should learn from life, and what one means by virtue.

METAMORPHOSIS

As Haydn Mason has observed, the essential unity of *L'Ingénu* is 'of an evolutionary nature, a metamorphosis'.[16] Indeed the Ingénu himself is aware that his own story is a modern version of ancient myth: 'Je serais tenté, dit-il, de croire aux métamorphoses, car j'ai été changé de brute en homme' (317). Just as Candide and the Homme aux quarante écus begin as ciphers and are gradually humanized in the course of their respective *contes*, so too Hercule de Kerkabon becomes 'one of us' — so much so that this man who starts out with simply a nickname ends up as a famous living contemporary whose anonymity must be preserved: 'l'Ingénu . . . a paru sous un autre nom à Paris et dans les armées, avec l'approbation de tous les honnêtes gens, et qui a été à la fois un guerrier et un philosophe intrépide' (347). Like M. André a year later in *L'Homme aux quarante écus*, he may even be a friend of the narrator's.

The Ingénu's education is presented as a progression from fable to actuality and from superstition to enlightenment — like the history of a nation: 'Je m'imagine que les nations ont été longtemps comme moi, qu'elles ne se sont instruites que fort tard' (317). Spared the

---

[16] 'The Unity of Voltaire's *L'Ingénu*', 97.

mind-warping fictions of French education (294, 325) 'il voyait les choses comme elles sont' (325) and is a quick learner (288). He is unmoved by the pretensions of Lower Brittany (287, 296) and debonair in the midst of its noisy social whirl (287). After one night in the place he would seem already to have matured when he makes his hosts a gift of his lucky talisman (291): smile as the recipients may at his naïvety, the 'petit brimborion' appears to be more suited to their intellectual level than his (though it turns out to be true that, having relinquished this charm, its donor will never again be as happy). The Ingénu's encounters with the New Testament and the sacraments of baptism and marriage confirm his intellectual superiority.

Like France itself in the 1760s, the Ingénu then undergoes the transition from a Jesuit to a Jansenist educational system. During his religious instruction in preparation for baptism the abbé de Saint-Yves is obliged to resort to a 'jésuite bas-breton' for advice on the more ticklish points which the straight-thinking Ingénu raises; but in the end only supernatural agency is effective: 'Enfin la grâce opéra' (295). His education then continues in prison under the tutelage of the Jansenist Gordon, a man who counts on 'la grâce efficace'. Voltaire now indulges in lively parody of Pascal: for here the two prisoners are, 'séparés de l'univers entier' (312), locked in a 'cachot' (320), and condemned to gaze into the void rather than at the wondrous spectacle of the stars (319). Their 'divertissement', however, is education, and once more the Ingénu displays his 'bons sens naturel' (318) and confounds his new adviser with the soundness of his judgement. There may be a touch of Rousseau in Gordon's amazement ('il n'écoute que la simple nature': 318), but Voltaire's message is clear. Curiosity, common sense, a willingness to concede error (295), and the courage of one's convictions (320), are all the qualifications one needs for the metamorphosis from brute into man.

And openness to experience. As in *Jeannot et Colin*, geometry, modern philosophy, history, astronomy, and literature are presented as the ideal curriculum (314–21). Since Jeannot never learns these subjects, we never find out whether the curriculum is adequate. In *L'Ingénu*, however, it is evident that they need to be complemented by life. Thus the Ingénu finds Molière and Racine superior to Corneille because the latter leaves him unmoved. Molière's *Tartuffe*, on the other hand, is relevant to his own situation (and Gordon's), as is the tragic love depicted by the author of *Phèdre*, *Andromaque*, and

Iphigénie. Similarly with novels: 'Il lut quelques romans nouveaux; il en trouva peu qui lui peignissent la situation de son âme. Il sentait que son cœur allait toujours au-delà de ce qu'il lisait' (326).

This is a crucial point. Here, as during Candide's visit to Pococur-anté's library, we are being told that the most valuable response to a work of art is not one of admiration based on received notions of good taste (as with *Rodogune*) but one which involves the receiver both intellectually and emotionally in the subject: both 'l'esprit' and 'le cœur'. By extension, life itself is the best educator. The end of *L'Ingénu* shows that the many surprises which have befallen the hero have rendered him circumspect and judicious. Where originally he literally leapt into the story and to the reader's (and Mlle de Kerka-bon's) attention (286), now he looks before he leaps: 'il avait appris à joindre la discrétion à tous les dons heureux que la nature lui avait prodigués, et le sentiment prompt des bienséances commençait à dominer dans lui' (341). Whether such discretion is an undivided blessing remains to be seen, but at least there is some evidence that the Ingénu's new accommodation with the ways of the Old World has not compromised his essential moral integrity: 'L'Ingénu, repre-nant son caractère, qui revient toujours dans les grands mouvements de l'âme, déchira la lettre [from Vadbled] par morceaux et les jeta au nez du courier: "Voilà ma réponse"' (344).[17]

In exactly parallel fashion Mlle de Saint-Yves is also educated by life. Like the Ingénu she first appears in the story as a cipher or stereotype: the nubile ward playing opposite the Ingénu's socially unsuitable foundling. Her pedigree is all, as the punning quasi-canine description suggests: 'jeune Basse-Brette, fort jolie et très bien élevée' (287). Her perfection is 'fabulous':

Cependant, comme elle était bien élevée et fort modeste, elle n'osait con-venir tout à fait avec elle-même de ses tendres sentiments; mais s'il lui échappait un regard, un mot, un geste, une pensée, elle enveloppait tout cela d'un voile de pudeur infiniment aimable. Elle était tendre, vive et sage. (299–300)

But there is irony in this insistence on how 'sage' and 'bien élevée' she is, for she knows nothing about life and is not in the least wise (though she may be well-behaved). Indeed it would seem that her curriculum to date has had but one objective, the prohibition of sex:

---

[17] Cf. also his spontaneous desire to kill Saint-Pouange (347).

'et en effet, [l'Ingénu] l'épousait [*sic*], si elle ne s'était pas débattue avec toute l'honnêteté d'une personne qui a de l'éducation' (302). Like the Ingénu she is then incarcerated — in a convent — where she undertakes her own education. The male chauvinism of the day, of course, dictates that, like Emma Bovary ninety years later: 'elle s'était bien formée dans son couvent par les romans qu'elle avait lus à la dérobée' (323). Despite the model of Mme du Châtelet, not for her the masculine world of geometry and metaphysics. But, as with the Ingénu, even her bookish instruction needs to be complemented by life. When Saint-Pouange makes his 'propositions délicates', the art of feigned innocence (328) merely exacerbates her predicament. Being unfaithful in order to be faithful is something they never taught her back in Saint-Malo.

Gender stereotypes are the one 'system' which *L'Ingénu* actually perpetuates, as becomes clear when the narrator makes the parallel between the Ingénu and Mlle de Saint-Yves explicit:

Ce n'était plus cette fille simple dont une éducation provinciale avait rétréci les idées. L'amour et le malheur l'avaient formée. Le sentiment avait fait autant de progrès en elle que la raison en avait fait dans l'esprit de son amant infortuné. Les filles apprennent à sentir plus aisément que les hommes n'apprennent à penser. Son aventure était plus instructive que quatre ans de couvent. (333)

For all that some modern readers may find this stereotyping unacceptable, however,[18] it plays an important role in the allegory of education contained in *L'Ingénu*. Part of this allegory concerns the important question of 'sensibilité'. While 'sensibilité' is here presented as a female preserve, it is notable, for example, that Gordon's metamorphosis ('il était changé en homme, ainsi que le Huron') is presented as a progression from cold, unfeeling moral austerity to warm humanity: 'l'âpreté de ses anciennes opinions sortait de son cœur' (337). Whereas on his first appearance in the story his *caritas* was the result of religious instruction and expressed itself in portentous sermonizing (312), by the end he has evolved sufficiently to condone Mlle de Saint-Yves's actions: 'Le vieux Gordon l'aurait condamnée dans le temps qu'il n'était que janséniste; mais étant devenu sage, il l'estimait et il pleurait' (343). Moreover he has

---

18 Elsewhere in the story Voltaire seems to send it up: e.g. 'car il faut convenir que Dieu n'a créé les femmes que pour apprivoiser les hommes' (324); 'Nous autres, pauvres femmes, nous avons besoin d'être conduites par un homme' (329).

learnt that greatest of Voltairian lessons: that moral aphorisms are no answer to the problems of living (or dying): 'Gordon se garda bien de lui [the suicidal Huron] étaler ces lieux communs fastidieux' (345). Like the Ingénu and Mlle de Saint-Yves, Gordon has learnt to accommodate himself to life: to face it on its own terms without the preconceptions of religious instruction, superstition, or the rules of polite society. He has opened his heart to experience and grown accordingly: 'par l'esprit et par le cœur.'

'SENSIBILITÉ'

While Gordon shows that men do have a heart, it is evidently Mlle de Saint-Yves who is at the centre of the story's debate of the issue of 'sensibilité'. The reader's response to this debate hinges on whether he or she thinks Mlle de Saint-Yves excessive in her reaction to what she has done.

Voltaire has a lot of fun with 'sensibilité' in *L'Ingénu*. This major current in eighteenth-century life and letters is omnipresent, with the vocabulary of sensibility—'sentiment', 'sentir', 'sensibilité', 'bon', 'bonté', 'cœur', 'attendri', etc.—appearing several times on almost every page. From the beginning it is foregrounded and parodied. Thus the Prior is 'très bon' (285), especially because he can hold his drink. Mlle de Kerkabon's character is 'bon et sensible': she is a devout pleasure-seeker (286). The hearts of brother and sister alike warm to the memory of the Prior's absent brother, not least because 'notre frère, qui avait beaucoup d'esprit, aurait fait assurément une grande fortune' (286). Not for the first time, the recognition scene comes in for some Voltairian parody,[19] as the two siblings fight over the portraits handed to them by the Ingénu (292). And so it continues. Mlle de Kerkabon 'était si bonne personne; . . . elle lui [the Ingénu] demanda, avec beaucoup de bonté . . .', while what this good lady of 45 really feels is that she would rather like to be 'married' (289). The plight of the Huguenots is moving, but the Ingénu is plainly naïve if he thinks he can persuade the King because 'il est impossible qu'on ne se rende pas à cette vérité quand on la sent' (309).

This evidence could be multiplied, and almost any page taken at random will provide examples of the vocabulary of sensibility being

---

[19] Cf. *Zadig*, 100–1, and *Candide*, 160, 177.

used to colour the story with the strong hue of the sentimental novel.
One needs to be aware of this before considering the vexed issue of
Mlle de Saint-Yves's death, for it is clear that the send-up of the
sentimental novel continues throughout the story, albeit in less self-
evident fashion towards the end. Thus it may seem plausible for
Mlle de Saint-Yves to faint on hearing the news from Père Tout-à-
tous that the Ingénu is in the Bastille. But when the lovers are finally
reunited, there is comical excess (334): 'Les deux amants se voient,
et tous deux s'évanouissent. La belle Saint-Yves resta longtemps sans
mouvement et sans vie.' She regains consciousness momentarily to
exclaim: 'Ah! je ne suis pas digne d'être sa femme' whereupon 'elle
retomba encore en faiblesse. Quand elle eut repris ses sens', etc.
Hereafter most of the characters are variously lachrymose or suicidal;
there is much talk of courage and virtue; adversaries are reconciled
(336); and even Saint-Pouange turns up in time to repent, as any
self-respecting villain in a *conte moral* should.

The possibility that the death of Mlle de Saint-Yves ought not to
be taken fully at its tragic face value was first proposed by Roger
Laufer, but it has not commanded quite the support it deserves.[20]
Laufer's essential point is this:

La mort de la 'respectable infidèle' est infiniment triste, mais elle n'est,
comme tous les malheurs qui pleuvent sur les protagonistes du roman, que
la conséquence d'un malentendu [. . .] Voltaire ne refuse pas de nous api-
toyer sur son sort, à condition que nous haussions les épaules, car elle seule
l'a voulu, en prenant sa vertu au tragique.[21]

The implications of 'malentendu' and the shrug of the shoulders are
highly questionable and, as will be seen, it is quite possible to draw
other conclusions from the anti-sentimental reading which Laufer
proposes. For him Mlle de Saint-Yves has simply failed to understand the way of the world, which Voltaire and any 'honnête homme'
will recognize with an urbane smile. Laufer's argument, however,
relies heavily on the unsustainable assertion that Vadbled's letter
(which proposes essentially that 'mistakes will happen' and which
the Ingénu tears up in proper indignation) is a reflection of Voltaire's
point of view.[22]

---

[20]   See esp. Haydn Mason's disagreement with Laufer in 'The Unity of Voltaire's
L'Ingénu', 95.
[21]   Roger Laufer, *Style rococo, style des lumières* (Paris, 1963), 103.
[22]   *Style rococo*, 106.

Nevertheless the idea that Mlle de Saint-Yves is both genuine and wrong is a fruitful one, even if rather difficult to present without apparent callousness. Clearly her 'virtual rape'[23] is a dramatic and unacceptable example of 'l'infâme': in this case, the abuse of ecclesiastical and political position for personal gratification. Furthermore, in this story which celebrates liberty, it evidently seems even more reprehensible that a woman should lose freedom over her own body. Undoubtedly Voltaire does lay it on sentimentally thick in the concluding chapters of this *conte*, and it would be a heartless reader indeed who felt no compassion at all for Mlle de Saint-Yves in her plight.

But other essential questions remain. How real is her dishonour? Is it sufficient to warrant her death? To what extent is she responsible for her own death? Do we blame her for letting her mind get the better of her body? Or do we blame an ideology that can so inculcate notions of noble human virtue (Corneille, Rousseau, the sentimental novel, the *conte moral*) that a young woman who has just saved two lives can believe that she is dishonoured?

In one sense *La Nouvelle Héloïse* has killed her (just as later, for different reasons, Walter Scott's novels 'kill' Emma Bovary). Fictions like Rousseau's create a moral pressure, apparently based on fact, which warps the capacity of individuals morally to assess their own actions with accuracy. *L'Ingénu* in effect subverts the sentimental novel to protect us from the consequences which prove so fatal to Mlle de Saint-Yves. It has already been seen that the vocabulary of sentiment is frequently a cover for perfectly normal (but ideologically proscribed) sexual desire. As Laufer notes, Mlle de Saint-Yves's own 'sensibilité' has a sensual subtext. As in other *contes*, notably *Candide*, Voltaire resorts to the pun, or 'double entendre', not only to entertain us but also to remind us of the reality of human motivation. The possible anatomical and sexual connotations of the words 'la plus belle attitude du monde' (291), 'étendue' (298, 303), 'une vertu mâle et intrépide'(302), 'l'énormité du procédé' (303), 'déchirée' (333) and 'déchirements' (345), 'jouirait' (333), 'enivrée' and 'pénétrée' (333), all offer the possibility of an alternative, physiological rather than sentimental, reading of the story. Which should we choose? Is 'sensibilité' actually another word for sexual desire? An indication of Voltaire's own answer to this question may be

²³ Mason, 'The Unity of Voltaire's *L'Ingénu*', 95.

afforded by his summary of the six volumes of Richardson's fashionable sentimental novel *Pamela*: 'Ce n'est qu'une petite fille qui ne veut pas coucher avec son maître à moins qu'il ne l'épouse.'[24] So much for finer feelings.

L'Ingénu is not as cynical as this, but the narrator goes beyond the pun in his efforts to indicate that Mlle de Saint-Yves is perhaps on the wrong track. While she lies 'à demi renversée sur un sopha' and (product of a sheltered upbringing that she is) 'croyant à peine ce qu'elle voyait', the narrator comments: 'Le Saint-Pouange . . . n'était pas sans agréments, et aurait pu ne pas effaroucher un cœur moins prévenu. Mais Saint-Yves adorait son amant et croyait que c'était un crime horrible de le trahir pour le servir' (328). 'Prévenu', 'croyait que c'était un crime': is this the 'voice' of Saint-Pouange and other 'libertins', or is it Voltaire's own? Subsequently the narrator is quite categoric: 'A ce mot de "vertu", des sanglots échappèrent à la belle Saint-Yves. Elle ne savait pas combien elle était vertueuse dans le crime qu'elle se reprochait' (335). From the external evidence of *Cosi-Sancta*[25] and the article 'Acindynus' in the *Dictionnaire philosophique* it would seem that this is indeed Voltaire's point of view. It is also the Ingénu's: 'Qui? vous, coupable! lui dit son amant; non, vous ne l'êtes pas; le crime ne peut être que dans le cœur, le vôtre est à la vertu et à moi' (343).[26] One may or may not share this view; what matters is the way in which Voltaire shows a human being convinced of her own moral worthlessness against all empirical evidence to the contrary. Mlle de Saint-Yves dies because she believes in 'notions', not facts; and that is a tragedy.

---

[24] D15668 (29 May 1769, to Thiriot). Cf. D15605 (24 Apr. 1769, to Mme du Deffand). Cf. also his summary of Richardson's *Clarissa*: 'il est cruel pour un homme aussi vif que je le suis, de lire neuf volumes entiers, dans lesquels on ne trouve rien du tout, et qui servent seulement à faire entrevoir que Mlle Clarisse aime un débauché nommé M. de Lovelace' (D8846: 12 Apr. 1760, to Mme du Deffand). The rape of Clarissa, of course, is directly comparable with Saint-Pouange's treatment of Saint-Yves, not least in that both are 'excused' by advisers with reference to St Augustine.

[25] Meaning 'quasi-saint'. Mlle de Saint-Yves's lack of a Christian name and the recurrent reference to her as simply 'Saint-Yves' emphasize her potential sanctity; and a story which begins with a spoof on St Dunstan and delights in the possible onomastic connotations of the historical Saint-Pouange is clearly seeking to redefine traditional notions of saintly virtue.

[26] Cf. Voltaire's sketch for a first version of *L'Ingénu*: 'Se marie, ne veut pas que le m[ariage] soit un sacrement, trouve très bon que sa femme soit infidèle parce qu'il l'a été' (see *RC*, 968). Cf. also the phoenix's plea to Formosante on behalf of the erring Amazan in *La Princesse de Babylone* (403).

LANGUAGE AND INTERPRETATION

Language and interpretation play a key role in *L'Ingénu*, not least in the dénouement. Here Mlle de Saint-Yves is persistently distraught at what she perceives to be the disparity between her actions and the terminology of virtue. The recurrent use of the 'double entendre' has demonstrated to the reader how slippery language can be, and yet Mlle de Saint-Yves has absolute faith in its meanings. Prior to her sobs at the word 'vertu', the word 'femme' is sufficient temporarily to rouse her from her swoon (334). Later it is the word 'épouse': 'A ce mot d' "épouse", elle soupira, le regarda avec une tendresse inexprimable, et soudain jeta un cri d'horreur' (343). Much is made of these labels of conjugality, and the advice of the altogether slippery Jesuit Tout-à-tous might suggest, by counter-example, that one ought not to abuse them: 'Premièrement, ma fille, ne dites jamais ce mot, "mon amant"; il a quelque chose de mondain qui pourrait offenser Dieu. Dites: "mon mari"; car, bien qu'il ne le soit pas encore, vous le regardez comme tel, et rien n'est plus honnête' (330). But what are the accurate words in any context? Why should not 'épouser' mean to make love rather than to undergo a religious ceremony since it is the former activity, both physically and emotionally, which presumably matters. In the context of the narrative, this view of the question is classed as 'savage', yet, as the Ingénu points out, this term too is more relevant to the surface of things than to the reality beneath: 'Mes compatriotes d'Amérique ne m'auraient jamais traité avec la barbarie que j'éprouve; ils n'en ont pas d'idée. On les appelle "sauvages"; ce sont des gens de bien grossiers, et les hommes de ce pays-ci sont des coquins raffinés' (313).[27]

Indeed the narrator himself finds language a problem, as he endeavours to tell an 'histoire véritable' without succumbing to the lies embedded in the language at his disposal. Thus he abdicates responsibility for grand moral terms through the dialogic device of quotation: 'Qui peut perdre à vingt ans son amant, sa vie, et ce qu'on appelle l' "honneur", sans regrets et sans déchirements?' (345). 'Amant' and 'vie' speak for themselves; but honour? In the very next sentence he repeats the device, for he himself lacks the means to

---

[27]   A similar point is made in respect of body language and the ceremony of the bow. A quaint custom observed by courteous mountains (285) and overlooked by uncouth English raiders (286), it is performed by the Ingénu only when he means it (for Mlle de Saint-Yves: 294).

convey grief: 'Elle sentait toute l'horreur de son état, et le faisait sentir par ces mots et par ces regards mourants qui parlent avec tant d'empire.' Once more, as at the end of *Micromégas, Histoire d'un bon brahmin*, and *Le Blanc et le noir*, there is the suggestion that silence or parrot-like quotation are more authentic than moral abstraction: 'Nulle langue n'a des expressions qui répondent à ce comble des douleurs; les langues sont trop imparfaites' (342).

The importance of language in the thematic texture of *L'Ingénu* is signalled right at the beginning of the story when Lower Breton society enquires how the Huron comes to speak French and what various Huron terms are for tobacco, eating, and making love. Like so many other aspects of life in the story, language is presented both as a source of myth, pretension, and provincial prejudice ('on convint que, sans l'aventure de la tour de Babel, toute la terre aurait parlé français': 289),[28] and as susceptible of enlightened development and application: 'dès que j'ai pu m'exprimer intelligiblement, je suis venu voir votre pays' (288). Most important of all, one of the consequences of 'la multiplicité des langues' (289) is that different nations see things differently. Thus the Huron language has no word for 'inconstance' (290). As Abacaba is said to prefer the Ingénu 'à tous ses amants' (290), monogamy would seem not to be the Hurons' strong suit; and doubtless Huron mores are such that the very issue of sexual fidelity or infidelity does not arise. Linguistic usage is determined by the practice of living.

But it is no accident that 'inconstance' should be the word singled out to illustrate the lack of 'fit' between languages, since the whole dénouement will turn on the question of constancy. Mlle de Saint-Yves's sensitivity to conjugal tags shows clearly that linguistic usage may just as easily determine the practice of living as *vice versa*. Worse still than the Bastille is the prison-house of language. Mlle de Saint-Yves is conditioned to interpret words in a particular way because of her upbringing, her supposed 'éducation'. Real experience should ideally free her from these preconceptions as it has complemented her convent education in other respects, but in the end she is unable to break out of the bondage of other people's interpretations of the world which she herself inhabits.

Yet the story shows how, as Flaubert later put it: 'Il n'y a pas de

---

[28] Cf. Mlle de Kerkabon: 'j'avais toujours cru que le français était la plus belle de toutes les langues après le bas-breton' (288).

vrai. Il n'y a que des manières de voir.'[29] Paris and the provinces are apparently worlds apart in *L'Ingénu*, and for René Pomeau this makes the story a forerunner of the nineteenth-century Realist novel.[30] But the differences between Lower Brittany and the metropolis may be differences of style rather than substance. Spying, religious bigotry, and arbitrary incarceration in prison and convent are equally present in both places. Père Tout-à-tous, the Jesuit confessor, seems, as his name suggests,[31] to be a casuist who provides convenient interpretations and moral commentaries to suit every eventuality, proving himself thus, at least etymologically, another Pangloss or Pansophe. He will even quote St Augustine, the Jansenists' favoured authority, if he has to: for him this is a guarantee of his sincerity (331)! But how different is he from the Prior? The latter, too, is eclectic in his sources, which range from St Augustine to Rabelais, and this eclecticism makes him universally popular: 'aussi tout le monde disait du bien de lui' (286). His vows have not prevented him from being 'aimé . . . autrefois de ses voisines' (285), just as Mlle de Saint-Yves's Parisian chaperone may well have 'befriended' Tout-à-tous: 'Abandonnez-vous à lui', she advises her protégée in yet another 'double entendre', 'c'est ainsi que j'en use; je m'en suis toujours bien trouvée' (329).

Furthermore, how different is Mlle de Saint-Yves herself in Paris from the young lady who willingly used her charms on the Ingénu to dissuade him from riverine baptism? On that occasion a shake of the hand (accompanied by a furtive lowered gaze to see, as it were, 'de quoi il s'agissait': 297) was sufficient to secure her ends (298). Saint-Pouange asks more than a shake of the hand, but the principle at stake might be thought (if only by a literal-minded 'ingénu') to be pretty much the same. Indeed the two incidents are united in the recurrent use of the word 'crédit' (298, 303, 335, 337). Whether one

---

[29] In a letter to Léon Hennique, 2–3 Feb. 1880.
[30] *Romans et contes*, 321.
[31] The name is borrowed from D'Alembert's *Sur la destruction des Jésuites en France* (1765) which Voltaire had helped to publish. D'Alembert was turning to polemical account one of the rules of the Jesuit order: 's'oublier soi-même pour être tout à tous', which derives from I Cor. 9: 22: 'I am made all things to all men, that I might by all means save some.' Given my argument at this point it is tempting to think that Voltaire may also have had in mind Pascal's *Pensées*: 'Chacun est un tout à soi-même, car, lui mort, le tout est mort pour soi. Et de là vient que chacun croit être tout à tous. Il ne faut pas juger de la nature selon nous, mais selon elle' (L. 668).

is in Paris or up to one's neck in the River Rance, life is a process of bargaining, of give-and-take. The moral contrast between Paris and Lower Brittany is much less clear-cut, therefore, than may at first appear. It all depends on one's point of view. The capital may be a whorehouse,[32] but it is also a centre of culture and learning. Lower Brittany may be quaint and genial, but considerable power is dangerously vested in dimwits like the 'bailli' and his son. This ambiguity is typical of the story as a whole, which demands to be read with great care if the reader is not to end up like the Ingénu reading Rabelais (in translation . . .) and Shakespeare:

'Je vous avoue, dit l'Ingénu, que j'ai cru en deviner quelque chose, et que je n'ai pas entendu le reste.' L'abbé de Saint-Yves, à ce discours, fit réflexion que c'était ainsi que lui-même avait toujours lu, et que la plupart des hommes ne lisaient guère autrement. (293)

TEXTUAL POLITICS

This incident is the first of several in the story which raise the issue of what one might call textual politics. *L'Ingénu* presents a society in which despotism governs by means of the *lettre de cachet*, a text signed by the ultimate secular authority (the King) and then countersigned by a powermonger to outlaw an individual's beliefs and behaviour without further reference to that central authority. The Bible is the ecclesiastical equivalent of the *lettre de cachet*, being a text which is invested with ultimate authority and then used, arbitrarily, to dictate belief and behaviour. The Ingénu reads the New Testament literally (i.e. honestly and freely) and is amazed to discover the disparity between its narrative and the lessons preached in its name: 'Je m'aperçois tous les jours qu'on fait ici une infinité de choses qui ne sont point dans votre livre, et qu'on n'y fait rien de tout ce qu'il dit' (301). Texts are instruments of powerplay in which the 'truth' of the text counts for nothing against the power relations within which the text is sent and received. The Ingénu goes to Versailles 'combl[é] de certificats' (307); but the ministry official only pretends to read them before giving the standard ministry response to such applications for a military commission. The Prior,

---

[32]   Saint-Preux's Parisian experience in *La Nouvelle Héloïse* is ironically echoed in Mlle de Kerkabon's belief that the Ingénu is probably hiding in a brothel (322).

too, leaves home armed with 'lettres de recommendation pour le père de La Chaise' (322), but he does not even manage to find a reader for them. Like the Ingénu before him, indeed, he has great difficulty in being seen, let alone read or listened to, by anyone. The powerful ecclesiastical figures on whom he ventures to call are all closeted with ladies on 'theological business' (322); feminine charms are the best 'lettres de recommendation' of all. Which, indeed, is just what Mlle de Saint-Yves already dimly realizes before she sets out for Versailles (323): physical allure is more powerful even than a *lettre de cachet*. As her Parisian chaperone informs her: 'Votre présence, d'ailleurs, ou je me trompe fort, fera plus d'effet que les paroles de votre frère' (327).

Letters play a crucial role in this story. *La Nouvelle Héloïse*, of course, actually consists of letters, but *L'Ingénu* has no need to be an epistolary *conte* (like the *Lettres d'Amabed* after it) in order to echo the famous second sentence of Rousseau's first preface (which Laclos later used as an epigraph to *Les Liaisons dangereuses*): 'J'ai vu les mœurs de mon temps, et j'ai publié ces lettres.' The apparatus of political oppression depends not only on the *lettre de cachet*, but on an epistolary spy network linking Paris to the provinces. The 'bailli' informs on the Ingénu in a letter to Louvois; the Jesuit spy in Saumur informs on him in a letter to Père de La Chaise. In receiving these letters both the secular and the ecclesiastical arms of authority 'interpret' the Ingénu in ways which repress the truth underlying his actions (but which the narrative of *L'Ingénu* itself reveals). When they are obliged (by Saint-Pouange's deal with Mlle de Saint-Yves) to concede that they 'misinterpreted' him, the result is Frère Vadbled's letter, a masterpiece of fiction: 'sa prison n'était qu'une méprise, ... ces petites disgrâces arrivaient fréquemment ... il ne fallait pas y faire attention' (344). With the consummate insincerity of Jesuits like Père Tout-à-tous and the one who welcomes the Prior 'à bras ouverts' (322), Vadbled rewrites *L'Ingénu* as a story of everyday incompetence. The Ingénu's response is all the more authentic for being non-verbal. 'L'Ingénu ... déchira la lettre par morceaux et les jeta au nez du courrier' (344).

What, then, of Voltaire's own version of events? Confined within language, and unable to resort to Babouc's statue or the Ingénu's physical violation of epistolary 'fable', he purports nevertheless to be providing us with an 'histoire véritable'. Constrained by the power relations operating within the France of 1767, he has resorted to a 'disingenuous' historical allegory of the present. The Ingénu, while reading the Bible, 'ne douta point que le lieu de la scène ne fût en Basse-Bretagne'; and such is his emotional involvement in the narrative that he is all set to 'couper . . . le nez et les oreilles à Caïphe et à Pilate si jamais il rencontrait ces marauds-là' (295). By a comic reversal we sophisticated readers must interpret *L'Ingénu* as he interprets the New Testament, believing it to be relevant to the present (not only 1767 but also now) and ultimately prepared to stand up to such religious and political oppression (Caiaphas and Pilate) as we may encounter. In so far as the Ingénu (with his 'air martial et doux' (286) and his final metamorphosis into 'un guerrier et un philosophe intrépide' (347)) is the role model advocated by this *conte*, the 'truth' of this 'histoire véritable' would seem to consist in the need to cultivate militant good sense.

The 'truths' which the story explicitly proclaims, however, are more problematic. Like many of Voltaire's *contes*,[33] *L'Ingénu* ends on an aphoristic note which appears reassuringly to shed retrospective light on the significance of what has gone before. In keeping with the double-barrelled nature of the story we are provided with two aphorisms, which are apparently mutually exclusive and yet each of which has its measure of truth: '[Gordon] prit pour sa devise: "malheur est bon à quelque chose". Combien d'honnêtes gens dans le monde ont pu dire: "malheur n'est bon à rien!"' (347). In support of Gordon's motto one could point to the way in which both the Ingénu and Mlle de Saint-Yves have matured in adversity. For them to become human beings rather than juvenile leads in a sentimental adventure they needed to be moulded by misfortune. True 'civilization' requires both reason and sensibility to be tried in the fire of experience. Mlle de Saint-Yves grows up, yet she fails to make that crucial final step which would have allowed her independently to see that there was no dishonour in what she did. The Ingénu, on the other hand, comes to terms with life and wins 'l'approbation de tous les honnêtes gens' (347). Thus 'malheur est bon à quelque chose' may be true not only in the trivial sense that 'it is an ill wind that blows nobody any good' (Gordon would not have become the man he is had he not been thrown into the Bastille, etc.) but also in the

---

[33] Cf. *Cosi-Sancta, Le Monde comme il va, Histoire des voyages de Scarmentado, Les Deux Consolés, Candide, Jeannot et Colin, Les Oreilles du comte de Chesterfield, Histoire de Jenni*.

more profound, almost Christian sense that evil may ennoble man by testing his reason and tempering his sensibility. On the other hand, such a 'rationalization' of evil may be unsatisfactory. Mlle de Saint-Yves's death, the persecution of the Huguenots, the abuse of ecclesiastical and ministerial power, all are evidence of the unacceptable face of 'civilization'. At the same time the glibness of Gordon's aphorism is suspect, as demonstrated by the ease with which a plausible counter-aphorism can be coined. Moreover, the two final maxims follow closely on a blatant cliché: 'Le temps adoucit tout'; and it is this cliché which is employed to introduce, in mid-paragraph, the most perfunctory of conclusions. A moment ago, the Ingénu was plunged in grief and ready to kill Saint-Pouange; now, 'Mons de Louvois', the Minister for War, has realized his officer potential and turned him into an ornament of this corrupt society. The narrative rhythm of the *conte* reverts to the amused jauntiness which characterized its opening chapters; and when the reward of a box of chocolates is finally bestowed on Père Tout-à-tous, the poignancy of Mlle de Saint-Yves's death has been entirely dispelled. For all that the Ingénu is said to cherish her memory until his dying day, the cavalier nature of this abrupt transition from sentiment to irony suggests that he has in some way been absorbed by the system. His metamorphosis has gone so far that he has become unrecognizable: he is 'l'Ingénu, qui n'était plus l' "ingénu" ' (337). But while time may have proved a great healer to the protagonists, the reader's sense of loss and outrage at Mlle de Saint-Yves's death has had no such opportunity to abate. What is more, she died because her actions did not fit with her preconceived notions of virtue. Why then should we seek to accept any aphorism as the gospel according to *L'Ingénu*? Should we not consult our own lives?

For in fact each of the final aphorisms is carefully presented as the result of personal experience. We can infer why Gordon has chosen his motto; and yet we can also envisage circumstances in which trustworthy witnesses 'ont pu dire' a motto which is its antithesis. As the story itself has demonstrated, both in the account of Mlle de Saint-Yves's death and in the implicit comparison of Paris and the provinces: 'il n'y a pas de vrai. Il n'y a que des manières de voir.' For such a 'manière de voir' to be authentic, it must be based not on any preconceived religious or moral system but on the facts of life. To put it in Voltaire's own terms: the only 'histoire véritable' is 'une histoire vraisemblable'.

That we should read texts in this way is the lesson which the
Ingénu learns from his study of literature in the Bastille. Surprised
to learn that Corneille's *Rodogune* is reputed to be the greatest French
tragedy, when he personally has found it much less moving and
memorable than the plays of Racine, he modestly concedes the possibility of his being in error before nevertheless honestly proclaiming
his independent judgement:

> Après tout, c'est ici une affaire du goût: le mien ne doit pas encore être
> formé; je peux me tromper; mais vous savez que je suis assez accoutumé à
> dire ce que je pense, ou plutôt ce que je sens. Je soupçonne qu'il y a souvent
> de l'illusion, de la mode, du caprice, dans les jugements des hommes. J'ai
> parlé d'après la nature: il se peut que chez moi la nature soit très imparfaite;
> mais il se peut aussi qu'elle soit quelquefois peu consultée par la plupart des
> hommes. (320)

The humorous adoption of a Rousseauist voice should not be
allowed to obscure the serious point which is being made here: the
worth of a work of art depends not on the articles of classical taste
but on the intellectual and emotional response of the reader. Similarly, when it comes to novels, the Ingénu resorts once more to the
criteria of real life:

> Il lut quelques romans nouveaux; il en trouva peu qui lui peignissent la
> situation de son âme. Il sentait que son cœur allait toujours au-delà de ce
> qu'il lisait. 'Ah! disait-il, presque tous ces auteurs-là n'ont que de l'esprit et
> de l'art.' (326)

Again the emphasis is on genuine emotional reaction as opposed to
dispassionate admiration for cleverness.

Here, perhaps, is the real lesson of *L'Ingénu*. Charles Rollin, the
Jansenist pedagogue, had set forth in his *Traité des études* (1726–8)
how best to 'enseigner et étudier les belles-lettres par rapport à
l'esprit et au cœur' (as the subtitle has it). Rollin was one of Voltaire's
villains not just for being a Jansenist but for suborning 'belles-lettres'
for the inculcation of a pious and blinkered morality. In so far as
Voltaire's *contes* are intended to instruct as well as to entertain, then
their primary purpose is to encourage in the reader a robust independence both of intellect and — here now for the first time in *L'Ingénu*
— of feeling. But how to encourage independence of feeling?

It might be said that, before *L'Ingénu*, each of Voltaire's *contes*
unequivocally dictates the same emotional response: namely,

detached amusement. This response is still being called forth in *L'Ingénu*, where indeed it is said to be a key antidote to 'l'infâme'. L'Ingénu's portrait of the ideal Minister of War ends by extolling 'cette gaieté d'esprit' because this 'belle humeur est incompatible avec la cruauté' (341). But in *L'Ingénu* Voltaire explores for the first time the possibility of affecting the reader emotionally. His first move is to undermine the 'fables' of sentiment by sending up the sentimental novel. His second, in the Ingénu's comments on Racine and Corneille, is to encourage the reader subsequently to relate the emotions of the protagonists (with which he is made to empathize) to his or her own. The final move is to leave the reader in that state of emotional ambivalence which good tragedy creates: 'ce mélange de compassion et d'effroi qui enchaîne toutes les puissances de l'âme' (345). While this phrase is used of those observing the Ingénu's grief, it is also characterizes our response to Mlle de Saint-Yves: pity for her suffering, horror that she should have such an exaggerated notion of virtue.

It is no accident that the final stages of *L'Ingénu* should be presented as if they were scenes in a play. Partly Voltaire is calling attention to his very efforts to move us, as if anxious to avoid the charge of covert emotional manipulation which he himself levels at the sentimental novel. But he is also genuinely trying to move us, not to sentimentality but to a blend of different reactions whose very complexity, as with intellectual ambiguity, is a sign of their authenticity. *L'Ingénu* is designed to stir not fine sentiments but mixed feelings.

In this way *L'Ingénu* is a politically radical text because it seeks to wean us — both intellectually and emotionally — from slavish dependence on the power of the book. It denounces the fictions which cloak the power strategies of Church and State alike, and it warns of the murderously inhuman consequences of some versions of the bourgeois moral code. It tries to makes us see and feel the world as it really is: a dangerous market-place of competing 'fables' in which the key to freedom and justice, however difficult these may be to achieve, is the raised eyebrow of the sceptic and the steady gaze of an Ingénu. This is what makes it an 'histoire véritable' and one perhaps to justify another of its mottos: 'La lecture agrandit l'âme.'

II

'L'univers en raccourci'

La Princesse de Babylone and Les Lettres d'Amabed

On se forme beaucoup par les voyages.

(524)

Complex and ambivalent though the conclusion of L'Ingénu may be, the story as a whole presents a fairly clear contrast between fable and history. Beginnings are miraculously straightforward: be it the two hagiographical paragraphs with which the story opens, or the stereotypes upon which the leading characters are based, or the mythical national origins which the Ingénu ridicules in his essay on ancient history. Middles and endings, however, are more problematic, as fiction is replaced by fact: whether it be the relatively precise historical account of late-seventeenth-century France, or the metamorphosis of foundling and marriageable maiden into 'honnête homme' and tragic heroine, or the scarcely veiled reality of life in contemporary France. So frank is L'Ingénu in its portrayal of the moral muddle of existence that it cannot bring itself to decide what, quite, it should think about so-called civilization. Certainly it is foolish to condemn all civilization out of hand as being a perversion of God's purpose and a corruption of man's essential self: natural man does need to be educated and polished if he is to fulfil his potential. But where does one draw the line between valuable adaptation and fruitful compromise, on the one hand, and, on the other, a cynical conformism which simply permits the speedier gratification of man's baser instinctual drives for power and physical pleasure?

In the three stories which follow L'Ingénu, both this opposition between fable and history and these questions about civilization continue to dominate. In L'Homme aux quarante écus, as we have seen,[1] various 'fables' (economics, statistics, militarism, agricultural theory, geological and biological hypotheses about the origins of life and

---

[1] See above, Ch. 2.

the universe) are 'exploded' by juxtaposition with the facts of life; while the values of urbane, 'civilized' enlightenment (discerning study, story-telling, conversation, supper-parties) are presented without ambivalence. Education is once more at a premium, and its consequence the humanizing transformation of a cipher into a friend of the author. As in *L'Ingénu*, the power of the book is replaced by the open invitation to the reader to add his or her voice to the polyphony of its text.

In *La Princesse de Babylone* and *Les Lettres d'Amabed* there is a similar retreat from ambivalence in respect of the values of 'civilization', as both stories seek to present the virtues of enlightenment on a universal basis. The voyage of reason now resembles the annual progress of a mildly left-wing world historian bent on surveying the dominions of his concern. Along the way, as in so many of Voltaire's *contes*, the fabulous is undermined by being taken for real; and the real is less excusable (in the *Lettres d'Amabed*) or more remarkable (in *La Princesse de Babylone*) for seeming so utterly incredible.

Ostensibly (and yet again) a text translated from another language (388), *La Princesse de Babylone* was composed between April and early August 1767 and published in March 1768 one month after *L'Homme aux quarante écus*.[2] Superficially it is a *conte oriental* told in the manner of Ariosto: more profoundly, it is a story about the function of narrative in fostering Enlightenment values.

Whereas *L'Homme aux quarante écus* abandons the 'romanesque', and thus reveals the skeletal structure of a typical Voltairian *conte* all the more clearly, *La Princesse de Babylone* embraces familiar 'romanesque' clichés the better to smother them in ridicule. Thus, as P. C. Mitchell has shown, it undermines implausible fiction by raising rather literal-minded questions of practicality.[3] The amphitheatre seats five hundred thousand spectators, for example, but forty thousand youngsters are able to dole out the refreshments 'sans confusion' (351–2). The 'prodigieuses armées que l'Orient vomit de son sein' seem all the more impressive to the 'roi de la Bétique' when he prosaically compares them to 'nos petits corps de vingt à trente mille soldats, qu'il est si difficile de vêtir et de nourrir' (409).

---

[2] For which Voltaire professed a preference. See D14897 (30 Mar. 1768, to Mme du Deffand).
[3] 'An Underlying Theme in *La Princesse de Babylone*', *SVEC* 137 (1975).

More broadly, *La Princesse de Babylone* pokes fun at a number of literary traditions. *The Iliad* is but the story of 'une vieille femme fort libertine qui s'était fait enlever deux fois' (369). As to chivalric romance, the fact that in *La Princesse de Babylone* it is the woman who pursues the man for most of the story (in order to assure him of her constancy) provides a new slant on the figures of the 'princesse lointaine' and the knight errant, as does Amazan's restless travelling every time a lady threatens to take him to bed. As in *Zadig* (73), the excesses of the Oriental style are disdained (354), while the theme of 'la destinée' becomes a blatant disguise for narrative convenience. The paths of Amazan and Formosante cross in mid-Channel: 'Ah, s'ils l'avaient su! Mais l'impérieuse destinée ne le permit pas' (394) – and nor did the plot. The pastoral tradition also receives a passing blow, as it turns out that Amazan is only a shepherd (359). This problem of unsuitability of rank, familiar in parvenu narratives, is temporarily overcome thanks to a Jesuitical lady-in-waiting who interprets the term as a metaphor for 'king' (because a king fleeces his subjects) and to Formosante, for whom 'berger' and 'amant' become synonymous. Thus: 'c'est depuis ce temps-là que les noms de "berger" et d' "amant" sont toujours employés l'un pour l'autre chez quelques nations' (366).

Here, as frequently elsewhere in the story, Voltaire is mocking the way in which fabulous origins are attributed to present phenomena. Banal adages are given an ancient, literal, oracular source: for example, 'Quand on ne marie pas les filles, elles se marient elles-mêmes' (369). Metaphors are repeatedly literalized in order to mock the attitude of mind which sees truth in primitive error:

> Vivre éternellement dans les cieux avec l'Etre suprême, ou aller se promener dans le jardin, dans le paradis, fut la même chose pour les hommes, qui parlent toujours sans s'entendre, et qui n'ont pu guère avoir encore d'idées nettes et d'expressions justes. (372)

Thus the metaphorical sense of the oracle which predicts that Formosante 'ne sera mariée que quand elle aura couru le monde' (359) is rejected by the Babylonian authorities, yet the oracle will prove literally true. Also, ironically, its implication of sexual promiscuity becomes the real motive for Formosante's journey, superseding the ostensible purpose of pilgrimage (367). By the same token Voltaire invites us to see metaphor where others see literal truth. Thus an 'ancien oracle' has decreed that Formosante shall belong to 'celui qui tendrait l'arc de Nembrod' (350); but the substitution of the word 'bander' for 'tendre' adds a typically Voltairian level of 'double entendre' to what follows.

In the textual politics of Babylon, oracles play a key role; and, as in *L'Ingénu* and *L'Homme aux quarante écus*, we see how the interpretation of such an authoritative source comes to depend on the extratextual realities of political powerplay. Thus the oracle requiring Formosante to be a flibbertigibbet is exempted from the normal rule of oracular exegesis that 'la raison doit se taire devant eux' (359) on the ground that 'cet oracle n'avait pas le sens commun' (360). When the interpretation of the cleverest and youngest minister (that a pilgrimage is being celestially recommended) prevails, cabinet discussion is motivated by the self-interest of would-be male chaperones.

Like oracles, fables are also supposedly authoritative sources of explanation. In *La Princesse de Babylone* Voltaire is demonstrating just how dangerous it is to accept such authority, since allegedly historical precedent can be used to justify all manner of present practice. Not far from his mind, of course, is the Bible, which was then still thought by many to offer a reliable history of the world,[4] and which had just been used to kill the chevalier de La Barre (399). As later, and more explicitly, in *Le Taureau blanc*, Voltaire here casts doubt and ridicule on the plausibility of the biblical narrative. In particular his account of the Garden of Eden suggests not only that it was not primordial but also that it is a myth comparable with the other myths which it later inspired ('des Champs-Elysées, des jardins des Hespérides et de ceux des îles Fortunées': 372). Similarly, in this land of metempsychosis, 'la résurrection . . . est la chose du monde la plus simple' (373).

Faced with such lies, the lesson of *La Princesse de Babylone* is the very opposite of the Babylonians' 'suicide philosophique' ('la raison doit se taire devant eux'). First, it points out how limited our knowledge of the earliest times actually is: 'Tout ce qu'on en savait [i.e. de Canope], c'est que la ville et l'étoile étaient fort anciennes; et c'est tout ce qu'on peut savoir de l'origine des choses, de quelque nature qu'elles puissent être' (411). Second, it shows how a pretence at such knowledge can be abused by people in power. This is exem-

---

4 See J. H. Brumfitt, *Voltaire Historian* (Oxford, 1958), 85–6, and Mitchell, 'An Underlying Theme', 36.

plified most explicitly (and closest to home) when, during his visit to France, Amazan comes across Jansenist 'parlementaires':

> ... les conservateurs d'anciens usages barbares contre lesquels la nature effrayée réclamait à haute voix; ils ne consultaient que leurs registres rongés des vers. S'ils y voyaient une coutume insensée et horrible, ils la regardaient comme une loi sacrée. C'est par cette lâche habitude de n'oser penser par eux-mêmes, et de puiser leurs idées dans les débris des temps où l'on ne pensait pas, que, dans la ville des plaisirs, il était encore des mœurs atroces. (399)

As in *L'Ingénu* and *L'Homme aux quarante écus*, 'fables' are mythical inventions employed as instruments of oppression and fanatical intolerance. Voltaire's reader, on the other hand, must dare to think for him- or herself.

Third, and by way of contrast, the *conte* itself is presented as an instrument of tolerance and reconciliation. In particular we see how the phoenix uses story-telling as an antidote to Formosante's outraged reaction on finding her much-pursued and supposedly faithful Amazan deep in exhausted sleep by the side of his Parisian 'fille d'*affaire*' (403). Unlike in *Les Deux Consolés*, where examples prove no consolation because they are irrelevant to the circumstances of the bereaved, the phoenix's tales strike home. The result is a rejection of the inhumanly one-sided interpretation of Amazan's lapse,[5] an acknowledgement of mixed feelings, and, above all, peace of mind. Narrative speaks to Formosante's heart; and it replaces the turbulence of moral outrage with the resigned, loving acceptance of human fallibility.

The ideal text, therefore, is not one which hankers after mythical origins or sends the likes of the chevalier de la Barre to his execution; but one which, like the *conte*, examines the facts of the present within a balanced moral framework and provides 'exemples' with which to instil tolerant humanity in the heart of its reader. Like a latter-day oracle it aspires somehow or other to get itself read without being travestied by false interpretations and poor sequels: 'Muses! ... Empêchez que les continuateurs témeraires ne gâtent par leur fables les vérités que j'ai enseignées aux mortels dans ce fidèle récit' (413). If not an 'Histoire véritable' like *L'Ingénu*, the translated 'mémoires' (388) of which *La Princesse de Babylone* purportedly consists do at

---

5 Cf. that of Mlle de Saint-Yves. See above, Ch. 10, n. 26.

least provide a 'fidèle récit' — as well, of course, as a 'récit' about fidelity. Or rather they provide a 'récit' about life, which, in the words of the oracle, is a 'Mélange de tout; mort vivant, infidélité et constance, perte et gain, calamité et bonheur' (368). This might be a summary not only of *La Princesse de Babylone* but also of *L'Ingénu*. As the example of the phoenix's sweet-talking of Formosante demonstrates, however — and as the serpent will show in *Le Taureau blanc* — the *conte* not only encourages independence of thought: it also beguiles. As Voltaire warms our heart with his playful mockery of literary tradition, we are at the same time being taken, if not for a ride, then at least on a world tour designed to foster an Enlightenment world-view. The itinerary is carefully calculated. Babylon, the starting-point, represents an ideal past as envisaged by unthinking conservatives for whom 'things ain't what they used to be'. Its gardens are finer than those of Sémiramis and since then, of course, as we all know: 'tout commençait à dégénérer chez les hommes et chez les femmes' (350). Formosante herself is more beautiful even than the subsequent statues of Praxiteles, for she was the paragon of beauty to be imitated. Babylon is the imaginary world of the 'good old days'.

Next comes Voltaire's own version of paradise, the 'pays des Gangarides'. 'La seule contrée de la terre où les hommes soient justes' (364), this Oriental Eldorado has it all. It is home to Amazan, our Enlightenment hero, 'le plus parfait des hommes' (364), who spends his life 'à faire du bien, à cultiver les arts, à pénétrer les secrets de la nature, à perfectionner son être' (366). It is a land of plenty (and especially large diamonds); its inhabitants are healthy vegetarians, with whom, consequently, the animal kingdom is prepared to converse; and it is a nation of equals. Religious worship is one perpetual thanksgiving, and its best preachers are parrots, who may presumably be relied on to repeat the simple truth of God's creation without adding sectarian complication (365).

Babylon is a false paradise. Its ruler is a usurper, dependent on the fictitious praise of courtier and historiographer alike (349); and its philosophy of complacent hedonism 'n'a jamais été démentie que par les faits' (352). The 'pays des Gangarides' is simply fabulous: a land about which 'Les fables de votre ancien Locman' provide 'un témoignage éternellement subsistant' (363–4). As to the real world, the nearest thing to paradise appears to be China, which, like France, has just got rid of its Jesuits but also, unlike France, is governed by 'le monarque de la terre le plus juste, le plus poli et le plus sage' (379). This glimpse of enlightened rule on earth is provided by the first place in which Formosante nearly catches up with Amazan: the second, Scythia (Tartary), provides its opposite, the very epitome of non-civilization. The voyage of reason presented by *La Princesse de Babylone* thus proceeds by repeated antithesis, and the lesson to be learnt is made explicit:

Dès qu'elle fut en Scythie, elle [Formosante] vit plus que jamais combien les hommes et les gouvernements diffèrent et différeront toujours jusqu'au temps où quelque peuple plus éclairé que les autres communiquera la lumière de proche en proche après mille siècles de ténèbres, et qu'il se trouvera dans des climats barbares des âmes héroïques qui auront la force et la persévérance de changer les brutes en hommes. (381–2)

Reminiscent of the metamorphosis of the Ingénu, this universal process of enlightenment is thus here presented in a series of geographical contrasts. The next staging-posts are 'l'empire des Cimmériens' (i.e. Russia), Scandinavia, and Sarmatia (Poland), each providing an example of how a Scythia can become a China: Russia being notable because 'La première de ses lois a été la tolérance de toutes les religions, et la compassion pour toutes les erreurs' (384–5); Scandinavia because 'Ici la royauté et la liberté subsistaient ensemble par un accord qui paraît impossible dans d'autres Etats' (385); and Poland because its ruler is both 'un philosophe' and 'un excellent pilote', whose conciliatory style brings order in the midst of potential anarchy. Germany, Batavia (Holland), and Albion complete this picture of achievable terrestrial perfection, the second being marred only by the frigidity of its women, and the last by the drunkenness of its lords. This section of the story is rounded off by the impromptu lecture given by the English Member of Parliament, who provides an account of how his country evolved from a state of quasi-Scythian primitivism into 'ce pays si recommendable' (390). Amazan concludes: 'que l'Albionien, qui lui avait fait présent de l'univers en raccourci, n'avait point eu tort en disant qu'on était mille fois plus instruit sur les bords de la Tamise que sur ceux du Nil, de l'Euphrate et du Gange' (393).

Unlikely as it may seem that an English Member of Parliament should come to epitomize the Voltairian *conte*, this one has presented 'l'univers en raccourci' just as *La Princesse de Babylone* itself does. Moreover the Englishman's concluding assessment of his account might stand as a statement of the Voltairian ideal not only in the *conte* but in his writing of history: 'Voilà au vrai l'état où nous sommes. Je ne vous ai caché ni le bien, ni le mal, ni nos opprobres, ni notre gloire; et je n'ai rien exagéré' (392).

While some may find the device of the world tour (or 'l'univers en raccourci') laborious, it is nevertheless an important means whereby the reader of *La Princesse de Babylone* is manipulated into an acceptance of its philosophy. Not only does the move from one country to another allow the list of Enlightenment virtues to be leavened with anecdote (and the familiar easy laughter at national stereotypes), but also the order of their appearance permits an important insidious effect. The visions of realizable progress in Protestant states are followed by a series of biting satires on Catholic awfulness (in Venice, Rome, Paris, and Spain) so that it seems that the further Amazan and Formosante travel away from the 'pays des Gangarides', the worse things get. Far from Christianity returning man to the bliss of an original paradise, popish perversions represent a geographically situated outer darkness from which Amazan and Formosante are more than eager to hurry home to Babylon.

This return to the start brings the story full circle, and where we began with a tournament and a feast, we end with conquests and a wedding breakfast. The veiled history of modern Europe gives place once more to the fable of Amazan, newly crowned King of Babylon. Much has happened, but has anything changed? As befits a story which laughs at fable in the name of a new historical sense of human progress, there is a certain temporal ambiguity about *La Princesse de Babylone*. Its opening chapters place the action in a period many centuries before Praxiteles and thirty thousand years after Babylon was built. In anticipation of the fun to be had with biblical chronology in *Le Taureau blanc*, the phoenix declares himself to be 'vingt-sept mille neuf cents années et six mois' old (363): by the time he reaches Cimmeria, he is a whole month older (385). Yet for all the insistence on apparent chronological precision in the story, the ancient names of Scythia, Batavia, and Albion do not, of course, conceal the anachronistic survey of the eighteenth-century political scene which the story provides. What in fact Voltaire has done is to mock the timelessness of fable with pseudo-ancient-historical learning and then to substitute his own symbolic chronology of progress towards Enlightenment. As in *Candide*, this illusion of chronology involves a movement from one paradise to another.

From the point of view of Amazan this movement begins in the impossible perfection of the Gangarides, leads first (because of sexual attraction) to the false paradise of Babylon, then to the fallen states of China and Europe, and finally back to the new paradise of Babylon in which legitimacy is restored to the throne and sexual constancy secured by marriage. From the point of view of the reader, as we have seen, the journey leads from specious Babylonian hedonism, via a glimpse of Gangaride perfection, to the good news and bad news of the contemporary situation. And then? The story of Amazan ends in a flurry of references to idyllic, unproblematic narrative: 'Chacun sait', 'On se souvient qu[e] ...', 'On n'ignore pas qu[e] ...', 'Ces prodiges ne sont-ils écrits dans le livre des chroniques d'Egypte?' (412). Amazan himself will live happily ever after in the land of heroes. But, in a most original departure from narrative convention, Voltaire reminds us of the world in which we live: a world of traducement and pedantry and pederasts, of prejudiced critics called Coger, Larcher, and Fréron. 'Je vous recommande ma *Princesse de Babylone*' (414), says the plaintive, clean-living, philanthropic author, anxious to look after the interests of his impecunious typesetter ('chargé d'une nombreuse famille': 413) and most implausibly keen to give his publisher a New Year's gift. In the fallen world of the present, the only way to ensure that this vulnerable *Princesse de Babylone* will flourish is for it to be falsely accused[6] – like Formosante herself.

The final invocation to the muses in *La Princesse de Babylone* completes a sequence of self-reference which has been running parallel to the main plot. As we have seen, the virtues of the land of the Gangarides are epitomized in the narrative skills of the phoenix, who instils peace and tolerance in the heart of his listener. Beyond the Ganges, however, lies a world of sexual and military aggression, represented by Formosante's warring suitors. This fallen, post-Gangaridian world is the realm of the informing blackbird (376), in which 'what a little birdy told me' is believed but the pacific exploits of Catherine the Great (385) and the probity of Amazan's anti-love-letters are incredible. Where the phoenix achieved a successful blend of pleasure and instruction, now writing seems to fall into opposed categories: that of the 'plus graves auteurs de l'antiquité, lesquels n'ont jamais conté de fables, et ... les professeurs qui ont écrit

---

[6] Cf. the 'Approbation' at the beginning of *Zadig*.

pour les petits garçons' (411); and that of the *conte libertin*, which Formosante finds so unsatisfactory:

La princesse fit acheter chez Marc-Michel Rey tous les contes que l'on avait écrits chez les Ausoniens et les Velches, et dont le débit était défendu sagement chez ces peuples pour enrichir les Bataves; elle espérait qu'elle trouverait dans ces histoires quelque aventure qui ressemblerait à la sienne, et qui charmerait sa douleur. Irla lisait, le phénix disait son avis, et la princesse ne trouvait rien dans *La Paysanne parvenue*, ni dans *Tansaï*, ni dans *Le Sopha*, ni dans *Les Quatre Facardins*, qui eût le moindre rapport à ses aventures. (388)

This division is reflected in Paris itself (399), where one half of the population are 'sombres fanatiques' and the other a superficial bunch of singing and dancing 'oisifs'. Gone are the days of the Grand Siècle: 'La vraie poésie, c'est-à-dire celle qui est naturelle et harmonieuse, celle qui parle au cœur autant qu'à l'esprit, ne fut connue de la nation que dans cet heureux siècle' (399–400).

'Au cœur autant qu'à l'esprit': perhaps, as in *L'Ingénu* (and in *L'Homme aux quarante écus* and *Le Taureau blanc*), only the *conte* can now achieve this happy blend of entertainment and instruction which both warms the heart and broadens the mind. The great themes of art and literature have been debased: female beauty is now represented by a 'Vénus aux belles fesses' (350); chivalric valour has become a form of play-acting at fairground carousels (356). Perhaps the subject of man's progress towards enlightenment can fill the void; and perhaps the *conte* can replace the oracles of religious dogma with the constantly resurrected art of a narrative that breeds tolerance. For the 'druides rechercheurs antropokaies' of this world, of course, the phoenix is simply 'le diable, déguisé en gros oiseau doré' (406). The literary equivalents of these agents of the Spanish Inquisition are Fréron and his Jansenist friends. Voltaire begs them to denounce his *conte* as 'hérétique, déiste, et athée'; only then will it live, by breathing the oxygen of publicity. Where once Voltaire's *contes* used to conclude with a visit from the angels, now they end on a note of devilish self-advertisement. The man whose books the Parlements repeatedly condemned to be burned now proclaims his intention to rise repeatedly from the ashes — in the golden plumage of the *conte*.

Les Lettres d'Amabed first appeared in 1769 in a three-volume miscellany of Voltairian works harmlessly entitled *Les Choses utiles et agré-*

ables. Useful and agreeable as Voltaire's latest *conte* may have been, this anodyne description gives little indication of the seamy nature of the story contained within. For in *Les Lettres d'Amabed* Voltaire comes closest to anticipating some of the calmer moments in de Sade's *Justine ou les malheurs de la vertu.* Foreseeing another popular success, the Cramers brought out a separate edition very soon afterwards, but the *conte* was not generally well received. Diderot, in particular, found it 'sans goût, sans finesse, sans invention', 'un rabâchage' of stale anti-clerical 'polissonneries', which offered 'nul intérêt, nulle chaleur, nulle vraisemblance, force ordures, une grosse gaieté'. Though no lover of religion, he wrote: 'je ne la hais pas assez pour trouver cela bon.'[7] Subsequent readers have tended to concur.

A first version of the *conte* seems to have been composed some fifteen years earlier (December 1753–January 1754) and to have reflected Voltaire's distress at the treatment of Mme Denis by the henchmen of Frederick the Great. New preoccupations then caused him to recast it during 1768, in particular his polemical strategy of asserting the historical priority and moral superiority of Indian religion in order to diminish Jewry (and thus Christianity). The epistolary form, unique among Voltaire's *contes* (if one excepts the uni-epistolary *Lettre d'un turc*), derived from the 1750s version but continued, in 1769, to provide both a reminder of Montesquieu's *Lettres persanes* and an ironically 'soft porn' alternative to such portraits of virtue as Richardson's *Pamela* (translated into French by Prévost in 1742). Indeed Voltaire felt that his own work was altogether better value for money: 'dans les six tomes de *Paméla* il n'y a rien . . . et *Les Lettres d'Amabed* sont le tableau du monde entier depuis les rives du Gange jusqu'au Vatican'.[8]

As in *La Princesse de Babylone*, therefore, Voltaire once more offers his reader an account of 'l'univers en raccourci'. And, sure enough, we are offered glimpses of Bombay, Aden ('ou Eden', which they do not visit), the mouth of the Zambezi, the land of the Hottentots, Angola, Lisbon, Malta, Sicily, and finally Rome. But whereas in the former story Voltaire uses the chronological insouciance of the fable to present a panorama of the contemporary world, here he reverts to the technique employed in the *Histoire des voyages de Scarmentado* and *L'Ingénu* and situates the story at a very precise historical

---

[7]   Quoted in *RC*, 1115.
[8]   D15668 (29 May 1769, to Thiriot).

moment: 1512–13. As the *Essai sur les mœurs* shows, he considered this period crucial for a number of reasons. Specifically he chose it because of the transition from the papal reigns of Alexander VI (characterized by crime and debauch: 520) and war-loving Julius II (521) to that of Leo X, patron of the arts and advocate of tolerance. More generally he wanted to display all the manifold seeds of the imminent Reformation: clerical abuse, monastic strife, the sale of indulgences. The first decades of the sixteenth century also saw the Portuguese colonization of Goa, and for Voltaire this represented the first occasion on which war had been waged not so much to gain territory as to corner the commodities market. In the business of colonial oppression God soon follows mammon, and, with telescopic historical licence, the Inquisition's subsequent arrival in Goa (soon after its establishment in Portugal in 1557) is brought forward forty-five years, thus permitting a strong contrast between the practical effects of original Indian religion and those of 'upstart' Christianity.

As a *conte historique*, therefore, *Les Lettres d'Amabed* employs the same polemical devices of antithesis and chronological order as *La Princesse de Babylone* to present the Church of Rome in a poor light. Unlike Christendom which arrogantly claims an ancient pedigree, Indian civilization actually is the oldest: but, as wise Shastasid enjoins: 'Ne nous glorifions pas d'être les plus anciens; et songeons à être toujours les plus justes' (479). Thus Christianity appears as a form of decadence, a debasing of earlier virtues: peaceable vegetarian teetotallers have been conquered by randy, drunken carnivores in fancy dress. Quaint as Oriental ways may be, with their months of the mouse, the rhinoceros, and the ewe, no less risible – and far more pernicious – are these disputatious monks with names like Fa tutto and Fa molto, these 'espèces de singes élevés avec soin pour faire des tours de passe-passe devant le peuple' (515). Once again the supposedly fabulous world of the East seems eminently sensible and credible; while the behaviour of the Catholic Church beggars belief. As Amabed remarks in open-mouthed and increasingly titil-lated astonishment: 'Tout ceci est un enchantement' (523).

Like *L'Ingénu*, *Les Lettres d'Amabed* is also attributed to a most unlikely source. Being supposedly 'traduites par l'abbé Tamponnet', this indictment of clerical depravity has been made available to French readers by the Sorbonne theologian who had contributed so energetically to the campaign to ban publication of the *Encyclopédie*. No doubt Voltaire was also tickled by the potential puns in such a name, since these would serve (like so many aspects of *Les Lettres d'Amabed*) to undermine the venerability of the Church. Oriental forms of address may seem flowery to the point of insincerity, but what of the truth which underlies Western titles? Thanks to some specious etymology, a cardinal is no better than a 'gond de porte' (525),[9] particularly as those depicted in the story seem perpetually to bend over backwards (in doctrine as in bed). The Pope himself, needless to say, is a 'vice-Dieu' (*passim*), or just plain 'vice' (496).

That the *Lettres d'Amabed* should itself be a translation is all the more appropriate for a text which places so much emphasis on the unreliability of language. Church authority is based on the Bible, and yet such vestiges of the truth as this 'livre . . . bien étrange' (480) may once have contained have since been filtered through so many languages — Greek (483), Syriac, and Arabic (479) — that it amounts to little more than a collection of unreliable fables. Worse, it seems positively pornographic in many of its pages, and both Amabed and Adaté blush to learn of such holy practices as incestuous troilism and the sodomization of angels (501–2). How can so many innocent Goans be butchered in the name of such a text as this?

Once again Voltaire uses the literary medium to undermine our faith in words. Where Frère Vadbled wrote in *L'Ingénu* that imprisonment without trial was a minor mishap, so here it is brushed aside as a 'facétie' (515). Where Adaté sees 'cette épouvantable inhumanité', Fa tutto speaks merely of 'ces petites sévérités' (490). Indian and Italian each have their own linguistic version of events: 'fosse', 'monstres', 'anthropophages', says the one; 'prison', '*inquisitori*', says the other (485). Indeed even among the Italians themselves there is disagreement, and the conflict between the Dominicans and the Franciscans is summed up as a 'dispute sur le sens des paroles' (500).

The whole story is, of course, a parody of religious conversion; and this conversion is essentially a linguistic process. Fa tutto begins by teaching Amabed and Adaté Italian, and their lesson in the conjugation of the verb 'aimer' (478) prefigures their subsequent permutation of sexual partnerships. Essentially the two protagonists undergo an anti-metamorphosis, a process of reverse enlightenment

---

[9]   Because 'cardo' in Latin means door-hinge (though, of course, 'cardinal' actually derives from 'cardinalis' (= principal)). Note also the implicit reference to Paul de Gondi, Cardinal de Retz.

whereby their original, clear-sighted Indian perception of things is gradually obfuscated by a Catholic interpretation of the world. They learn the language of hypocrisy which can transform monstrous depravity into the most congenial of pastimes. What at first seems to be a 'galimatias infernal', a 'mélange incompréhensible d'absurdités et d'horreurs, d'hypocrisie et de barbarie' (491) becomes a fairytale world of ceaseless pleasure.

One of the more effective aspects of the *Lettres d'Amabed* is the way in which the epistolary form is used to convey this gradual loss of innocence. Indeed one reason why it is unjust to Voltaire to dismiss this *conte* as a rehash of previous polemical concerns and devices is that he has given them a new, effective, and entertaining slant. Not only is the voyage of reason now a journey into unreason, but the technique of the innocent observer is turned on its head. Where Candide and Montesquieu's Persians maintain moral distance from the astonishing world in which they live, Voltaire's Indian travellers are recuperated by the system which at first seems so strange. In the early letters we see Amabed naïvely and unsuspectingly telling Shastasid, his wise tutor, all about Fa tutto. His writing reflects 'mon âme, qui s'ouvre toujours devant toi' (477); and Shastasid responds with knowing caution. Halfway through the story, both correspondents are fully in the picture: 'J'ai tout su, et tu sais tout' (498), writes Amabed upon his release from prison.[10] In the remaining letters Amabed gradually becomes a less diligent letter-writer, and party-going seems increasingly to prevent him from putting 'pinceau' to 'planche' (503). When we learn at the end that no further letters by Amabed have been found anywhere, again it is clear that Voltaire is not merely rehashing the old technique of a 'lost manuscript' and an inconclusive ending (in the manner of *Zadig*). The absence of further letters demonstrates that epistolary honesty has finally been defeated by the unspeakable activities which Amabed, Adaté, and Déra have engaged in with the two young cardinals at their country house: 'Je ne sais comment te conter ce qui nous est arrivé, je vais pourtant essayer de m'en tirer' (525). Amabed's way out is silence: the silence of guilt, the shamed refusal to tell Shastasid another word.

---

[10] He also comments on the part Adaté has played in his release in terms which recall the plight of Mlle de Saint-Yves and the false suspicion surrounding the Princesse de Babylone: 'Charme des yeux n'a point été coupable; elle ne peut l'être. La vertu est dans le cœur, et non ailleurs' (498).

Hence, and in another new variation on a previous device (cf. the end of *La Princesse de Babylone*), the narrator's confident assertion that *Les Lettres d'Amabed* cannot be prolonged in any spurious sequel. Amabed is a changed man: 'je me sens déjà tout autre' (517). Like so many of Voltaire's heroes he has learnt through travel: 'On se forme beaucoup par les voyages' (524). He has learnt to modify his earlier opinions: 'En vérité je doute que Maduré soit plus agréable que Roume [*sic*]' (523); and he has sought to accommodate himself to the world as he finds it: 'Je crois que le plus sage est de rire comme les autres, et d'être poli comme eux' (515). Indeed he has found final happiness at a supper-party (524–5). Amabed's metamorphosis is a travesty of the process of enlightenment as depicted in most of Voltaire's other *contes*. Accordingly, where many *contes* end on an inconclusive note, inviting the reader to turn from the provisional answers of Voltaire's fiction to the facts of his or her own life, *Les Lettres d'Amabed* stops dead. There is nothing more to say. Amabed has lost the power to communicate: 'Je ne sais comment te conter'. Indeed he seems to have forgotten his own language, for his translation of Ariosto 'en indien' in the penultimate letter is simply gobbledegook:

> Modermen sebar eso
> La te ben sofa meso.

The lines of Ariosto, that *conteur* 'par excellence', remind the reader of Fa tutto's convenient description of rape as an act of 'charité' (490), and provide a final indictment of monks as 'si ingorda e si crudel canaglia [such a greedy, cruel rabble]'. Amabed's 'translation' is neither 'Indian' nor anagrammatic. If anything it resembles a garbled tonic scale, no more comprehensible but infinitely more suspect than 'le glossement dont [les Hottentots] se servent pour se faire entendre au lieu d'un langage articulé' (504).

Les Lettres d'Amabed thus ends by drawing the line between what may or may not be narrated. Given what has gone before, one may feel that it is rather late in the day for discretion. In his enterprising article on this *conte*, Robin Howells has argued from a Bakhtinian point of view that the various themes of language, sexuality, slaughter, consumption, immersion, and penetration combine and overlap in this story to 'offer a carnivalesque vision of the world in which ambiguity and paradox are celebrated, violence liberates and conversion is the material principle'. 'Unable to resolve these tensions', he concludes, 'the text ends by re-representing them as ritual.'[11] For Howells the apparent moral and didactic basis of the *conte* (the satire on Catholicism) sits ill with the final *mise-en-abyme* whereby all Rome laughs at Machiavelli's *La Mandragola*. In this play a man, wishing to sleep with his neighbour's wife, employs a monk to seduce her. As Amabed himself remarks: 'On se moque, tout le long de la pièce, de la religion que l'Europe professe' (520). For Howells this reveals a Rome (and hence, because of the evident parallel, *Les Lettres d'Amabed* itself) which 'knows its own ignorance, though cynically pretending to know reality. It knows the world-process, though it puts a gloss on it. Its response is laughter and ceremony.' Thus (and here comes Bakhtin): 'Positive festivity emerges from negative satire.'[12]

But this, precisely, is to read *Les Lettres d'Amabed* the way Amabed reads Rome; and, as we have seen, his 'conversion' is the story of an anti-metamorphosis, of a journey into unreason. If we look at Amabed's reaction to Machiavelli's play, we see that a choice of responses to such theatrical delight is offered: 'De tels plaisirs te paraîtront peut-être indécents, mon cher et pieux Shastasid. Charme des yeux en a été scandalisée; mais la comédie est si jolie que le plaisir l'a emporté sur le scandale' (520). Entertaining (and 'indécent') as *Les Lettres d'Amabed* is, should we allow the comedy to outweigh the scandal? Clearly Shastasid, the wise representative of 'original' Indian enlightenment, is most unlikely to see the funny side; and Adaté has at least one cruel memory to give her pause. And so do we have several. For the whole of *Les Lettres d'Amabed* is a shocking indictment of the Catholic Church, and if it appears debonair in its depiction of what Howells calls the 'world-process' with its sexual 'five-siders' in the country,[13] its primary polemical purpose in so doing is an implicit take-off of the Bible. For, as Voltaire is constantly pleased to relate, the Old Testament is full of two-siders and three-siders of every sort, not to mention prophets eating the odd dung sandwich (501). Halfway through the story, Amabed is still 'Indian' enough to be shocked by the whoredoms of Aholah and Aholibah:

[11]   R. J. Howells, 'Processing Voltaire's *Amabed*', *British Journal for Eighteenth-Century Studies*, 10 (1987), 154.
[12]   Ibid. 161, 159.
[13]   Ibid. 159.

Il y a bien pis. Ce savant homme [Fa molto] nous a fait remarquer deux sœurs Oolla et Ooliba. Tu les connais bien, puisque tu as tout lu. Cet article a fort scandalisé ma femme. Le blanc de ses yeux en a rougi. J'ai remarqué que la bonne Déra était tout en feu à ce paragraphe. Il faut certainement que ce franciscain Fa molto soit un gaillard. Cependant il a fermé son livre dès qu'il a vu combien Charme des yeux et moi nous étions effarouchés, et il est sorti pour aller méditer sur le texte. (501-2)

Here the Bible is a source of 'gaillardises' which can sexually excite (Déra), perhaps even to the point of onanism (Fa molto). The 'unconverted' Indians blush and take exception. When it comes to sodomy with angels, Amabed is so 'épouvanté' and 'saisi d'horreur' that he is almost reduced to silence ('ma plume frémit comme mon âme . . . le dirai-je?': 502). Here the threatened silence is a sign of his scandalized 'propreté' and 'grande pudeur' (501): later it will be a sign of his ignoble shame.

This incident at Sodom is also highlighted in the third of Voltaire's *Homélies prononcées à Londres en 1765*. Here Voltaire comments sarcastically that this passage from the Book of Genesis is 'une pierre de scandale pour les examinateurs qui n'écoutent que leur raison'. One must remember, he continues with similar irony, that 'c'était la manière d'écrire de tout l'Orient. Les paraboles furent si longtemps en usage que l'auteur de toute vérité, quand il vint sur la terre, ne parla aux Juifs qu'en paraboles.'[14] The homily ends with a brilliant tongue-in-cheek satire on the art of convenient interpretation. We must be ready sometimes to read the Bible in figurative as well as literal terms. Otherwise 'nous serions révoltés et indignés à chaque page':

Edifions-nous de ce qui fait le scandale des autres; tirons une nourriture salutaire de ce qui leur sert de poison. Quand le sens propre et littéral d'un passage paraît conforme à notre raison, tenons-nous-en à ce sens naturel. Quand il paraît contraire à la vérité, aux bonnes mœurs, cherchons un sens caché dans lequel la vérité et les bonnes mœurs se concilient avec la Sainte Ecriture. C'est ainsi qu'en ont usé tous les Pères de l'Eglise; c'est ainsi que nous agissons tous les jours dans le commerce de la vie: nous interprétons toujours favorablement les discours de nos amis et de nos partisans; trait-erons-nous avec plus de dureté les saints livres des Juifs, qui sont l'objet de notre foi? Enfin, lisons les livres juifs pour être chrétiens; et s'ils ne nous rendent pas plus savants, qu'ils servent au moins à nous rendre meilleurs.[15]

---

[14] *Mélanges*, 1151.
[15] *Mélanges*, 1155.

This withering scorn at those who would have their exegetical cake and eat it is a useful pointer to the principal direction of the polemic in *Les Lettres d'Amabed*. 'Scandale' is the word which keeps recurring both in the *conte* and in Voltaire's contemporary remarks on biblical interpretation. For Amabed the scandal of Rome fades beneath the enchantment of comedy. But for Voltaire and for readers of *Les Lettres d'Amabed* 'qui n'écoutent que leur raison', the scandal of Rome and the farcical pornography of its sacred writ must remain foremost in the mind.

These *Lettres d'Amabed* are no less wondrous in their content than the epistles of St 'Pual' (500), which Amabed reads with Fa molto. Being 'un des grands saints de la religion italienne et portugaise' (501), St Paul is someone whom Amabed would much like to imitate: 'dussé-je acheter cette gloire par cent quatre-vingt-quinze coups de verges bien appliqués sur le derrière' (501). Presumably the reason that Amabed writes no more letters at the end of this *conte* is that, as he himself might have said in another language, 'I am abed' — abed, and well and truly 'retourné' (487) in the fond clutches of his two cardinals, Sacripanté and Faquinetti. Perhaps they have been good enough to administer the required 'coups de verges' by which this 'disenlightened' hero will be, like St Paul but in a different sense, 'ravi au troisième ciel' (500). If *Pot-pourri* was Voltaire's answer to the Gospels and the Acts of the Apostles, *Les Lettres d'Amabed* are his version of the Epistles, his very own 'Epîtres sur l'infâme'.

12

Totem and Taboo

Le Taureau blanc

Il concluait que sagesse vaut mieux qu'éloquence.

(550)

If *Les Lettres d'Amabed* is Voltaire's version of St Paul's epistles, then *Le Taureau blanc* is his answer to the Old Testament. Begun perhaps as early as 1766[1] and composed further in 1771–2, it was completed during 1773 and first published in three instalments in the *Correspondance littéraire* in November and December 1773 and January 1774. As has long been recognized,[2] the story reflects Voltaire's preoccupation with biblical criticism, from his reading of the Benedictine Dom Calmet[3] to his own polemical commentaries in the *Dictionnaire philosophique* and, most especially, in the *Questions sur l'Encyclopédie* (1770–2), and *La Bible enfin expliquée* (1776). Superficially *Le Taureau blanc* seems little more than an entertaining send-up of the Old Testament. It contains within one story many of the jokes and biblical absurdities which had studded Voltaire's anti-clerical writing (and no doubt also his conversation) for several decades, and combines them in a *faux naïf* tale of a young Princess's forbidden love for Nebuchadnezzar during the period when the Babylonian king had the misfortune to be turned into a bull. By the time *Le Taureau blanc* was published, the anti-Christian campaign of Voltaire and the younger generation of deists and atheists had succeeded to the point where the Old Testament was hardly a very

---

[1] *Zadig and other stories*, ed. Mason, 43. See also Haydn Mason, 'A Biblical "Conte philosophique"': Voltaire's *Taureau blanc*' in E. T. Dubois *et al.* (eds.), *Eighteenth-Century French Studies. Literature and the Arts* (Newcastle, 1969).

[2] See *Le Taureau blanc*, ed. René Pomeau (Paris, 1957), pp. xxxv–xlvii.

[3] Known for his *Commentaire littéral sur tous les livres de l'Ancien et du Nouveau Testament* (24 vols, 1707–16) and a *Dictionnaire historique, critique, chronologique, géographique, et littéral de la Bible* (4 vols, 1720–1; rev. edn., 1730).

daunting target any more. Nevertheless the authority of the Old Testament as an historical document is once again implicitly rejected by the presentation of many of its more famous and often miraculous moments as mere fables, akin to the metamorphoses of Ovid. Hence the concentration on animals and, the white bull apart, on animals which speak. As with the 'pays des Gangarides' in *La Princesse de Babylone*, Voltaire depicts a pre-Enlightenment world[4] in which the marvellous is an everyday occurrence (even if for the venerable Mambrès metamorphosis is not quite what it used to be: 542). By locating the action in Egypt, Voltaire is able to draw on and debunk a tradition of more or less implausible fictions: for the noble savage and the knight errant, now read 'the wise Egyptian'.[5] At the same time he is able to lump Egyptian mythology and Old Testament prophecy together in such a way that he both diminishes the Jewish tradition (and again, therefore, ultimately Christianity) and questions the primacy of Egypt as a 'cradle of civilization'.

By way of a contrast with the 'wisdom' of Old Testament prophets and Egyptian sages, Voltaire presents modern enlightenment in the guise of two ironic self-portraits: Mambrès and the Serpent. Here is Mambrès, coming up to his thirteen-hundredth birthday, a bit slow on the uptake now but still a wily and cogitative bird once he gets going. With all the wisdom of his years he exploits and manipulates the religious beliefs of King Amasis and the people of Tanis to his own ends. In one way, of course, he acts no differently from the Jesuit confessors in *L'Ingénu*, using a position of religious and political authority for personal ambition. But, as with Voltaire, Mambrès's ambition is a humanitarian one, and in this respect he provides a portrait of Voltaire, the Patriarch of Ferney, saving the victims of 'l'infâme' by manipulating public opinion and outwitting a corrupt and bigoted judiciary in the Parlements. As for the Serpent, he too

---

4 Cf. the Ingénu's comments on the early history of nations: 'Je ne vois, avant Thucydide, que des romans semblables aux *Amadis*, et beaucoup moins amusants. Ce sont partout des apparitions, des oracles, des prodiges, des sortilèges, des métamorphoses, des songes expliqués, et qui font la destinée des plus grands empires et des plus petits Etats: ici des bêtes qui parlent, là des bêtes qu'on adore, des dieux transformés en hommes, et des hommes transformés en dieux' (317–18). As Amadis and Amaside anagrammatically recall the chivalric romances of *Amadis de Gaule*, so *Le Taureau blanc* presents the pre-Thucydidian world in action. The comparison between ancient historiography and *Amadis de Gaule* derives from Voltaire's earlier contact with Bolingbroke: see Brumfitt, *Voltaire Historian*, 43.
5 On this Egyptian tradition see *Le Taureau blanc*, ed. Pomeau, pp. xlviii–l.

seems a little over the hill, and in Amaside he has a very demanding audience. Not for her 'Les contes qu'on pouvait faire à la quadrisaïeule de la quadrisaïeule de ma grand-mère' (553). The fashion, in literature, as in all things, has moved on, threatening to leave an ageing author looking decidedly 'passé'.

For René Pomeau the Serpent fails the test of his new readership, for his two tales (about King Gnaof and about the three prophets) are 'lourdement significatifs au détriment de la fiction'. What we have here, he claims, is 'du Voltaire fatigué'.[6] While several critics have praised the polished wit of *Le Taureau blanc*,[7] there seems to be general agreement that this *conte* lacks the polemical punch of earlier works and does indeed reflect a measure of Voltairian fatigue: 'on cherche en vain ici la critique de la justice, les attaques contre l'Inquisition, les jésuites et le Parlement . . .'.[8]

In vain? Once again it is necessary to defend Voltaire against the charge that his later *contes* reflect a waning in his powers. In the case of *Le Taureau blanc* it seems particularly ironic that critics should have contented themselves with the surface of the *conte* when it contains the most significant statement of a 'poetics' of the *conte* to be found anywhere in Voltaire's works, and one which specifically warns against superficiality. Indeed, when Amaside tells the Serpent that she is bored by all these Old Testament tales, one wonders if Voltaire himself is not aware of the impending charge of senescent repetitiveness. Amaside's famous prescription then follows:

Je veux qu'un conte soit fondé sur la vraisemblance, et qu'il ne ressemble pas toujours à un rêve. Je désire qu'il n'ait rien de trivial ni d'extravagant. Je voudrais surtout que, sous le voile de la fable, il laissât entrevoir aux yeux exercés quelque vérité fine qui échappe au vulgaire. (553)

It seems difficult not to conclude that Voltaire has placed this passage as an incitement to his readers to look further than the surface of *Le Taureau blanc*. The silliness of the Old Testament has already been

---

[6] See *Le Taureau blanc*, ed. Pomeau, p. lx.

[7] Pomeau (*Le Taureau blanc*, p. lxix) points especially to the 'ballet parodique' of literary styles: official court terminology, ecclesiastical unction, 'marivaudage', the registers of fairy-tale and epic, etc. For an informative study of how the 'general conflict of the tale can be characterized as an opposition between human and divine language in which analytic discourse triumphs over revelation', see Maureen F. O'Meara, '*Le Taureau blanc* and the Activity of Language', *SVEC* 148 (1976), 117.

[8] *RC*, 1150.

exposed as obvious and old-hat. Where then is the 'vérité fine qui échappe au vulgaire'?

Without wishing to condemn the critical consensus as being necessarily 'vulgaire', one might propose two such 'vérités': the one political, the other concerning the function of the *conte*. Why, one must ask, has Voltaire chosen the story of Nebuchadnezzar's seven-year metamorphosis as the backbone of his plot? One answer would be, of course, that it offered rich comic potential and particularly suited the purpose of taking the topoi of fable literally. But why, more especially, has Voltaire chosen to end his story with the phrase: 'Vive notre grand roi qui n'est plus bœuf!'? *Le Taureau blanc* is a story about power being usurped (by the inhuman Amadis who would behead his own daughter) and of a king who is restored to his throne when he ceases to be 'bœuf' (i.e. 'stupide, grossier tant de corps que d'esprit').[9] May not the king be Louis XV, whose royal power had been temporarily usurped by the Jansenist-dominated Parlements (who are willing to behead a chevalier de La Barre and his young, innocent equivalents)?

For seven years had elapsed between the 'rebellion' of the Rennes Parlement in 1764 and Maupeou's exile of the Paris Parlement in January 1771 and his sweeping reforms of the magistrature announced on 23 February. The Parlements represented the party of the nobility, whose power had been steadily growing ever since the Regent had restored the Parlements' right to remonstrate in 1715. For Voltaire and the other *philosophes* they were the enemy of reform (while enlightened absolutism represented, in the absence of modern democracy, the best chance for progress).[10] Conflict between crown and magistrature came to a head in 1764 when the Parlement at Rennes supported the Etats provinciaux (of clergy, nobility, and bourgeoisie) in their refusal to levy the royal *corvée*. When La Chalotais and five other officials were arrested, other Parlements remonstrated with the King. This led in turn to the so-called *séance de flagellation* on 3 March 1766, when the King addressed the Paris Parlement and sought to reassert his authority, and to the appointment of Maupeou as Chancellor in September 1768. By his

---

[9] See *RC*, 1184, n. 1 to p. 561.
[10] Cf. D12937 (16 Oct. 1765, to D'Alembert): 'On ne s'était pas douté que la cause des rois fût celle des philosophes; cependant il est évident que des sages qui n'admettent pas deux puissances, sont les premiers soutiens de l'autorité royale.' See Gay, *Voltaire's Politics*, 89.

support for the unlovable Maupeou (and the desertion of the enlightened Choiseul which this entailed) Voltaire brought considerable odium upon himself, but it shows just how deeply he was opposed to the Parlements and how concerned about the threat which he saw them as posing to the political stability of France. He continued to support Maupeou and was delighted when the latter, having precipitated a crisis with the Paris Parlement, decided in 1771 to deprive one hundred and sixty-five of its magistrates of their posts and to propose a series of wide-ranging reforms.[11]

These reforms, involving among other things the replacement of the Paris Parlement by six separate councils, were thought a considerable advance by Voltaire. With his *lit de justice* on 13 April, Louis XV gave his full support to Maupeou's programme, and the troubled seven-year period which had begun in Rennes was seemingly at an end. As Peter Gay writes: 'At last it seemed possible that the counter-revolution of the robe nobility might be stopped, and that a bureaucratic absolutism, rational and modern, might be imposed on the country. This was Maupeou's aim, and Voltaire's as well.'[12] No wonder, then, that Voltaire should have proceeded to write a *conte* in which he seeks to praise the reigning monarch. No wonder, too, that his bull should be white, for that was the colour of royalty. Thus *Le Taureau blanc* ends on a note of celebration that kings are corrigible:

> Et depuis ce fut une coutume dans Babylone que, toutes les fois que le souverain (ayant été grossièrement trompé par ses satrapes, ou par ses mages, ou par ses trésoriers ou par ses femmes) reconnaissait enfin ses erreurs et corrigeait sa mauvaise conduite, tout le peuple criait à sa porte: 'Vive notre grand roi qui n'est plus bœuf!' (561)

The implication that Louis XV has been led into error by satrap and mistress alike is presumably sufficient to explain why the 'vérité fine' of *Le Taureau blanc* had to be quite so veiled.

The other 'vérité fine' which it is possible to discern in *Le Taureau blanc* concerns the nature of story-telling. As mentioned above, René Pomeau finds the Serpent's two tales unduly obvious in their message: the King Gnaof story illustrating the lubricity of priests, the account of the three prophets demonstrating that one can have too

---

[11]	On the Crown's struggle with the Parlements and Voltaire's support for Maupeou, see Gay, *Voltaire's Politics*, 312–33.
[12]	Ibid. 326.

much of a good thing. Nothing is pleasurable without variety. But this is to underestimate the guile of the story-teller, who is, after all, 'le plus prudent et le plus subtil des animaux' (556). The point of the Serpent's stories lies not in their message but in their effect on Amaside. After all the tired tales from the Old Testament, which bore her, the story about King Gnaof lulls her further into a false sense of security. The Serpent's narrative ploy is evidently to get her to ask him what the priest whispered into the Queen's ear; but this ruse is so blatant that she at once 'voi[t] où cela mène':

ce conte est trop commun; je vous dirai même qu'il alarme ma pudeur. Contez-moi quelque fable bien vraie, bien avérée et bien morale, dont je n'aie jamais entendu parler, pour achever 'de me former l'esprit et le cœur', comme dit le professeur égyptien Linro [i.e. Charles Rollin]. (554)

Promising now to tell her a story 'qui est des plus authentiques', the Serpent embarks on the tale of the three prophets. With its traditional and relatively unveiled message, this lulls Amaside yet further by its seeming irrelevance to her own situation; so much so that she drops her guard and is beguiled into uttering the forbidden name of Nebuchadnezzar. For its devilish narrator, the real point of his 'authentic' story consists in manipulating his listener's vicarious interest in the sex life of a king and exploiting her readiness to interrupt his narrative (about which this most gentlemanly serpent has warned her: 538). By these means he induces her to break a taboo and to speak the unspeakable. Thus he precipitates the crisis which wise Mambrès had sought to forestall and which only the ageing prophet's superior foresight will in the end resolve to the benefit of his loose-tongued ward. With an art similar to that of the Serpent, Mambrès manipulates the Egyptians' faith in their own totem, the bull-god Apis, and thereby enables Nebuchadnezzar to survive his taurine septennium intact.

Le Taureau blanc thus provides an object-lesson in the importance of story-telling.[13] We are shown a world of linguistic taboo, ruled over by Harpocrates the god of silence: wisdom is defined as the ability to 'commander à votre langue' (528). Amaside must not utter her lover's name, and her ladies-in-waiting are sworn to silence (which they keep for a whole day: 533); the bull cannot speak; the

[13] On this aspect of the story see also Thomas M. Carr jun., 'Voltaire's Fables of Discretion. The Conte Philosophique in *Le Taureau blanc*', *Studies in Eighteenth-Century Culture*, 15 (1986).

witch of Endor is forbidden to reveal the identity of her silent charge
(531). At court, the well-bred are tongue-tied, while boors are garrulous (533), as garrulous as the raven from the ark ('une bête si difficile
et si bavarde': 547), who is as much of a tell-tale (556) as the blackbird
in *La Princesse de Babylone*. This is a realm not of ancient civilization
but of primitive superstition, in which not only bulls, but ewes, cats,
crocodiles, goats, and even onions (558), assume totemic significance. Through the art of story-telling the Serpent undermines this
system by seducing his listeners into acknowledging and acting upon
the truth.

The biblical account of the Garden of Eden thus takes on a new
significance. That, too, was a world of prohibition; but the Serpent's
guile has liberated man from the chains of ignorance by seducing
woman:

je lui donnai le meilleur conseil du monde. Elle m'honorait de sa confiance.
Mon avis fut qu'elle et son mari devait se gorger du fruit de l'arbre de la
science. Je crus plaire en cela au maître des choses. Un arbre si nécessaire
au genre humain ne me paraissait pas planté pour être inutile. Le maître
aurait-il voulu être servi par des ignorants et des idiots? L'esprit n'est-il pas
fait pour s'éclairer, pour se perfectionner? Ne faut-il pas connaître le bien
et le mal pour faire l'un et pour éviter l'autre? Certainement on me devait
des remerciements. (536)

In the world of eighteenth-century France, where censorship
imposes its own taboos and Christianity holds the people in thrall
to totemic fables, Voltaire's *contes* are like apples plucked from the
Tree of Knowledge and handed to his readers by the Serpent himself
that they, too, should to dare to know and dare to speak the truth.
The oblique art of story-telling is the polemicist's most effective
weapon against 'l'infâme'. Where Daniel changed a man into a bull,
and Mambrès a bull into a god (559), Voltaire once more seeks to
effect the metamorphosis of his reader into a human being.

13
Anglicans and Academics
Aventure de la mémoire, Eloge historique de la raison, Les Oreilles du comte de Chesterfield, and *Histoire de Jenni*

Les gens de lettres qui ont rendu le plus de services au petit nombre d'êtres pensants répandus dans le monde sont les lettrés isolés, les vrais savants renfermés dans leur cabinet, qui n'ont ni argumenté sur les bancs des universités, ni dit les choses à moitié dans les académies.

(*Dict. phil.*, 254)

AVENTURE DE LA MÉMOIRE

Voltaire's last four *contes* were all published in 1775, some three years before his death. Of these *Aventure de la mémoire* may have been thought of first, since the 'bel axiome' (566) with which it ends is Voltaire's revised version of a subject set by the abbé Coger for a Latin prize at the Sorbonne in 1772. Once more, therefore, we find Voltaire writing against the text of an author who represents his ecclesiastical enemy: Père Quesnel of *L'Ingénu* and the abbé Tamponnet of *Les Lettres d'Amabed* have been replaced by yet another opponent of the *philosophes*. In this case, whereas Coger's discourse-topic proposes that modern philosophy is the enemy of God and King alike, Voltaire uses the medium of the *conte* to stress the importance of memory to both man and his muse and to show that modern (empiricist) philosophy is more conducive to social stability than the Cartesianism of the academic and theological establishment. By revising Coger's prize subject *Aventure de la mémoire* becomes a subversive, vernacular entry in the cleric's stuffy competition.

At first sight this *conte* seems a rather dated and superfluous affirmation of Voltaire's lifelong rejection of Cartesian innate ideas and his acceptance of Lockian epistemology. Knowledge derives from sense impressions which, being retained in the memory, permit of comparison and evaluation and, ultimately, of human understanding: 'la mémoire est le seul instrument par lequel nous puissions joindre deux idées et deux mots ensemble' (563). Mnemosyne is thus not only the goddess of memory and mother of the muses, but also in effect the goddess of enlightenment and literature. Thanks to a rapid history of human thought this recognition of the importance of memory is presented as belonging to universal, age-old wisdom, from which Cartesianism constitutes a weird, if temporary, aberration. Human foolishness being what it is — and since quite self-evidently 'un Anglais' (564) cannot be right — Descartes's chimeras have been adopted by an unholy anti-Lockian alliance of 'la Nonsobre' (the Sorbonne), 'liolisteois' ('loyolistes', or Jesuits), 'séjanistes' (Jansenists), and 'dicastériques' (magistrates in the Parlements).

The refutation of the Cartesian 'system' which Voltaire here imagines is, as usual, both narrative and empirical: let the muses take memory away, and then let us see how human beings fare on the meagre basis of the innate. The witty account of the resultant chaos ends with clever, self-referential irony: memory is restored, and the ogres revert to type. The Parlements do some remonstrating; the Jansenists record the event in their notorious gazette; the Jesuits intrigue at court; and poor old Coger, 'tout ébahi de l'aventure' (566), treats his Fifth Year to a nice Latin saw. In their desire to correct the human race, the muses had preferred this practical 'moyen de les éclairer' because 'les satires ne corrigent personne, irritent les sots et les rendent encore plus méchants' (564). Presumably Voltaire, with wry and elderly wisdom, envisages his *Aventure de la mémoire* as having just as little effect on its readership as the muses' experiment in amnesia.

Having played the devil in *Le Taureau blanc*, Voltaire here chooses to occupy the Olympian heights — and to turn his attention to other animals. A horse, perhaps of Trojan provenance, has overheard the proscription of Locke: 'ce cheval . . . qui avait du sens aussi bien que des sens, en parla un jour à Pégase dans mon écurie; et Pégase alla raconter aux Muses cette histoire avec sa vivacité ordinaire' (564). Who, then, is this narrator whose stable contains Pegasus, the symbol of poetic inspiration?[1] Is he simply a writer well placed to drink the 'blushful Hippocrene'? Or is he Bellerophon riding to victory against the Chimera (not only of Cartesianism but the monstrous

---

[1] Cf. Voltaire's *Dialogue de Pégase et du vieillard* (1774) in which Pegasus describes himself as 'ton coursier du Parnasse' (l. 6) and calls on the old man to cease cultivating his garden for a time and devote himself to the arts. When he refuses, Pegasus exclaims: 'Eh bien, végète et meurs' (l. 205). See Mol., x. 195, 205.

'infâme')? Or is he simply an old man looking down from the summit of his eighty years and calling on his younger readers to *remember*: to remember the lessons of the past and to remember the gifts of the muses, 'qui depuis cent ans avaient singulièrement favorisé le pays longtemps barbare où cette scène se passait' (564). True to his Olympian persona, Voltaire offers a pseudo-Greek fable, a modern myth of anarchy and unreason to frighten his Establishment readers. With memory departed, Parlement magistrates go uncaressed by their wives; the 'bonnet carré' of a Sorbonne theologian becomes a chamber-pot; and, worst of all, the servants have quite forgotten the 'marché qu'ils avaient fait avec leurs maîtres' (565). Class barriers are trampled under foot as sexual instinct rules supreme; and language, reduced by oblivion to mere 'sons informes' (565), is powerless to protest. And, greatest of disasters, the supper-party is off: 'personne ne savait plus comment il fallait s'y prendre' (565).

As in *Le Taureau blanc*, hindsight tempts one to see in this *conte* a foretaste of the Revolution. At the very least it reflects the deep, if lightly worn, unease of a man with a longer memory than most. He knew how great the cultural glories of the Grand Siècle had been, and how (in his view) his own century had fallen artistically short. He knew, too, both from his own experience and from his extensive work as a historian just how hard-won and precarious were the achievements of civilization over barbarism. Beneath the veil of an anti-Cartesian fantasy he has an urgent message to convey: 'Imbéciles ... ressouvenez-vous que ... sans la mémoire il n'y a point d'esprit' (566). With the wisdom of his years he warns that 'Non magis musis quam hominibus infensa est ista quae vocatur memoria' (566). But who listens to old men, especially if they speak in Latin?

ELOGE HISTORIQUE DE LA RAISON

Eloge historique de la raison, with its subtitle 'Prononcé dans une académie de province par Ma ...', continues in the same mock-academic vein as *Aventure de la mémoire*. Written late in 1774, its tone is far removed from the octogenarian anxiety of the latter *conte* and reflects instead a decidedly sanguine view of contemporary France. Following the death of Louis XV in May, the early months of his successor's reign were notable for the rise to power of Turgot. He was eventually dismissed in May 1776, and the Parlements were able to regain the influence which Maupeou had denied them. For the moment, however, Turgot offered a vision of tolerance and intelligent reform sufficient to console Voltaire for Maupeou's earlier dismissal – and sufficient for Reason and her daughter Truth to decide to tarry amongst the French (575).

Where Erasmus had written his *Praise of Folly* (567), Voltaire here offers his own 'Praise of Reason', presenting it with further wry self-deprecation as if addressed (by 'Ma[dame Raison]' herself?) to a provincial academy. Doubtless the heavy-handed allegory is in keeping with the pomposity of such occasions, and the requirement of elaborate flattery is nicely evoked in the description of Pope Clement XIV's cook as being 'après vos confesseurs, messieurs, l'homme le plus désoeuvré de sa profession' (569). Witticisms are to hand, albeit infrequently: 'Rien n'est si désagréable que d'être pendu obscurément' (569). But contentment makes poor writers, and Voltaire is no exception: or, as Reason herself declares: 'Je suis aujourd'hui trop heureuse' (575). For *Eloge historique de la raison* is in effect *La Princesse de Babylone* without the fun. The fiction of a spoken eulogy is scarcely exploited, either to comic or polemical ends; while the device of a voyage of reason, here at its most explicit, is here also at its most pedestrian. Beyond the odd joke about taking refuge in a well, the narrative offers no more than an allegorized history of European enlightenment from Caesarian barbarism to current Gallic commitment to progress. Along the road we meet Clement XIV, Maria Theresa, and Stanislas Poniatowski, each of them gallantly lighting their own particular local darkness. Such intellectual delight as the journey may afford derives more from guessing the identities beneath the fictional masks than from any entertainingly carnivalesque behaviour; and the former may be attenuated by the need, more than ever, to resort to learned footnotes. There are fleeting, mocking echoes of the Gospels: 'Les disciples de leurs premiers apôtres' (568); 'quelques semences des fruits qu'elles portent toujours avec elles, et qu'elles avaient répandues, germèrent sur la terre; et même sans pourrir' (569): but this mockery is much less concerted than in *Les Lettres d'Amabed* or *Le Taureau blanc*. The idea of an eight-page 'Bible of Enlightenment', telling of the early prophets of reason and proclaiming the Coming of Turgot, is a promising one, but Voltaire has not done it the justice that he might.

   Eloge historique de la raison is instructive in that it shows clearly where Voltaire's strengths as a *conteur* lie. When he is attacking and debunking and generally writing 'against', be it a person, or an institution, a genre or a particular text, then he is at his most powerful. But when he is writing 'for' and abandons the open-ended, provisional, sceptical format that leaves it to the reader to make the final decisions, then he is at his least persuasive. It is true that Reason's final remark strikes a note of caution which historical hindsight again (as with *Aventure de la mémoire*) allows the modern reader to invest with prophetic significance: 'jouissons de ces beaux jours; restons ici, s'ils durent; et, si les orages surviennent, retournons dans notre puits.' But Reason is here being little more than greyly sensible. The fact remains that when Voltaire seeks to support a 'system' (here of enlightened royal absolutism) rather than to undermine one with digs and common sense, then his *contes* risk falling into that category which he most abhorred: 'le genre ennuyeux'.[2] In the case of the *Éloge* one can at least be grateful that 'la Raison n'est pas prolixe' (568).

LES OREILLES DU COMTE DE CHESTERFIELD

Voltaire's penultimate *conte*, however, runs no such risk of belonging to 'le genre ennuyeux'. *Les Oreilles du comte de Chesterfield et le chapelain Goudman* was composed between 1773 and 1775. This 'comte de Chesterfield' was Philip Dormer Stanhope, the fourth Earl (1694–1773), diplomat, government minister, opponent of Walpole, Enlightenment luminary, and author of the famous *Letters to his son*, which Voltaire described to Mme du Deffand as perhaps 'le meilleur livre d'éducation qu'on ait jamais fait'.[3] The deafness from which the Earl suffered for many years serves as the pretext for this story of a Chaplain Goudman, a benignly named Anglican clergyman in search of a benefice, who finds himself as much a plaything of fate as did once Zadig.

Since the *conte* begins and ends (with a neat symmetry to offset the fragmentary nature of its centre) by referring to 'la fatalité qui gouverne toutes les choses de ce monde', the theme of free will and destiny is once more at the forefront of Voltaire's preoccupations.

---

[2] 'tous les genres sont bons, hors le genre ennuyeux' (from the 1738 preface to *L'Enfant prodigue* (1736), Mol., iii. 445).

[3] D19075 (12 Aug. 1774). This work also has an important bearing on the *Histoire de Jenni*. See René Démoris, 'Genèse et symbolique de l'*Histoire de Jenni, ou le sage et l'athée* de Voltaire', *SVEC* 199 (1981), 93–6.

As in *Il faut prendre un parti* (1772) he returns with sympathy to some Leibnizian arguments about the nature of God, in particular that He is subject to the laws of logic.[4] Sidrac tells Goudman (as Jesrad told Zadig) that for the chaplain to have married Miss Fidler: 'Il aurait fallu un monde tout différent du nôtre . . . Tout est enchaîné, et Dieu n'ira pas rompre la chaîne éternelle pour mon ami Goudman' (585). When Goudman objects that this makes the Almighty as much of a slave as he, Sidrac's response recalls the *Essais de théodicée* in the clearest terms:

Il est esclave de sa volonté, de sa sagesse, des propres lois qu'il a faites, de sa nature nécessaire. Il ne peut les enfreindre, parce qu'il ne peut être faible, inconstant, volage comme nous, et que l'Etre nécessairement éternel ne peut être une girouette. (586)

But whether we are all 'les marionnettes de la Providence' (584) is only one of the several issues which this *conte* addresses, and indeed, for all the serious echoes of Leibniz, it is given a fairly flippant treatment. In the manner of Cleopatra's nose, the Earl of Chesterfield's ears have played a crucial part in the Chaplain's fate by sparing him from marriage to Miss Fidler while yet ultimately securing for him both the desired living and the extra-conjugal favours of his syphilitic sweetheart. Given the arbitrariness with which these matters are finally resolved, the story offers a more lighthearted response to this metaphysical conundrum than the end of the 1752–3 version of *Zadig*, but the degree of bafflement remains the same.[5]

The eponymous ears point to another central theme in this *conte*, the value of conversation. In many of Voltaire's stories it is the eyes which serve as the most telling anatomical symbol of the struggle between reason and folly. From the one-eyed 'crocheteur' and the nearly blinded Zadig to Memnon and Pangloss, blindness and insight are favourite Voltairian poles. Here we have deafness and conversation. As has been noted several times, the supper-party constitutes the epitome of enlightened civilization for Voltaire. It provides a

---

[4] See Barber, *Leibniz in France*, 208. Barber's principal thesis is that Voltaire came in old age to hold views which 'are strikingly similar to those of the philosopher [Leibniz] whom he had so little understood and whose views, distorted by professed disciples, he had so long and so bitterly opposed' (243).

[5] Cf. E. D. James, 'Voltaire on Free Will', *SVEC* 249 (1987), who reaches a different conclusion after comparing it with the 1748 version.

pacific and pleasurable social activity in which anecdote and opinion may be exchanged to the mutual benefit of the participants. *L'Homme aux quarante écus* imitates its structure and proclaims its virtues: here the shared meal is the means of converting a priest into a 'philosophe' (580). As Sidrac says to Goudman: 'Venez dîner avec moi . . . nous causerons, et votre faculté pensante aura le plaisir de se communiquer à la mienne par le moyen de la parole, ce qui est une chose merveilleuse que les hommes n'admirent pas assez' (581). In a similar manner the Voltairian *conte* engages us in a dialogue with itself and makes us open our ears and our minds.

The structure of *Les Oreilles du comte de Chesterfield* reflects these dialogic delights. It begins in the first-person (of Goudman), but then moves to the third-person as an anonymous 'recording' narrator takes over and proceeds to present the ensuing conversations *verbatim*. Embedded in these conversations is M. Grou's first-person narrative describing his visit to Tahiti, making this *conte* the Voltairian equivalent of Diderot's *Supplément au voyage de Bougainville*.[6] Thanks to M. Grou, the *conte* is able to provide not only a journey round a number of philosophical issues but also another helping of 'l'univers en raccourci' to place beside those of *Candide*, *La Princesse de Babylone*, and *Les Lettres d'Amabed*. Grou himself 'a fait le tour du monde' (586) and so is able to contribute generously to a conversation which at once represents the Enlightenment ideal of unparochial broadmindedness and also pokes fun at what Voltaire knows to be the formula of so many of his own *contes*:

Le lendemain, les trois penseurs dînèrent ensemble; et, comme ils devenaient un peu plus gais sur la fin du repas, selon la coutume des philosophes qui dînent, on se divertit à parler de toutes les misères, de toutes les sottises, de toutes les horreurs qui affligent le genre animal, depuis les terres australes jusqu'auprès du pôle arctique, et depuis Lima jusqu'à Méaco. Cette diversité d'abominations ne laisse pas d'être fort amusante. C'est un plaisir que n'ont point les bourgeois casaniers et les vicaires de paroisse, qui ne connaissent que leur clocher, et qui croient que tout le reste de l'univers est fait comme Exchange-Alley à Londres, ou comme la rue de la Huchette à Paris. (587)

The spectacle of the universal problem of evil is now a diverting and educational antidote to the blinkered, deaf world of the parish pump.

---

[6] Of which the first version dates from 1772 and a revised version from 1778–9. Bougainville's own account of his voyage (15 Nov. 1766 to 16 Mar. 1769) entitled *Voyage autour du monde* appeared early in 1771.

As befits a story which calls on us to wonder at 'le moyen de la parole', the nature of language itself comes under scrutiny. As has already been seen, many of Voltaire's *contes* play more or less critically with the slipperiness of words, and this story is no exception. As Goudman, the dutiful reader of Locke, observes: 'Tous nos discours, à ce qu'il me semble, ont été fondés sur des équivoques' (582). Part of the delight of conversation — and of the *conte* — lies in exploiting these 'équivoques'. When Grou comments that 'Pour des anthropophages, j'avoue qu'on en regorge' (588) or hesitates to praise the alluring Queen of Tahiti as 'la première reine . . . des deux hémisphères' (590), the globe-trotting doctor is exhibiting a well-informed and original 'esprit'. This 'esprit' (from the Latin 'spiritus' meaning 'breath', as Goudman informs us: 582) is real and valuable: it breathes life into the conversation. 'Âme', on the other hand, from 'anima', is paradoxically a dead word, a term of metaphysical fiction which Sidrac professes not to understand. As Goudman accepts: 'Il est, au fond, ridicule de prononcer des mots qu'on n'entend pas' (582).[7]

At the same time Voltaire revels in using words whose meaning is all too clear. One of the principal unifying features in this story which appears so disparate is the constant juxtaposition of the spiritual and the physiological. This is true of the protagonists as a whole, of course, since the work turns on encounters between a clergyman and two physicians. But it is also present at other levels of the text and is introduced at the very beginning when Goudman goes in search of a living or 'cure' only to be dispatched to the Earl's doctor for a physical cure. Goudman has complained of 'pauvreté', the first syllable of which has presumably put his deaf interlocutor in mind of urinary need. Hence Sidrac 'se met incontinent [how else?] en devoir de me sonder' and proposes the removal of a gallstone: 'si j'ai la pierre, il me taillera très heureusement'; which in turn prompts further punning since this means that 'milord . . . avait voulu, selon sa générosité ordinaire, me faire tailler à ses dépens'. The stock situation of an impecunious man of the cloth being in need of sartorial assistance has received a novel, and physiological, twist.

This adumbrates the final set-piece conversation of the story (fol-

---

7   The etymologies of 'esprit' and 'âme' are examined at length by Voltaire in his article 'Esprit' in the *Dictionnaire philosophique*. See Mol., xix. 14–16.

lowing the debates on the nature of the soul and the question of freedom), which addresses the question: 'quel est le premier mobile de toutes les actions des hommes' (592). Goudman and Grou provide answers (respectively, 'l'amour et l'ambition' and 'l'argent') which have been illustrated at length in Voltaire's previous stories, notably *Candide*. Sidrac's reply is more basic: 'la chaise percée.' Where we began with a man applying for a cure of souls, we end with a philosophy of life in which the crucial element is the avoidance of constipation. Accordingly the 'mot de Cambronne' finally makes its appearance in the Voltairian *œuvre*, as we discover that what the business of life all comes down to in the end are 'ces intestins, s'il m'est permis de le dire . . . remplis de merde' (592). Not that we should be surprised, for between the initial diagnosis of faulty micturation and this final paean to morning defecation comes the lurid dismissal of the soul on the grounds of anatomical implausibility: 'je n'ai jamais pu comprendre comment un être immatériel, immortel, logeait pendant neuf mois inutilement caché dans une membrane puante entre de l'urine et des excréments' (583).[8]

'Vessie', 'cul', 'merde', 'prépuce', 'Phallus', 'les vaisseaux spermatiques': Voltaire's linguistic candour is particularly insistent in *Les Oreilles du comte de Chesterfield*. Indeed the 'oreilles' themselves also have the slang sense of 'testicules'.[9] Sidrac may be right that bowel motions are 'le premier mobile de toutes les actions des hommes', but the story itself suggests that sexual desire may be no less moving. Goudman is motivated by his fancy for Miss Fidler, while giving the Queen of Tahiti the pox would seem to be one of the perks of being a circumnavigator (591). In Tahiti sex is a very public affair; but whereas physicians like Sidrac reduce all human life to the physiological, the aptly named ruler Princess Obéira presides over a 'fête sacrée' (590) in which virginity is sacrificed in the most spiritually uplifting (and well-attended) of ceremonies.

'C'est à vous d'en tirer les conséquences' (590), remarks Grou at the end of his colourful traveller's tale. One possible conclusion is that the Tahitians are indulging in just the sort of practical worship which Sidrac himself advocates (586). Another is perplexity that God or 'ce qu'on appelle "la nature"' should have allowed life to be

---

[8] A favourite reflection of Voltaire's. Cf. *L'Homme aux quarante écus*, 443, and *Histoire de Jenni*, 637.
[9] See *RC*, 1206.

poisoned at source by venereal disease: 'c'est la plus énorme et la plus détestable de toutes les contradictions' (591). *Les Oreilles du comte de Chesterfield* presents many such contradictions between noble human aspiration and the sordid facts of life which bring men and women low. Should we conclude from the story as a whole, like Sidrac, that the answer to living is a balanced diet and bed at ten o'clock: 'Buvez chaud quand il gèle, buvez frais dans la canicule; rien de trop ni de trop peu en tout genre; digérez, dormez, ayez du plaisir, et moquez-vous du reste' (594)? Should we accept that we are not only puppets on the strings of an inscrutable 'fatalité' but also mere physical cogs in a gigantic, well-regulated machine: 'Animaux, végétaux, minéraux, tout me paraît arrangé avec poids, mesure, nombre, mouvement. Tout est ressort, levier, poulie, machine hydraulique, laboratoire de chimie, depuis l'herbe jusqu'au chêne, depuis la puce jusqu'à l'homme, depuis un grain de sable jusqu'à nos nuées' (579)? For the soul, that Christian answer to the nightmare of 'l'homme-machine', has been discredited and finds no place in 'le seul livre de métaphysique raisonnable qu'on ait jamais écrit' (582: i.e. Locke's *Essay Concerning Human Understanding*).

But the wit and learning of *Les Oreilles du comte de Chesterfield* give the lie to such materialism. Voltaire's 'ghost in the machine' is 'esprit' (582): and this *conte* demonstrates how the physiological entity transcends its diurnal need to evacuate and procreate by achieving humanity in the amusing and instructive intercourse of the table. Like *L'Homme aux quarante écus* it contains much discussion of the miracle of conception and birth (579–80; 583–4; 588–90), at the same time as it traces the 'birth' and development of a *philosophe* (here Sidrac's education of Goudman). Thus, in the new religion of Enlightenment, it fulfils a sacred role since, as Goudman himself says: 'Travailler à faire naître une créature raisonnable est l'action la plus noble et la plus sainte' (590). Sidrac and later Goudman quote several of Voltaire's own works as if they were gospel (579, 584); and Goudman ends up 'un des plus terribles prêtres de l'Angleterre' (595). As with Freind in the *Histoire de Jenni*, Voltairian deism has become fictionally synonymous with Anglicanism; and the Voltairian *conte* proclaims the new Jerusalem: 'Nous sommes dans un siècle de raison; nous trouvons aisément ce qui nous paraît la vérité, et nous osons la dire' (582). It would appear to be located in the vicinity of St James's Park (580).

HISTOIRE DE JENNI

In the *Histoire de Jenni, ou le sage et l'athée*, on the other hand, the new Jerusalem is proclaimed by a fictional amalgam of an Oxford Professor of Chemistry and the Headmaster of Westminster School.[10] Written probably between December 1774 and the following April, Voltaire's final *conte* was published by the Cramers in June or July 1775. Since the story seeks to equate atheism with immorality, it is perhaps not surprising that the unbelieving editors of the *Correspondance littéraire* should have echoed Mme d'Houdetot's view that 'M. de Voltaire retombe en jeunesse'.[11] It might have been fairer to say that the *Histoire de Jenni* marked a return to middle-age, since both the content and setting of the story provide strong echoes of the *Traité de métaphysique* and the *Lettres philosophiques*. It is as if the aged *philosophe*, beset by visions of anarchy and godlessness in a modern, rapidly changing world, had gone back to his intellectual roots in order to reaffirm his own position with greater confidence. England, in the shape of Newton, Locke, and Samuel Clarke, is where his own independent voyage of reason had begun: and England is where it ends, the promised land of deism, a nation inhabited by the perfect Freind and the reformed characters of Jenni and Birton.

While Voltaire had been particularly conscious of the need to preserve a united front against 'l'infâme', the increasingly militant campaign of atheist *philosophes* (Diderot, Grimm, d'Holbach) was causing him much concern. This atheism had recently received its fullest expression in d'Holbach's *Système de la nature*, which appeared in 1770. For Voltaire this new 'system' was no more acceptable than the materialism which he had rejected forty years earlier in the *Traité de métaphysique*. There he had made plain how he found the atheist account of Creation intellectually inadequate. Here in the *Histoire de Jenni* (and through the mouthpiece of Freind) he rejects d'Holbach's

---

[10] Jenni's father, M. Freind is based largely on John Freind (1675–1728), one of the leading physicians of his time. He was appointed to the Oxford Chair in 1704, but resigned to serve the Earl of Peterborough as doctor in Spain during the War of the Spanish Succession. He was elected to the Royal Society in 1712 and subsequently became MP for Launceston in 1722. His brother Robert, eight years his senior, was an Anglican clergyman and Headmaster of Westminster School. Unlike the fictional Freind they were not in any way related to William Penn (1644–1718), the Quaker and founder of Pennsylvania.

[11] Grimm *et al.*, *Correspondance littéraire* xi. 97.

thesis (expounded by Birton) that 'la nature fait tout, . . . la nature est tout' by proclaiming once more that 'tout est art sans aucune exception!' (632). The order in the universe cannot be the result of blind chance; it bespeaks a divine intelligence.

The dialogue between Freind and Birton is clearly the most important part of this *conte*, and in it Voltaire rehearses many of the religious issues and arguments which had preoccupied him since at least the 1730s.[12] Comparison with some earlier works reveals differences of emphasis and approach, but Voltaire's essential deist position remains much the same. Unlike in the *Traité de métaphysique* Clarke's metaphysics (in particular his version of the first cause argument) is soft-pedalled (630); the question whether matter is eternal or was created by God at a fixed moment is now left in abeyance (635). But the argument from design is once more asserted with conviction and is summarized in Freind's declaration: 'Pour savoir s'il est un Dieu, je ne vous demande qu'une chose, c'est d'ouvrir les yeux' (631). The problem of evil is handled in a number of ways by Freind, but his main strategy is to minimize physical evil and to stress the degree of human responsibility for both physical and moral evil: 'Tout le physique d'une mauvaise action est l'effet des lois générales imprimées par la main de Dieu à la matière; tout le mal moral de l'action criminelle est l'effet de la liberté dont l'homme abuse' (645). Physical evil is dismissed as 'accidents qui ont attaqué quelques roues de la machine de cet univers' (638), while the particular evil of disease is attributed in large measure to human abuse (for example, the pox, alcoholism). Such moral evils as war and colonial exploitation are clearly acknowledged, and the old Optimist argument that 'les maux particuliers forment le bien général' (642) is rejected. But the blame for such evils is laid squarely at the feet not of God but of human beings and their 'détestable usage de la liberté que ce grand Etre leur a donnée' (642).

Some aspects of the Birton–Freind dialogue appear to suggest that Voltaire's position has altered more radically. While Freind defines freedom in the Lockian form which Voltaire had adopted a quarter of a century earlier ('c'est-à-dire . . . la puissance d'exécuter leurs volontés': 642), the emphasis on the abuse of freedom as the principal reason for evil suggests not only an orthodox Christian outlook but also a return to the libertarian views expressed in the

---

[12]   For a fuller account see Pomeau, *La Religion de Voltaire*, 391–427.

Traité de métaphysique and rejected in the late 1740s. Moreover, when Freind speaks of 'la voix de votre conscience' (648) which instils a knowledge of good and evil in every human heart, he seems to be coming close not only to Rousseau (in particular the *Profession de foi du vicaire savoyard*) and to Christianity itself, but also to the concept of innate ideas which the empirical Voltaire had spent a lifetime denigrating. The possibility of divine punishment in an after-life is not rejected (because there is no evidence to the contrary), while the logic of the Pascalian wager (which Voltaire had scorned in the *Lettres philosophiques*) is adopted as a basis for ethics: 'Le meilleur parti que vous ayez à prendre est d'être honnête homme tandis que vous existez' (650).

Do Freind's statements constitute a change in Voltaire's position? Of course, it may be that Freind is not Voltaire's mouthpiece and that he is simply voicing the doctrine one might expect of an Anglican clergyman. But Freind is no orthodox Anglican, as his implicit denial of the divinity of Christ (607) suggests. Moreover Voltaire himself had come increasingly to acknowledge the value of Christ as a moral teacher. It does therefore seem that while Birton voices many of Voltaire's doubts, Freind represents his attempt to present a coherent deist position (though, as Freind himself says: 'Dieu me garde de faire un système': 651).

What one finds in the *Histoire de Jenni* is the Voltaire who wrote 'Si Dieu n'existait pas, il faudrait l'inventer'.[13] On the metaphysical level God had to exist (rather as on the political level so did the King) to guarantee order. Voltaire's belief in progress was founded on his faith in reason and in man's capacity to understand the world he lives in and to improve both it and himself. Take away the clock-maker, and you are left with blind nature and an irrational universe. Thus, unlike Diderot for example, he was loath to countenance the idea of nature as some kind of permanent laboratory of trial and error. On the moral and social level God had again to exist as a guarantee of order. As Freind says: 'La croyance d'un Dieu rémunér-ateur des bonnes actions, punisseur des méchantes, pardonneur des fautes légères, est donc la croyance la plus utile au genre humain' (653). Not for Voltaire the belief of Diderot and others that man-

---

[13] In the *Epître à l'auteur du livre des Trois Imposteurs* (1769), l. 22. The previous two lines read: 'Si les cieux, dépouillés de son empreinte auguste, / Pouvaient cesser jamais de le manifester'. See Mol., x. 403.

made laws, however unwieldy, could on their own regulate human behaviour for the greater good. What was needed was a celestial bogeyman to frighten the lower orders into submission.

To a modern eye this misanthropic conservatism sits ill with the image of Voltaire the great champion of tolerance and justice. Yet there is no doubt that it was the potential social consequences of atheism, more even than what he perceived as its metaphysical implausibility, which exercised the master of Ferney in his last years. The *Histoire de Jenni* is thus a desperate attempt to persuade his readership not only of God's existence but of the beneficial effects of a deist ethos. Such is this desperation that the literary quality of the *conte* may have suffered; but for the same reason the *conteur*'s art of persuasion is here all the more manifest. What makes the *Histoire de Jenni* interesting is the way in which Voltaire tries to use his trusty polemical devices against the grain of his own scepticism. But, as in the *Eloge historique de la raison*, it may turn out to be not quite his style to be on the side of the angels.

Like *Les Lettres d'Amabed* and *Les Oreilles du comte de Chesterfield*, the *Histoire de Jenni* is a story of conversion; not of a Brahmin into a very lapsed Catholic, or a priest into a *philosophe*, but of an atheist into a deist and a reprobate son into a gentleman. Central to these conversions is the figure of Freind, whose name, while historically founded, is as suggestive of English amiability as those of Chaplain Goudman (in *Les Oreilles*) and Dr Goodnatur'd Wellwisher, the putative author of the *Défense de milord Bolingbroke*.[14] In order to make friendly virtue sympathetic, Voltaire resorts to a series of contrasts which leave the reader (who, as ever, is also being converted) no other character with whom to identify but Freind. Broadly, the excesses of Catholic libertinage (doña Las Nalgas and doña Boca Vermeja) and theology (don Inigo y Medroso y Papalamiendo) are balanced by the excesses of atheist debauch (Mme Clive-Hart) and cynicism (Birton). As occupant of the sensible middle ground between these extremes, this hero, whom one might consider in fact rather excessively virtuous, thus becomes the very embodiment of his own (and, apparently, the Angel Gabriel's) maxim: 'Rien de trop' (640).

So, too, on the stylistic level Freind represents the voice of reason.

---

[14] See Démoris, 'Genèse et symbolique', 105–11, for an account of name symbolism in *Histoire de Jenni*.

In this most polyphonic of texts his level tones are contrasted with the casual wit of doña Las Nalgas and the sentimental excess of M. Sherloc, the supposed author of the *conte* as a whole. One might wish, perhaps, that Jenni's Spanish admirer had been entrusted with greater narrative responsibilities, for, as M. Sherloc himself recognizes: 'C'était une femme qui ne manquait pas d'un certain esprit, que les Espagnols appellent "agudeza"' (600). But the narrative strategy of the *Histoire de Jenni* is such that her (eminently Voltairian) narrative is decried as being 'trop libre et trop naïve': 'de tels écrits ne vont point jusqu'au cœur du sage' (598). Here Voltaire is explicit in his intention to persuade emotionally as well as (or even rather than) intellectually; which is exactly how Freind proposes to persuade Birton. He rejects the assistance of Clarke's metaphysical arguments because 'ils sont plus faits pour vous éclairer que pour vous toucher: je ne veux vous apporter que des raisons, qui peut-être parleront plus à votre cœur' (630).

But there is more than one way of appealing to the heart. Freind's approach seems the more acceptable by virtue of the contrast with the pompous and effusive style of M. Sherloc. As with Jenni's father, Voltaire may here have had a historical figure in mind: namely, Thomas Sherlock (1678–1761), Dean of Chichester and later Bishop of London, a Christian apologist and author of several works denouncing atheism. In order to win us over to Freind's side, his potential priggishness is made to fade into acceptability beside the absurdity of M. Sherloc's melodramatic sensibility:

Ecrasé de tant de coups si rapides et si multipliés, l'esprit bouleversé par des soupçons horribles que je chassais et qui revenaient, je me traîne dans la maison de la mourante [Miss Primerose] . . . Dévoré de ces pensées, j'entre en frissonnant . . . A ce mot, j'avoue qu'un torrent de larmes coula de mes yeux. (620)

Compared with these effusions Freind's repeated display of the stiff upper lip seems positively welcome rather than implausible or merely dull.

Unlike Freind M. Sherloc is also a rather peremptory expositor. Having been asked for details about Freind and his 'étrange fils', he assures his imaginary correspondent (in the first paragraph of the *conte*) that 'Vous serez aussi étonné que je l'ai été, et vous partagerez tous mes sentiments'. When he then introduces doña Las Nalgas's 'récit très fidèle', he observes with equal certainty: 'Vous la lirez sans scandale comme un portrait fidèle des mœurs du pays' (598). M. Sherloc would seem to be an army man who is used to being obeyed, even by his readers; whereas, by contrast, Freind's subsequent persuasion of Birton seems all the more subtle and courteous.

One further function of M. Sherloc is to voice an uncompromising condemnation of atheism. In the manner of an eighteenth-century Colonel Blimp, he displays a robust vocabulary of denunciation: 'une vie débordée et crapuleuse', 'leurs débauches', 'un nommé Warburton, méchant garnement très impudent', 'Un autre fou nommé Needham . . . Cet animal . . .' (614). M. Sherloc may apparently be anxious to convince his correspondent of the veracity of his narrative, not only in the reference to doña Las Nalgas's 'récit très fidèle' (597) but also in his insistence on the reliability of his sources: Freind's conversation with the Bachelier is offered in a 'précis fidèle . . . rédigé par Jacob Hulf, l'un des secrétaires de milord' (610–11), while he himself has dutifully sat down 'dans un coin' (629) and taken notes throughout the conversation between Birton and Freind. Yet this concern for the truth is belied by his taste for hyperbole, be it in his tear-jerking account of his visit to Miss Primerose or in his blustering condemnation of atheist delinquents. Or in his description of women, for M. Sherloc is also a hearty misogynist: 'On dit que c'est dans leurs cœurs que toutes les contradictions se rassemblent. C'est sans doute parce qu'elles ont été pétries originairement d'une de nos côtes' (617).

When, therefore, M. Sherloc proclaims that 'Le grand secret est de démontrer avec éloquence' (627), we may suspect that he understands this complimentary remark about Freind's powers of persuasion rather differently from its object. For Freind himself is shown to be eloquent in a much more convincing manner. Addressing the House of Commons in defence of the Earl of Peterborough's conduct of the Spanish Campaign, he produces a 'discours ferme et serré, sans aucun lieu commun, sans épithète, sans ce que nous appelons des phrases'. Instead of hectoring his audience into submission, he persuades through restraint and accuracy: 'on l'écoutait en silence; on ne l'interrompait qu'en disant: "Hear him, hear him: écoutez-le, écoutez-le" ' (613). Clearly he succeeds as much because of his manner as by his words, and he himself is very clear about the power of example: 'Les exemples corrigent bien mieux que les réprimandes' (616). Thus, by recommending mercy towards the Inquisitor Caracucarador, he succeeds in converting numerous Catalans to Anglicanism (602–3). His treatment of Jenni's creditor turns the latter into a paragon of generosity, while doubtless providing the young surgeon Cheselden with a role model for life (616). Freind's strategy of appealing to the heart is also Voltaire's, and in this cause, just as actions speak louder than words, so narrative convinces more readily than learned debate. Hence the importance of not dismissing the *Histoire de Jenni* as merely a dialogue masquerading as a *conte*. When we come to the central encounter between Freind and Birton, we have already been narratively persuaded of the former's moral worth and are now ready to side with him. Our allegiance is then reinforced as much by event as by argument, especially as we are led to identify with the reactions of Freind's audience. Thus at the first mention of 'ces mots d'infini, d'espace, d'Homère, de commentateurs' (630) they would all rather take a walk on deck; when they are presented with 'preuves ... plus palpables' (633), they are ready to accept Freind's case for the existence of God; but the imminence of a discussion of the problem of evil clearly calls for a cup of tea (635). These humanizing responses make us warm to Freind's lay companions: not for them the 'mots un peu scientifiques, que des gens nés sur les montagnes bleues ne pouvaient entendre aussi commodément que des docteurs d'Oxford et de Cambridge' (630).

As Voltaire knew, not every reader of the *Histoire de Jenni* would have an Oxford doctorate. The highbrow content of the Freind–Birton dialogue has to be leavened with humorous aside and comforting chapter division. The arguments employed by Freind may or may not stand up — and several do not — but if his lowbrow companions accept them, then we can safely follow their example. Most especially, of course, if even Birton accepts them, then they must be right. Birton's response indeed gives the game away: 'je crois en Dieu et en vous' (654). He has been persuaded by Freind's person more than by his arguments. As a result he becomes simply a less demonstrative version of the North American Indians who revere Freind for his lineage as if he were the son of God: 'Un fils de Penn! que je baise ses pieds et ses mains, et ses parties sacrées de la génération' (625–6). Freind has 'civilized' Birton just as his supposed grandfather civilized the Indians of Pennsylvania. The example of Parouba's good sense is thus a further narrative means of persuading us that atheists are unreformed savages.

Birton's conversion, of course, itself serves as an example to Jenni, and it causes this shadowy eponymous hero with a girl's name once more to accept paternal authority. Said to have been 'né sensible et avec beaucoup d'esprit' (617), Jenni first appears in the *conte* like a naked Adam, with arms and legs to match the Belvedere Apollo, the face of Adonis, and the trunk of Hercules (599). As in so many of Voltaire's *contes* this youthful paradise proves ephemeral, and the harmless temptations of the Spanish doñas are succeeded by corruption at the hands of the onomastically sinister Clive-Hart. This murderous and mannish Eve is the instrument of his Fall, from which he is finally redeemed by Freind, the 'fils de Penn', and restored to his proper place in the divine and social order of things. To be saved is to become a gentleman: 'Jenni et [Birton] sont aujourd'hui les plus honnêtes gens de l'Angleterre' (655).

Jenni's 'conversion', like Birton's, has been the result of a conversation, which, like the supper-party, is the Enlightenment equivalent of the Indians' pipe of peace (626). Indeed, following his encounter with Parouba, Freind 'trumps' the latter's reference to the 'calumet de l'adoration' by summoning up 'une trentaine de jambons, autant de grands pâtés et de poulardes à la daube, deux cents gros flacons de vin de Pontac ...' (626). Just as later Freind's astronomy lesson supplements Parouba's natural religion (646), so here Old World commensality replaces primitive Indian custom, and the civilized (and civilizing) Freind seems able to go one better even than the Almighty, who is powerless to reward English virtue with a heaven-sent consignment of best burgundy (645). Jenni's moment of grace comes, in the last chapter of the *conte*, in a final act of repentance as the memory of Primerose prompts him to confess his guilt to his father. In a remarkable Voltairian transformation of the theology of the Eucharist, Jenni's fallen state is presented as a lack of appetite: 'On soupa; mais Jenni ne put souper: il se tenait à l'écart' (654). Following his confession he is readmitted to the communion of 'honnêtes hommes', along with Birton and his atheist companions: 'L'excellent Freind leur a servi de père à tous' (655). God the Son has now become God the Father.

For throughout the story Freind seems to display many divine attributes, from his beneficence and seeming omnipotence to his refusal to interfere with the laws of nature:

Un bon père ne doit être ni le tyran de son fils, ni son mercure. La fornication entre deux personnes libres a été peut-être autrefois une espèce de droit naturel dont Jenni peut jouir avec discrétion sans que je m'en mêle; je ne le

gêne pas plus sur ses maîtresses que sur son dîner et sur son souper ...
(612)

By the same token Freind's description of a non-interventionist God
sounds almost like a self-portrait:

Sa providence générale serait ridicule, si elle descendait dans chaque moment
à chaque individu; et cette vérité est si palpable que jamais Dieu ne punit
sur-le-champ un criminel par un coup éclatant de sa toute-puissance: il laisse
luire son soleil sur les bons et sur les méchants. (645)

This is exactly how Freind responds to Jenni's duel with his creditor:
'Je lui demandai ... s'il ne ferait pas venir son fils chez lui, s'il ne
lui représenterait pas ses fautes. "Non, dit-il, je veux qu'il les sente
avant que je lui en parle"' (616).

The *Histoire de Jenni, ou le sage et l'athée* is thus an object-lesson
in the art of persuasion, and the reader, no less than Birton and
Jenni, is subjected to a number of insidious pressures. On the one
hand, we are led to see atheism as a form of savagery and even
bestiality (614, 652). It is identified as the diabolical cause of Jenni's
Fall from innocence, and it is associated with poison — in Clive-
Hart's murders and during the Italian Renaissance ('Il fut aussi commun d'empoisonner que de donner à souper': 652) — as well as disease: 'J'ai toujours remarqué qu'on peut guérir un athée' (653). It is
a perversion of free-thinking: 'l'athée est un homme d'esprit qui se
trompe, mais qui pense par lui-même' (653). At the same time we
are led to see Freind as both Christ and God. Indeed just as Freind
plays God to the atheists, so God is 'le seul frein des hommes puiss-
ants ... le seul frein des hommes qui commettent adroitement les
crimes secrets' (653). The *Histoire de Jenni* is thus Voltaire's Gospel
of Deism, in which God, both friend and 'frein', assumes a human
form and saves Everyman from 'l'athéisme et le fanatisme ... les
deux pôles d'un univers de confusion et d'horreur' (653). The teaching of this gospel is straightforward and differs not one iota from
the message of the *Lettres philosophiques* written forty years earlier:
'croyez un Dieu bon, et soyez bons. C'est tout ce que les grands
législateurs Locke et Penn demandent à leurs peuples' (653). M.
Sherloc, for his part, is in no doubt as to the final lesson we should
draw from the story: 'Vous conviendrez qu'un sage peut guérir des
fous.' Coming from him, that sounds like an order: but, this being
the last sentence of Voltaire's last *conte*, we may already have been
persuaded of the truth which it proclaims.

Conclusion

... les fables ont tout dit.

(Dict. phil., 272)

Speaking at the Sorbonne in December 1944 to mark the two hundred and fiftieth anniversary of Voltaire's birth, Paul Valéry reflected on the significance of this grand occasion:

Nous savons bien que l'objet profond de cette assemblée est moins de commémorer la naissance d'un homme illustre, de rendre hommage à cet homme et à son œuvre, si considérable et étincelante soit-elle, que d'exalter entre nous, Français, ce qui fut sa passion la plus constante et la plus généreuse, celle de la liberté de l'esprit. Nous savons ce que vaut cette liberté. Nous savons ce qu'elle coûte.

For Valéry, deep in the shadow of the Second World War, Voltaire's great virtue was to have defended humanity against inhuman ideology, to have fostered the humane by appealing to what is most essentially human:

Il invoque la raison, mais *il tire au cœur*. Qu'est-ce qui résisterait à l'alliance de la vérité et de la pitié? L'une et l'autre travaillent en l'homme ce qu'il a de plus humain, ce qui vit en lui quand il est libre d'être soi, quand il est sans haine et sans crainte . . .[1]

But compare Isaiah Berlin. In his collection of essays *The Crooked Timber of Humanity*, Berlin sets out his well-known opinion that the seeds of the Holocaust and twentieth-century totalitarianism are to be found in the eighteenth-century cult of reason. For him the rationalists' faith in systematic thinking and in the possibility of successful progress towards a perfect society blinded them to the needs and limitations of humanity and led in the following century to the German thought (Hegel, Marx, Nietzsche) which has, in its subsequent application (or misapplication), cast a massive blight over our own. Finding common ground between the reactionary Joseph de Maistre and libertarian Voltaire, Berlin writes:

---

[1] Valéry, 'Voltaire', in *Œuvres*, 2 vols. (Paris, 1957–60), i. 524, 525.

Their ideas may have strictly contradicted one another, but the quality of mind is often exceedingly similar . . . They stand for the dry light against the flickering flame, they are implacably opposed to all that is turbid, misty, gushing, impressionistic . . . They are ruthlessly deflationary writers, contemptuous, sardonic, genuinely heartless, and, at times, genuinely cynical. Beside their icy, smooth, clear surface Stendhal's prose is romantic, and Flaubert's writings are an imperfectly drained marsh. Marx, Tolstoy, Sorel, Lenin are — in the cast of their minds (not their ideas) — their true successors.[2]

Valéry and Berlin are eloquent modern spokesmen for the deeply antithetical reactions which have generally characterized the reception of Voltaire. On the one hand, there is Voltaire the human rights campaigner, the sceptic with a heart; on the other, the demonic monkey whom de Maistre himself created in *Les Soirées de Saint-Pétersbourg* and who so upset Mme de Staël and Victor Hugo. In every case, however, one notes the tendency to pass beyond the Voltairian text to Voltaire as the representative of some particular tendency. Of course, this says much for the stature of Voltaire as a historical figure; and it is a measure of Voltaire's profound engagement with the realities of his day — and of the enduring relevance of this engagement — that he, perhaps more than any other French writer (including Rousseau), should so continue to be treated as an ideological football. Or, as Voltaire himself preferred it, like some flying fish: 's'il s'élève un peu, les oiseaux le dévorent; s'il plonge, les poissons le mangent.'[3] But what conclusions can be drawn specifically from a consideration of his *contes*?

The present study has argued that Voltaire's cast of mind was essentially narrative and that his *contes* represent an ideal match of medium and mentality. *Pace* René Pomeau, they are not merely the peripheral outbursts of an irritable soul: nor are they simply, as Jacques Van den Heuvel would have it, quasi-confessional resolutions of inner turmoil.[4] Pomeau's view merely perpetuates eigh-

---

[2] 'Joseph de Maistre and the Origins of Fascism', in *The Crooked Timber of Humanity. Chapters in the History of Ideas*, ed. Henry Hardy (London, 1990), 91–174 (159). This essay was almost complete in 1960 and has since been only slightly revised (see p. x). The title of the volume is taken from Kant: '[A]us so krummem Holze, als woraus der Mensch gemacht ist, kann nichts ganz Gerades gezimmert werden.' (Out of timber so crooked as that from which man is made, nothing entirely straight can be fashioned.)

[3] *Dict. phil.*, 255 ('Lettres, Gens de lettres ou lettrés').

[4] See René Pomeau, *Voltaire par lui-même* (Paris, s.d. [1959]), 67: 'en marge de l'histoire, Voltaire a inventé des œuvres de fiction, tragédies, contes, facéties, qui sont les exutoires de son humeur'; and *Romans et contes*, ed. Pomeau: 'Voltaire n'écrit ses

teenth-century reluctance to grant intellectual weight to narrative fiction, while Van den Heuvel's heavily biographical approach occludes the question of reader response. Voltaire's *contes* were written above all to be read, and they constitute perhaps his most effective attempts to undermine the 'fables' by which men have sought to explain and govern the lives of others.

The Voltaire who emerges from these *contes* is 'ruthlessly deflationary' of humbug but ever mindful of human suffering, of the problem of evil. No less than Isaiah Berlin, Voltaire is an implacable opponent of German metaphysics; and, like Kant, he too is aware of 'the crooked timber of humanity'. As we have seen, his stories are all about the ways in which human experience exceeds every attempt to theorize about it or to legislate for it. The smoothness of their surface is not the smoothness of ice but of urbanity, of a wit that can indeed be contemptuous and sardonic, but also of a wit that warms to the complexity of human life, to its conflicts and its paradoxes, of a wit that also has the wit to eschew any 'final solution'.

It is certainly true that Voltaire opposed 'all that is turbid, misty, gushing, impressionistic', but with good reason. These are the 'fables' which his own narratives seek to destroy: obscurantist religion and superstition, the gush of baseless eloquence and harangue, the muddled, slipshod thinking of those who refuse or are unable to 'voir les choses comme elles sont'. His enemies are Berlin's enemies: the 'systems' by which the rationalists thought to explain the world and solve its problems, but at the expense of humanity itself. 'Je ne veux point être philosophe', says Dondindac in the *Dictionnaire philosophique*, 'je veux être homme';[5] and he speaks for Voltaire. Everywhere one looks in Voltaire's works, one finds a profound awareness of the limits of reason coupled with a deep-seated concern for the future of humanity. 'La philosophie ne rend point raison de tout', he repeats as once more he confronts the conundrum of matter.[6] Instead of producing metaphysical answers he seeks to establish a dialogue with his fellow human beings. 'Un livre doit

---

récits que par passades: comme si, en de certains moments, il lui fallait calmer ses irritations en leur ouvrant cette issue'. (12) Van den Heuvel, *Voltaire dans ses contes*, 10.

[5] *Dict. phil.*, 166 ('Dieu').
[6] *Dict. phil.*, 277 ('Matière').

être, comme un homme sociable, fait pour les besoins des hommes.'[7] The *Traité de métaphysique* begins not with 'S'il y a un Dieu' but with 'Doutes sur l'homme', and he tells Frederick quite categorically that 'l'humanité . . . est le principe de toutes mes pensées': 'C'est l'homme que j'examine.'[8] Of course, as Roland Barthes has argued, there are problems with this view of a humanist Voltaire. There is force in Barthes's contention that Voltaire's onslaught on 'systems' is a polemical device allowing him to present his own ideology as an independence of mind:

En opposant continûment intelligence et intellectualité, en se servant de l'une pour ruiner l'autre, en réduisant les conflits d'idées à une sorte de lutte manichéenne entre la Bêtise et l'Intelligence, en assimilant tout système à la Bêtise et toute liberté d'esprit à l'Intelligence, Voltaire a fondé le libéral-isme dans sa contradiction. Comme système du non-système, l'anti-intellectualisme élude et gagne sur les deux tableaux, joue à un perpétuel tourniquet entre la mauvaise foi et la bonne conscience, le pessimisme du fond et l'allégresse de la forme, le scepticisme proclamé et le doute ter-roriste.[9]

But can Voltairian scepticism be so easily dismissed as mere bour-geois liberalism, as the 'happy' proclamation of intellectual freedom while the masses remain sunk in abject poverty and ignorance? Although condemning Voltaire for his naïve, pre-Hegelian view of History, Barthes himself fails adequately to situate Voltaire in his historical context; and in tendentiously minimizing the stature of his opponents (the Church, the Jansenists, the Parlements) as prehistoric monsters doomed to destruction, he also minimizes the powerful and radical corrosiveness of Voltaire's irony. Voltaire's 'humanism' is not ideologically innocent, but nor is it simply bad faith.

And nor is it simplistic. To say that 'la raison consiste à voir toujours les choses comme elles sont' may seem so, and clearly such a definition of reason begs an enormous question. To a post-structuralist eye such an assertion of 'presence' seems positively quaint, yet Voltaire is simply arguing the need for intellectual rigour. As most of his *contes* demonstrate, it is far from easy to see 'how

---

[7] *Le Sottisier de Voltaire*, ed. Léouzon le Duc (Paris, 1880), 61.

[8] D1376 (c. 15 Oct. 1737).

[9] 'Le dernier des écrivains heureux' (originally published as the introduction to an edition of Voltaire's *Romans et contes* (Paris, 1958)), in Roland Barthes, *Essais critiques* (Paris, 1964), 100.

things are': the nature of Creation, the problem of evil, providence, these are some of the unsolved riddles with which the human mind must continue to grapple. For Voltaire reason consists first and foremost in seeing 'how things are not', in exposing the flaws in the theories and assumptions which his reader may be willing to accept. His scepticism — and his *contes* — constitute a thorough-going critique of all manner of assertions of the 'truth', and in this respect his writing is no different from another, more modern 'système du non-système', the deconstruction of Derrida. Voltairian reason is also a willed dissent, a dismantling of edifices: and in its own way it, too, would alert us to the snares and illusions of the word.

As we have seen, both in the paradigmatic *L'Homme aux quarante écus* and in most of the other *contes*, narrative maketh man. Voltaire's stories trace the emergence of a rich and provisional humanity from the ashes of exploded theories. At the same time, in constantly inviting his reader to do half the work, to see the 'vérité fine' beneath the plot, to 'translate' the allegory into his or her own reality, Voltaire is encouraging an attitude of mind quite contrary to the humble passivity with which the Christian must accept the word of God or the loyal subject obey a royal edict. Voltaire's texts encourage participation and debate. By their informality and pseudo-orality they subvert the very notion of a secular literary or philosophical canon: be it in the *conversazzione* at the end of *Micromégas*, or in Pococuranté's library, or at the home of Monsieur André, the 'graves auteurs' have a hard time of it, from Aristotle to Zoroaster. But the *conte* itself, a mere 'facétie' or 'rogaton', has no such pretensions. It is neither the slave nor the product of the Academy and all its neo-classical rules. It is candid.

At the same time the Voltairian *conte* subverts fiction itself. It shows that the worlds of chivalric romance and the Oriental tale are even further removed from reality than its own absurd Punch and Judy world with its only too visible puppeteer. It is the more real for being demonstrably unreal. It defamiliarizes the familiar, renders the world and its inhabitants strange, ready to be seen and judged afresh. We are offered succeeding images of the human condition, as it were, from both ends of a telescope or microscope: as, in turn, it enlarges (through exaggeration and accumulation) and reduces (by brevity and understatement) the specimens and behaviour under observation. It stimulates an adjustment of focus by the incongruous juxtapositions and combinations of the burlesque.[10] It undermines the univocity of language by puns and the literalization of metaphor. It manipulates our sense of time.[11]

As fictions denouncing fiction, Voltaire's *contes* are not only central to Voltaire's intellectual and polemical endeavours, they also belong squarely in the tradition of self-conscious ironic narrative which has dominated French and European fiction since the Renaissance. For, as the phenomenon of nineteenth-century realism recedes into the past, it has become possible to see this as an aberration rather than a culmination. It has been thought, and by some is still thought, that the imaginative creation of believable alternative worlds is the sole, proper, and unproblematic function of a novel. When Joyce could 'only' compose a novel (*Ulysses*) by pastiching Greek epic and sending up English period styles in chapter after chapter; when Proust could 'only' write a novel about how to write a novel; and when Gide, who could hardly bring himself to write a novel at all, writhed in self-conscious textual agony when he finally did; then the genre itself was duly pronounced 'dead'. But this self-reference is, as Bakhtin has persuasively argued,[12] the very life-blood of the novel. As a protean genre comparatively free from the prescriptions of neo-classicism, the novel has long been a forum for 'dialogue' between succeeding and conflicting discourses and registers, or ways of figuring the world in language. It is, as it were, a melting-pot of fictions, in which myths are constantly being demythified and reassembled, and in which the power or 'truth' of any particular novel's own discourse consists in the subtlety and provisionality with which this polyphony (or 'heteroglossia') is orchestrated. When Cervantes takes on the world of chivalric romance (in *Don Quixote*), or Flaubert dismantles the world of Walter Scott (in *Madame Bovary*), or Stendhal turns the ideology of the parvenu novel upside down (in *Le Rouge et le noir*), they are participating in a continuing process of renewal

---

[10] See R. J. Howells, 'The Burlesque as a Philosophical Principle in Voltaire's *contes*', in R. J. Howells *et al.* (eds.), *Voltaire and his World. Studies Presented to W. H. Barber* (Oxford, 1985).

[11] See Edwin P. Grobe, 'Discontinuous Aspect in Voltaire's *Candide*', *Modern Language Notes*, 82 (1967), and 'Aspectual Parody in Voltaire's *Candide*', *Symposium*, 21 (1967). See also R. A. Sayce, *Style in French Prose. A Method of Analysis* (Oxford, 1953), 119.

[12] See either *Esthétique et théorie du roman*, tr. Daria Olivier (Paris, 1978), or *The Dialogic Imagination. Four Essays by M. M. Bakhtin*, ed. Michael Holquist (Austin, Tex., and London, 1981).

and mental liberation from cliché and stereotype. They are heirs to Rabelais's carnival.

So, too, is the Voltairian *conte*. Of all eighteenth-century French fiction it comes closest, along with Diderot's *Jacques le fataliste*, to this tradition. The opposite tradition is represented by *La Nouvelle Héloïse*. In his second preface Rousseau describes his work as 'une longue romance, dont les couplets pris à part n'ont rien qui touche, mais dont la suite produit à la fin son effet'.[13] Here we see the beginnings of the nineteenth-century ploy of using length to create and sustain the reader's illusion that he is inhabiting a real, alternative world, a ploy which Balzac was to supplement with his device of recurring characters. Rousseau's strategy, clearly, is to lure the reader into the moral universe of his novel and, by sheer duration, to convince the reader first of the normality, then of the exemplary status, of his Swiss protagonists. Rousseau's novel fits the Bakhtinian scheme in so far as it takes on Samuel Richardson's 'mythical' equation of chastity and moral rectitude and presents an alternative ethos wherein the moral regeneration of a fallen woman constitutes a higher form of virtue.[14] But *La Nouvelle Héloïse* lies outside the ironic tradition because, precisely, it would persuade us that the world of Clarens is not a fiction.

Voltaire's *contes*, however, like the novels of Flaubert, Gide, and, to a limited extent, Stendhal, are notorious for keeping the reader at a distance. The puppet-like nature of the characters reduces our empathy because of their apparent lack of humanity:[15] hence in part the recurrent condemnation of a 'genuinely heartless' Voltaire. But whereas the belief that the human protagonists of a fiction are 'real' may have the effect of allowing the reader to use this consequent 'otherness' as an excuse for refusing further identification when the reading-process is at an end, the allegorical status of Voltaire's characters constantly throws us back on our own situation by requiring us to flesh out the symbolism with our own experience. It is easy enough for a complacent reader — however paternal or mercenary

---

[13] *Œuvres complètes*, eds. Gagnebin and Raymond, ii. 18.
[14] See Angelica Goodden, *The Complete Lover. Eros, Nature, and Artifice in the Eighteenth-Century French Novel* (Oxford, 1989), 6.
[15] Cf. Lessing's hypothesis in his *Abhandlungen über die Fabeln* that animals are traditionally used in fable not only to provide a form of easily identified shorthand for human character traits but also to minimize the reader's (or listener's) compassion so that the 'message' is the more clearly communicated for not being clouded by sentiment.

— to deny any possible resemblance to Goriot and Grandet; but how easily can one deny that Voltaire's Everyman (Zadig, Candide, the Ingénu) is a version of ourselves? As Pangloss and Cunégonde's brother exclaim upon being recognized by Candide and Cacambo: 'C'est nous-mêmes, c'est nous-mêmes' (224). But the humanity of Voltaire's *contes* lies not so much in the lessons which they allegorically contain as in the response which they seek to elicit in us. Like the phoenix in *La Princesse de Babylone*, or M. André, or the Serpent in *Le Taureau blanc*, the Voltairian *conte* performs a therapeutic as well as an educational function. Its comedy springs not from cruel dispassion but from spirited resilience; and its presentation of conflict is intended less to stir the partisan than to breed an attitude of judicious tolerance and a taste for plurality and relativity — in short, to 'former l'esprit et le cœur'. It would effect a cure from the diseases of prejudice, narrow-mindedness, and intellectual timidity by subjecting its reader to the skilfully modulated vicissitudes of narrative, to a massage of the mind. 'Tout homme peut s'instruire', declares milord Boldmind to comte Médroso (an agent of the Spanish Inquisition) in the *Dictionnaire philosophique*.[16] 'Il ne tient qu'à vous d'apprendre à penser', he tells Médroso after a few drinks: 'vous êtes né avec de l'esprit . . . osez penser par vous-même.' Such is the message of Voltaire's *contes*, just as it will be the message some nine years later of Kant's short essay 'Was ist Aufklärung?': 'Sapere aude'.[17]

In this essay Kant distinguishes between an enlightened ('aufgeklärten') age and an age of enlightenment ('Aufklärung'). Perhaps there never has been nor ever will be an enlightened age, but only — at best — a continuing process of enlightenment. Kant's caution against complacency has proved its worth, not least in the recent case of Salman Rushdie's *The Satanic Verses*. As Philippe Sollers has commented, the rise of Islamic fundamentalism has caught us napping in the West:

nous dormions un peu, il faut l'avouer . . . nous étions à peu près sûrs de notre Raison, nous préférions même ironiser sur elle, après tout les Lumières sont bien limitées, nos penseurs sophistiqués nous en ont montré le sim-

---

[16]   *Dict. phil.*, 261 ('Liberté de penser', which article dates from 1765).

[17]   'Was ist Aufklärung?', in Kant, *Werke*, 6 vols. (Frankfurt am Main, 1964), vi. 53–61: 'Sapere aude! Habe Mut, dich deines eigenen Verstandes zu bedienen! ist also der Wahlspruch der Aufklärung' (Dare to know! Have the courage to use your own mind! is thus the motto of the Enlightenment) (53).

plisme à côté de l'inconscient, de la déconstruction, de l'epistémê, de la structure, de la réévaluation du sacré ou du retour au Talmud (Sartre compris). Nous pouvions, n'est-ce pas, *nous payer ce luxe.*

Sollers is no bourgeois liberal, yet it is still the value of the human individual which he asserts against the new inquisitors. Why, he asks, have they chosen to attack not a philosophy or a revolutionary theory or a scientific idea but a *novel*, 'un ouvrage de *fiction* . . . une rêverie subjective'?

Mais justement: c'est l'individu qu'il s'agit désormais de nier, dans son langage même, et pour cela le contrôle ou l'exténuation de la littérature s'impose . . . Voulez-vous savoir ce qu'ils ressentent? Qu'un individu c'est un livre, un roman. Un tel 'objet' échappe, il se passe de *un à un*.[18]

Sollers's remarks point to the continuing relevance and value of Voltaire's scepticism, and in particular of his 'fallen fables'. Indeed if one looks at Rushdie's defence of *The Satanic Verses*, one finds him describing his own literary ambitions in terms which might have been penned by Voltaire himself:

The Satanic Verses celebrates hybridity, impurity, intermingling, the transformation that comes of new and unexpected combinations of human beings, cultures, ideas, politics, movies, songs. It rejoices in mongrelisation and fears the absolutism of the Pure . . . Throughout human history, the apostles of purity, those who have claimed to possess a total explanation, have wrought havoc among mere mixed-up human beings . . . What does this novel dissent from? Certainly not from people's right to faith, though I have none. It dissents most clearly from imposed orthodoxies *of all types*, from the view that the world is quite clearly This and not That. It dissents from the end of debate, of dispute, of dissent.[19]

Here, is Kant's 'crooked timber of humanity'. Here, *mutatis mutandis*, is Voltaire's *conte*: the mongrel genre, the hybrid of fable, Platonic dialogue, and allegorical journey, the enemy of 'pure' systems and tyrannical *doxa*, the tale of a Serpent, the Satanic *conte*.

Three centuries after the birth of Voltaire, the need for such literature is no less imperative than it ever was. 'Ah! s'il nous faut des fables, que ces fables soient du moins l'emblème de la vérité!' (318). As we read Voltaire's *contes* today, the quaint figures of the

---

[18] 'Journal', *L'Infini*, 28 (1989–90), 41–2.
[19] Salman Rushdie, 'In Good Faith', *Independent on Sunday*, 4 Feb. 1990.

mufti, the inquisitor, and the physiocrat begin all too rapidly to lose their antique air and to emerge as glaring emblems of a modern truth. Voltaire's fables of reason still have a story to tell.

VOLTAIRE'S CONTES

	Date of composition	Date of publication
Le Crocheteur borgne	?c.1715	1774
Cosi-Sancta	?c.1715	1784
Micromégas	?1738/9; 1750–1	1751
Le Monde comme il va	?1739; ?1746–7	1748
Zadig ou la destinée	1746–7	1748
Memnon ou la sagesse humaine	1748–9	1749
Lettre d'un turc	?late 1740s	1750
Songe de Platon	?1737/8; 1752/3–6	1756
Histoire des voyages de Scarmentado	1753–4	1756
Les Deux Consolés	1756	1756
Candide ou l'optimisme	1757–8	1759
Histoire d'un bon brahmin	1759	1761
Pot-pourri	1761–2; 1764	1765
Le Blanc et le noir	?1763–4	1764
Jeannot et Colin	?1763–4	1764
Petite digression	?1738; ?1766	1766
Aventure indienne	?1766	1766
L'Ingénu	?1764; 1766	1767
La Princesse de Babylone	1767	1768
L'Homme aux quarante écus	1767	1768
Les Lettres d'Amabed	?1753–4; 1768–9	1769
Le Taureau blanc	?1766; 1771–3	1773–4
Aventure de la mémoire	?1772	1775
Eloge historique de la raison	1774	1775
Les Oreilles du comte de Chesterfield	1773–5	1775
Histoire de Jenni ou le sage et l'athée	?1774–5	1775

SELECT BIBLIOGRAPHY

I. THE WORKS OF VOLTAIRE

A. Collected Editions

Œuvres complètes, ed. Louis Moland (52 vols.; Paris, 1877–85).
Les Œuvres complètes de Voltaire. The Complete Works of Voltaire, ed. T. Besterman, later W. H. Barber, later W. H. Barber and Ulla Kölving (Geneva, Banbury, and Oxford, 1968–   ).
Romans et contes, ed. Henri Bénac (Paris, s.d. [1949]).
Romans et contes, ed. René Pomeau (Paris, 1966).
Romans et contes, ed. Frédéric Deloffre and Jacques Van den Heuvel (Paris, 1979).
Romans et contes I. Zadig et autres contes, ed. Frédéric Deloffre in collaboration with Jacques Van den Heuvel (Paris, 1992)
Romans et contes II. Candide et autres contes, ed. Frédéric Deloffre in collaboration with Jacques Van den Heuvel (Paris, 1992)
Mélanges, ed. Jacques Van den Heuvel (Paris, 1961).
Œuvres historiques, ed. René Pomeau (Paris, 1957).

B. Individual Editions

Candide, ed. J. H. Brumfitt (Oxford, 1968).
Candide, ed. Christopher Thacker (Geneva, 1968).
Candide, ed. André Magnan (Paris, 1969; rev. edn. 1984).
Candide, ed. Jean Goldzink (Paris, s.d. [1989]).
Dictionnaire philosophique, ed. René Pomeau (Paris, 1964).
Essai sur les mœurs, ed. René Pomeau (2 vols.; Paris, 1963).
Le Philosophe ignorant, ed. J. L. Carr (London, 1965).
Le Sottisier de Voltaire, ed. Léouzon le Duc (Paris, 1880).
Le Taureau blanc, ed. René Pomeau (Paris, 1957).
Lettres philosophiques, ed. Frédéric Deloffre (Paris, 1986).
'L'Ingénu' and 'Histoire de Jenni', ed. J. H. Brumfitt and M. I. Gerard Davies (Oxford, 1960).
Traité de métaphysique (1734), ed. H. Temple Patterson (Manchester, 1937).
Zadig ou la destinée, ed. Georges Ascoli, edn. rev. Jean Fabre (2 vols.; Paris, 1962).
Zadig and other stories, ed. H. T. Mason (Oxford, 1971).

II. OTHER PRIMARY SOURCES

FONTENELLE, BERNARD LE BOVIER DE, *De l'origine des fables (1724)*, ed. J.-R. Carré (Paris, 1932).

—— *Entretiens sur la pluralité des mondes. Digression sur les anciens et les modernes*, ed. Robert Shackleton (Oxford, 1955).

—— *Nouveaux dialogues des morts*, ed. Jean Dagen (Paris, 1971).

GRIMM, FRÉDÉRIC-MELCHIOR, et al., *Correspondance littéraire, philosophique et critique* (16 vols.; Paris, 1877–82).

KANT, EMMANUEL, 'Was ist Aufklärung?', in *Werke* (6 vols.; Frankfurt am Main, 1964).

LEIBNIZ, GOTTFRIED WILHELM VON, *Essais de théodicée sur la bonté de Dieu, la liberté de l'homme et l'origine du mal*, ed. J. Brunschwig (Paris, 1969).

PASCAL, BLAISE, *Œuvres complètes*, ed. Louis Lafuma (Paris, 1963).

POPE, ALEXANDER, *Les Principes de la morale et du goût [Essay on Man]*, tr. abbé du Resnel, 2nd edn. (London, 1750).

ROUSSEAU, JEAN-JACQUES, *Œuvres complètes*, eds. Bernard Gagnebin and Marcel Raymond (4 vols.; Paris, 1959–69).

III. STUDIES ON VOLTAIRE

ADAMS, D. J., *La Femme dans les contes et les romans de Voltaire* (Paris, 1974).

BARBER, W. H., *Leibniz in France from Arnauld to Voltaire. A Study in French Reactions to Leibnizianism, 1670–1760* (Oxford, 1955).

—— 'The Genesis of Voltaire's *Micromégas*', *French Studies*, 11 (1957), 1–15.

—— *Voltaire: 'Candide'* (London, 1960).

BARTHES, ROLAND, 'Le dernier des écrivains heureux', in *Essais critiques* (Paris, 1964), 94–100.

BELAVAL, YVON, 'L'esprit de Voltaire', *SVEC* 24 (1963), 139–54.

BESTERMAN, THEODORE, *Voltaire*, 3rd edn. (revised) (London, 1969).

BETTS, C. J., 'On the Beginning and Ending of *Candide*', *Modern Language Review*, 80 (1985), 283–92.

BIANCO, JOSEPH, '*Zadig* et l'origine du conte philosophique. Aux antipodes de l'unité', *Poétique*, 17 (1986), 443–61.

BONGIE, LAURENCE L., 'Crisis and the Birth of the Voltairian "conte"', *Modern Language Quarterly*, 23 (1962), 53–64.

BONNEVILLE, DOUGLAS A., *Voltaire and the Form of the Novel* (Oxford, 1976) (= *SVEC* 158).

BOTTIGLIA, WILLIAM F., *Voltaire's 'Candide': Analysis of a Classic*, 2nd edn. (Geneva, 1964) (= *SVEC* 7a).

—— (ed.), *Voltaire. A Collection of Critical Essays* (Englewood Cliffs, NJ, 1968).

BROOKS, RICHARD A., *Voltaire and Leibniz* (Geneva, 1964).

BRUMFITT, J. H., *Voltaire Historian* (Oxford, 1958).

CAMBOU, PIERRE, 'Le héros du conte voltairien: sa genèse dans les *Œuvres historiques*', *Littératures*, 23 (1990), 89–101.

CARR jun., THOMAS M. 'Eloquence in the Defense of Deism. Voltaire's *Histoire de Jenni*', *Kentucky Romance Quarterly*, 25 (1978), 471–80.

—— 'Voltaire's Fables of Discretion. The Conte Philosophique in *Le Taureau blanc*', *Studies in Eighteenth-Century Culture*, 15 (1986), 47–65.

CARROLL, M. G., 'Some Implications of "vraisemblance" in Voltaire's *L'Ingénu*', *SVEC* 183 (1980), 35–44.

CASTEX, P.-G., *Voltaire: 'Micromégas', 'Candide', 'L'Ingénu'*, 2nd edn. (Paris, 1982).

CHERPACK, CLIFTON, 'Voltaire's *Histoire de Jenni*: A Synthetic Creed', *Modern Philology*, 54 (1956), 26–32.

CLARK, PRISCILLA P., '*L'Ingénu*: The Uses and Limitations of Naïveté', *French Studies*, 27 (1973), 278–86.

CLOUSTON, JOHN S., *Voltaire's Binary Masterpiece. 'L'Ingénu' Reconsidered* (Berne, Frankfurt am Main, and New York, 1986).

COULET, HENRI, 'La candeur de Candide', *Annales de la Faculté des Lettres et Sciences humaines d'Aix-en-Provence*, 34 (1960), 87–99.

CROCKER, LESTER G., 'Voltaire's Struggle for Humanism', *SVEC* 4 (1957), 137–69.

DÉMORIS, RENÉ, 'Genèse et symbolique de l'*Histoire de Jenni ou le sage et l'athée* de Voltaire', *SVEC* 199 (1981), 87–123.

FAUDEMAY, ALAIN, *Voltaire allégoriste. Essai sur les rapports entre conte et philosophie chez Voltaire* (Fribourg, 1987).

GAILLARD, POL, '*L'Ingénu. Histoire véritable*: analyse critique', *L'Information littéraire*, 34 (1982), 212–18.

GALLIANI, R., 'La date de composition du *Crocheteur borgne* par Voltaire', *SVEC* 217 (1983), 141–6.

—— 'La date de composition du *Songe de Platon* par Voltaire', *SVEC* 219 (1983), 37–57.

GAY, PETER, *Voltaire's Politics. The Poet as Realist*, 2nd edn. (New Haven, Conn., and London, 1988).

GERTNER, MICHAEL H., 'Five Comic Devices in *Zadig*', *SVEC* 117 (1974), 133–52.

GILOT, MICHEL, 'Fonctions de la parole dans *Candide*', *Littératures*, 9–10 (1984), 91–7.

GINSBERG, R., 'The Argument of Voltaire's *L'Homme aux quarante écus*: A Study in Philosophic Rhetoric', *SVEC* 56 (1967), 611–57.

GROBE, EDWIN P., 'Aspectual Parody in Voltaire's *Candide*', *Symposium*, 21 (1967), 38–49.

—— 'Discontinuous Aspect in Voltaire's *Candide*', *Modern Language Notes*, 82 (1967), 334–46.

HAFFTER, PIERRE, 'L'Usage satirique des causales dans les contes de Voltaire', *SVEC* 53 (1967), 7–28.

HELLEGOUARC'H, JACQUELINE, 'Mélinade ou la duchesse du Maine. Deux contes de jeunesse de Voltaire: *Le Crocheteur borgne* et *Cosi-Sancta*', *Revue d'histoire littéraire de la France*, 78 (1978), 722–35.

—— 'Genèse d'un conte de Voltaire', *SVEC* 176 (1979), 7–36.

—— '*Les Aveugles juges des couleurs*: interprétation et essai de datation', *SVEC* 215 (1982), 91–7.

HENRY, PATRICK, 'Sacred and Profane Gardens in *Candide*', *SVEC* 176 (1979), 133–52.

HIGHMAN, DAVID E., '*L'Ingénu*: Flawed Masterpiece or Masterful Innovation?', *SVEC* 143 (1976), 71–83.

HOWELLS, R. J., ' "Cette boucherie héroïque": *Candide* as Carnival', *Modern Language Review*, 80 (1985), 293–303.

—— 'The Burlesque as a Philosophical Principle in Voltaire's *contes*', in R. J. Howells *et al.* (eds.), *Voltaire and his World. Studies Presented to W. H. Barber* (Oxford, 1985), 67–84.

—— 'Processing Voltaire's *Amabed*', *British Journal for Eighteenth-Century Studies*, 10 (1987), 153–62.

JAMES, E. D., 'Voltaire on the Nature of the Soul', *French Studies*, 32 (1978), 20–33.

—— 'Voltaire on Free Will', *SVEC* 249 (1987), 1–18.

KOTTA, NUÇI, *L'Homme aux quarante écus'. A Study of Voltairian Themes* (The Hague and Paris, 1966).

KRA, PAULINE, 'Note on the Derivation of Names in Voltaire's *Zadig*', *Romance Notes*, 16 (1975), 342–4.

LANGDON, DAVID, 'On the Meanings of the Conclusion of *Candide*', *SVEC* 238 (1985), 397–432.

LEIGH, R. A., 'From the *Inégalité* to *Candide*: Notes on a Desultory Dialogue Between Rousseau and Voltaire (1755–1759)', in W. H. Barber *et al.* (eds.), *The Age of Enlightenment: Studies Presented to Theodore Besterman* (Edinburgh and London, 1967), 66–92.

LONGCHAMP ET WAGNIÈRE, *Mémoires sur Voltaire* (2 vols.; Paris, 1826).

McGHEE, DOROTHY MADELEINE, *Voltairian Narrative Devices as Considered in the Author's 'Contes Philosophiques'* (Menasha, Wis., 1933).

MAGNAN, ANDRÉ, *Voltaire. 'Candide ou l'optimisme'* (Paris, 1987).

MASON, HAYDN, 'Voltaire and Manichean Dualism', *SVEC* 26 (1963), 1143–60.

—— 'The Unity of Voltaire's *L'Ingénu*', in W. H. Barber *et al.* (eds.), *The Age of Enlightenment: Studies Presented to Theodore Besterman* (Edinburgh and London, 1967), 93–106.

—— 'A Biblical "Conte philosophique": Voltaire's *Taureau blanc*', in E. T. Dubois *et al.* (eds.), *Eighteenth-Century French Studies. Literature and the Arts* (Newcastle, 1969), 55–69.

MASON, HAYDN, 'Voltaire's "Contes": An "Etat présent" ', *Modern Language Review*, 65 (1970), 19–35.

——— *Voltaire* (London, 1975).

——— *Voltaire. A Biography* (London, 1981).

——— 'Voltaire et le ludique', *Revue d'histoire littéraire de la France*, 84 (1984), 539–52.

——— 'L'Ironie voltairienne', *CAIEF* 38 (1986), 51–62.

——— 'Contradiction and Irony in Voltaire's Fiction', in Robert Gibson (ed.), *Studies in French Fiction in Honour of Vivienne Mylne* (London, 1988), 179–90.

——— 'Voltaire's "Sermon" Against Optimism: The *Poème sur le désastre de Lisbonne*', in Giles Barber and C. P. Courtney (eds.), *Enlightenment Essays in Memory of Robert Shackleton* (Oxford, 1988), 189–203.

MERVAUD, CHRISTIANE, 'Sur l'activité ludique de Voltaire conteur: le problème de *L'Ingénu*', *L'Information littéraire*, 35 (1983), 13–17.

——— 'Voltaire, saint Augustin et le duc Du Maine, aux sources de *Cosi-Sancta*', *SVEC* 228 (1984), 89–96.

——— '*Jeannot et Colin*: Illustration et subversion du conte moral', *Revue d'histoire littéraire de la France*, 85 (1985), 596–620.

——— 'Voltaire et Fontenelle', in Alain Niderst (ed.), *Fontenelle. Actes du colloque tenu à Rouen du 6 au 10 octobre 1987* (Paris, 1989), 317–30.

MITCHELL, P. C., 'An Underlying Theme in *La Princesse de Babylone*', *SVEC* 137 (1975), 31–45.

MORTIER, ROLAND, 'Voltaire et le peuple', in W. H. Barber *et al.* (eds.), *The Age of Enlightenment: Studies presented to Theodore Besterman* (Edinburgh and London, 1967), 137–52.

MURRAY, GEOFFREY, *Voltaire's 'Candide': The Protean Gardener 1755–1762* (Geneva, 1970) (= *SVEC* 69).

MYLNE, VIVIENNE, 'Literary Techniques and Methods in Voltaire's *contes philosophiques*', *SVEC* 57 (1967), 1055–80.

——— 'Wolper's View of Voltaire's Tales', *SVEC* 212 (1982), 318–27.

NAVES, RAYMOND, *Voltaire* (Paris, 1966).

NIVAT, JEAN, '*L'Ingénu* de Voltaire, les jésuites et l'affaire La Chalotais', *Revue des sciences humaines*, 66 (1952), 97–108.

O'MEARA, MAUREEN F., '*Le Taureau blanc* and the Activity of Language', *SVEC* 148 (1976), 115–75.

——— 'Linguistic Power-Play: Voltaire's Considerations on the Evolution, Use, and Abuse of Language', *SVEC* 219 (1983), 93–103.

POMEAU, RENÉ, *Voltaire par lui-même* (Paris, s.d. [1959]).

——— 'Une esquisse inédite de *L'Ingénu*', *Revue d'histoire littéraire de la France*, 61 (1961), 58–60.

——— 'Voltaire conteur: masques et visages', *L'Information littéraire*, 13 (1961), 1–5.

—— *La Religion de Voltaire*, 2nd edn. (Paris, 1969).

—— 'De Candide à *Jacques le fataliste*', in *Enlightenment Studies in Honour of Lester G. Crocker* (Oxford, 1979), 243–51.

—— 'Un "bon sauvage" voltairien: l'Ingénu', *Studi di letteratura francese*, 7 (1981), 58–73.

—— *Voltaire en son temps. I. D'Arouet à Voltaire 1694–1734* (Oxford, 1985).

—— '*Les Lettres philosophiques* ou l'avènement de l'esprit voltairien', *Littératures*, 19 (1988), 87–99.

—— and MERVAUD, CHRISTIANE, *Voltaire en son temps. III. De la Cour au jardin 1750–1759* (Oxford, 1991).

PRINCE, GERALD, 'Candid Explanations', *Saggi e ricerche di letteratura francese*, 22 (1983), 183–97.

PRUNER, F., *Recherches sur la création romanesque dans 'L'Ingénu' de Voltaire* (*Archives des Lettres Modernes* (no. 30); Paris, 1960).

RAYNAUD, JEAN-MICHEL, 'Mimésis et philosophie: approche du récit philosophique voltairien', *Dix-huitième siècle*, 10 (1978), 405–15.

REISLER, MARSHA, 'Rhetoric and Dialectic in Voltaire's *Lettres philosophiques*', *L'Esprit créateur*, 17 (1977), 311–24.

RIDGWAY, RONALD S., *La Propagande philosophique dans les tragédies de Voltaire* (Geneva, 1961) (= *SVEC* 15).

—— *Voltaire and Sensibility* (Montreal and London, 1973).

SAREIL, JEAN, 'De *Zadig* à *Candide*, ou Permanence de la pensée de Voltaire', *Romanic Review*, 52 (1961), 271–8.

—— 'La Répétition dans les "Contes" de Voltaire', *French Review*, 35 (1961–2), 137–46.

—— *Essai sur 'Candide'* (Geneva, 1967).

—— 'Le Vocabulaire de la relativité dans *Micromégas* de Voltaire', *Romanic Review*, 64 (1973), 273–85.

—— 'Les Apologues de Voltaire', *Romanic Review*, 68 (1977), 118–27.

—— 'Le massacre de Voltaire dans les manuels scolaires', *SVEC* 212 (1982), 83–161.

SCHICK, URSULA, *Zur Erzähltechnik in Voltaires 'Contes'* (Munich, 1968).

SENIOR, NANCY, 'The Structure of *Zadig*', *SVEC* 135 (1975), 135–41.

SHERMAN, CAROL, *Reading Voltaire's 'Contes': A Semiotics of Philosophical Narration* (Chapel Hill, NC, 1985).

SHOWALTER jun., ENGLISH, 'The Theme of Language in Voltaire's Tales', *French Forum*, 14 (1989), 17–29.

SMITH, D. W., 'The Publication of *Micromégas*', *SVEC* 219 (1983), 63–91.

STAROBINSKI, JEAN, 'Le fusil à deux coups de Voltaire', *Revue de métaphysique et de morale*, 71 (1966), 277–91; reprinted in *Le Remède dans le mal. Critique et légitimation de l'artifice à l'âge des lumières* (Paris, 1989), 144–63.

—— 'Sur le style philosophique de *Candide*', *Comparative Literature*, 28 (1976), 193–200; reprinted in *Le Remède dans le mal. Critique et légitimation de l'artifice à l'âge des lumières* (Paris, 1989), 123–33.

STAROBINSKI, JEAN, '*Candide* et la question de l'autorité', in Jean Macary (ed.), *Essays on the Age of Enlightenment in Honor of Ira O. Wade* (Geneva, 1977), 305–12; reprinted in *Le Remède dans le mal. Critique et légitimation de l'artifice à l'âge des lumières* (Paris, 1989), 133–44.

TAYLOR, S. S. B., '*L'Ingénu*, the Huguenots and Choiseul', in W. H. Barber *et al.* (eds.), *The Age of Enlightenment: Studies Presented to Theodore Bester-man* (Edinburgh and London, 1967), 107–36.

—— 'Voltaire's Humour', *SVEC* 179 (1979), 101–16.

UNDANK, JACK, 'The Status of Fiction in Voltaire's *contes*', *Degré second*, 6 (1982), 65–88.

VAILLOT, RENÉ, *Voltaire en son temps. II. Avec Madame Du Châtelet 1734–1749* (Oxford, 1988).

VALÉRY, PAUL, 'Voltaire', in *Œuvres*, 2 vols. (Paris, 1957–60), i. 518–30.

VAN DEN HEUVEL, JACQUES, 'Le conte voltairien ou la confidence déguisée', *Table ronde*, 122 (1958), 116–21.

—— *Voltaire dans ses contes. De 'Micromégas' à 'L'Ingénu'*, 3rd edn. (Paris, 1967).

VARTANIAN, ARAM, '*Zadig*: Theme and Counter-theme', in Catherine Lafarge (ed.), *Dilemmes du roman. Essays in honor of Georges May* (Saratoga, Calif., 1989), 149–64.

VERNIER, FRANCE, 'Les Disfonctionnements des normes du conte dans *Candide*', *Littérature*, 1 (1971), 15–29.

VIROLLE, ROLAND, 'Voltaire et les matérialistes d'après ses derniers contes', *Dix-huitième siècle*, 11 (1979), 63–74.

WADE, IRA O., *Voltaire's 'Micromégas'. A Study in the Fusion of Science, Myth, and Art* (Princeton, NJ, 1950).

—— *Voltaire and 'Candide'. A Study in the Fusion of History, Art and Philosophy* (Princeton, NJ, 1959).

—— *The Intellectual Development of Voltaire* (Princeton, NJ, 1969).

WEIGHTMAN, J. C., 'The Quality of *Candide*', in E. T. Dubois *et al.* (eds.), *Essays presented to C. M. Girdlestone* (Newcastle, 1960), 335–47.

WILLIAMS, DAVID, *Voltaire: Literary Critic* (Geneva, 1966) (= *SVEC* 48).

—— 'Voltaire on the Sentimental Novel', *SVEC* 135 (1975), 115–34.

WOLPER, ROY S., 'Candide, Gull in the Garden', *Eighteenth-Century Studies*, 3 (1969), 265–77.

—— '*Zadig*, a Grim Comedy?', *Romanic Review*, 65 (1974), 234–48.

—— 'Voltaire's *Contes*. A Reconsideration', *Forum*, 16 (1978), 74–9.

—— 'The Final Foolishness of Babouc: The Dark Centre of *Le Monde comme il va*', *Modern Language Review*, 75 (1980), 766–73.

—— 'The Toppling of Jeannot', *SVEC* 183 (1980), 69–82.

—— 'The Black Captain and Scarmentado. Tyrant and Fool', *Eighteenth-Century Fiction*, 1 (1988/9), 119–31.

IV. GENERAL

AUERBACH, ERICH, *Mimesis. The Representation of Reality in Western Literature*, tr. Willard R. Trask, 2nd impr. (Princeton, NJ, 1968).

BAKHTIN, M. M., *Esthétique et théorie du roman*, tr. Daria Olivier (Paris, 1978).

—— *The Dialogic Imagination. Four Essays by M. M. Bakhtin*, ed. Michael Holquist (Austin, Tex., and London, 1981).

BARCHILON, JACQUES, 'Uses of the Fairy-Tale in the Eighteenth Century', *SVEC* 24 (1963), 111–38.

—— *Le Conte merveilleux français de 1690 à 1790: cent ans de féerie et de poésie ignorées de l'histoire littéraire* (Paris, 1975).

BARGUILLET, FRANÇOISE, *Le Roman au XVIIIᵉ siècle* (Paris, 1981).

BELAVAL, YVON, 'Le conte philosophique', in W. H. Barber *et al.* (eds.), *The Age of Enlightenment: Studies Presented to Theodore Besterman* (Edinburgh and London, 1967), 308–17.

BENNINGTON, GEOFFREY, *Sententiousness and the Novel. Laying Down the Law in Eighteenth-Century French Fiction* (Cambridge, 1985).

BERLIN, ISAIAH, *The Crooked Timber of Humanity. Chapters in the History of Ideas*, ed. Henry Hardy (London, 1990).

BRADY, PATRICK, *Rococo Style Versus Enlightenment Novel* (Geneva, 1984).

CASSIRER, ERNST, *The Philosophy of the Enlightenment*, tr. Fritz C. A. Koelln and James P. Pettegrove (Princeton, NJ, 1951).

COULET, HENRI, *Le Roman depuis les origines jusqu'à la Révolution* (2 vols.; Paris, 1967–8).

—— 'La distanciation dans le roman et le conte philosophiques', in *Roman et lumières au XVIIIᵉ siècle* (Paris, 1970), 438–47.

CRANSTON, MAURICE, *Jean-Jacques. The Early Life and Work of Jean-Jacques Rousseau 1712–1754* (London, 1983; repr. 1987).

—— *The Noble Savage. Jean-Jacques Rousseau (1754–1762)* (London, 1991).

FINK, BEATRICE C., 'The Banquet as Phenomenon or Structure in Selected Eighteenth-Century French Novels', *SVEC* 152 (1976), 729–40.

FRANCE, PETER, 'The Literature of Persuasion', in John Cruickshank (ed.), *French Literature and its Background* (6 vols.; Oxford, 1968–70).

—— *Rhetoric and Truth in France. Descartes to Diderot* (Oxford, 1972).

GODENNE, RENÉ, *Histoire de la nouvelle française aux XVIIᵉ et XVIIIᵉ siècles* (Geneva, 1970).

GOODDEN, ANGELICA, *The Complete Lover. Eros, Nature, and Artifice in the Eighteenth-Century French Novel* (Oxford, 1989).

GRIMSLEY, RONALD, *Jean D'Alembert (1717–83)* (Oxford, 1963).

GUENIER, NICOLE, 'Pour une définition du conte', in *Roman et lumières au XVIIIᵉ siècle* (Paris, 1970), 422–36.

HERTZBERG, ARTHUR, *The French Enlightenment and the Jews. The Origins of Modern Anti-Semitism* (New York, 1968; repr. 1990).

ISHERWOOD, ROBERT M., *Farce and Fantasy. Popular Entertainment in Eigh-teenth-Century Paris* (New York and Oxford, 1986).

LAUFER, ROGER, *Style rococo, style des 'lumières'* (Paris, 1963).

LOVEJOY, ARTHUR O., *The Great Chain of Being. A Study of the History of an Idea* (Cambridge, Mass., 1950).

LUONI, FLAVIO, 'Récit, exemple, dialogue', *Poétique*, 19 (1988), 211–32.

KENDRICK, T. D., *The Lisbon Earthquake* (London, 1956).

LANSON, GUSTAVE, *L'Art de la prose* (Paris, 1908).

MACDONALD ROSS, G., *Leibniz* (Oxford, 1984).

MARTIN, ANGUS, 'The Origins of the *Contes moraux*: Marmontel and Other Authors of Short Fiction in the *Mercure de France* (1750–1761)', *SVEC* 171 (1977), 197–210.

——— *Anthologie du conte en France 1750–1799. Philosophes et cœurs sensibles* (Paris, 1981).

MASON, HAYDN, *French Writers and their Society 1715–1800* (London and Basingstoke, 1982).

MAUZI, ROBERT, *L'Idée du bonheur dans la littérature et la pensée française au XVIIIe siècle* (Paris, 1960).

MAY, GEORGES, *Le dilemme du roman au XVIIIe siècle* (Paris, 1963).

MORTIER, ROLAND, 'Esotérisme et lumières. Un dilemme de la pensée du XVIIIe siècle', in his *Clartés et ombres du siècle des lumières. Etudes sur le XVIIIe siècle littéraire* (Geneva, 1969), 60–103.

——— 'Les "Philosophes" français et l'éducation publique', in his *Clartés et ombres du siècle des lumières. Etudes sur le XVIIIe siècle littéraire* (Geneva, 1969), 104–13.

MYLNE, VIVIENNE, *The Eighteenth-Century French Novel. Techniques of Illusion* (Manchester, 1965).

NIKLAUS, ROBERT, 'Diderot et le conte philosophique', *CAIEF* 13 (1961), 299–315.

——— 'Fontenelle as a Model for the Transmission and Vulgarisation of Ideas in the Enlightenment', in R. J. Howells *et al.* (eds.), *Voltaire and his World. Studies Presented to W. H. Barber* (Oxford, 1985), 167–83.

PREMINGER, ALEX (ed.), *Princeton Encyclopedia of Poetry and Poetics*, 2nd edn. (London and Basingstoke, 1975).

RUSHDIE, SALMAN, 'In Good Faith', *Independent on Sunday*, 4 Feb. 1990.

RUSTIN, M. J., '"L'Histoire véritable" dans la littérature romanesque du XVIIIe siècle français', *CAIEF* 18 (1966), 89–102, 254–62.

SAYCE, R. A., *Style in French Prose. A Method of Analysis* (Oxford, 1953).

SGARD, JEAN, 'Marmontel et la forme du conte', in J. Ehrard (ed.), *De l'Ency-clopédie à la Contre-Révolution: Jean-François Marmontel (1723–1799)* (Cler-mont-Ferrand, 1972), 229–37.

SOLLERS, PHILIPPE, 'Journal', *L'Infini*, 28 (1989–90), 36–56.

STAROBINSKI, JEAN, 'Le Mythe au XVIIIe siècle', *Critique*, 33 (1977), 975–

97; reprinted as 'Fable et mythologie aux XVIIe et XVIIIe siècles' in *Le Remède dans le mal. Critique et légitimation de l'artifice à l'âge des lumières* (Paris, 1989), 233–62.

SULEIMAN, SUSAN, 'Le récit exemplaire. Parabole, fable, roman à thèse', *Poétique*, 8 (1977), 468–89.

INDEX

Bold face figures denote an extended discussion.